Strategy after Deterrence

STRATEGY
AFTER
DETERRENCE

STEPHEN J. CIMBALA

PRAEGER

New York
Westport, Connecticut
London

Library of Congress Cataloging-in-Publication Data

Cimbala, Stephen J.
    Strategy after deterrence / Stephen J. Cimbala.
      p. cm.
    Includes bibliographical references and index.
    ISBN 0–275–93741–0
    1. Europe—Military policy.   2. North Atlantic Treaty
Organization.   3. United States—Military policy.   4. Deterrence
(Strategy)   5. Nuclear warfare.   I. Title.
UA646.C54   1991
355′.03354—dc20   90–39027

British Library Cataloguing in Publication Data is available.

Library of Congress Catalog Card Number: 90–39027
ISBN: 0–275–93741–0

First published in 1991

Praeger Publishers, One Madison Avenue, New York, NY 10010
An imprint of Greenwood Publishing Group, Inc.

Printed in the United States of America

The paper used in this book complies with the
Permanent Paper Standard issued by the National
Information Standards Organization (Z39.48–1984).

10 9 8 7 6 5 4 3 2 1

CONTENTS

ACKNOWLEDGMENTS

I gratefully acknowledge David Tarr for all that he has taught me about deterrence and arms control, and Jacob Kipp for doing the same service with regard to Soviet military studies. I have learned much from Kipp and other colleagues at SASO about Soviet military history and art, including David Glantz, Bruce Menning, Harry Orenstein, Graham Turbiville and Tim Sanz. With equal gratitude I acknowledge Chris Donnelly, Peter Vigor, and Maj. Peter Podbielski of the Royal Military Academy, Sandhurst, for invaluable assistance in identifying pertinent sources and for their encouragement. Raymond Garthoff, of the Brookings Institution, has provided helpful comments on draft manuscripts and useful references in Soviet military strategy, as has Ned Lebow on the subject of crisis management. Mary Glenn, Political Science editor at Praeger, has been generous with encouragement and support; Alda Trabucchi served as production editor, and Alice Vigliani was a very thorough copy editor. Finally, I am most in debt to my wife Betsy for her patience and understanding, and to my mother for making education a matter of first importance.

INTRODUCTION: DETERRENCE, DISSUASION, AND THE CHANGING CHARACTER OF EUROPEAN POLITICS AND STRATEGY

The year 1989 was one of profound political change in the Soviet Union and in Eastern Europe. Communist governments in Poland, East Germany, Czechoslovakia, and Hungary fell altogether or were forced into reluctant partnership with noncommunist opposition. The way for these developments in Eastern Europe was prepared in Moscow. Following the accession of Mikhail Gorbachev to the position of general secretary of the Communist Party of the USSR, the leadership of the Soviet Union embarked on a restructuring—*perestroika*—of its economy that had equally significant implications for political participation. Having argued that democratization was imperative in the citadel of world communism, the Soviet leadership could hardly reimpose the Brezhnev doctrine (Soviet military intervention to prevent the overthrow of existing communist regimes) on Eastern Europe. Quite the opposite was implied by the movement toward "reasonable sufficiency" and other manifestations of defensive military doctrine: The Politburo would no longer use the Red Army as a gendarmerie to bail out those rulers in Eastern Europe who were too incompetent to rule by consent or by coercion.

Obviously, U.S. and NATO strategy would be affected by all these developments. Most dramatically, the destruction of the Berlin Wall, which had stood since 1961 as a symbol of the division of Germany, now opened the door to a large political debate on the future of Germany: one or two? Military strategy in Washington, Brussels, and Moscow would, of necessity, be influenced strongly by the political upheavals taking place in Eastern Europe and in the Soviet Union from 1985 through 1989.

Additionally, Western Europe was undergoing important change. The European Community scheduled 1992 as the launching date for the creation of a truly integrated, trans-European market for capital, goods, and services. This was an unacknowledged leap over the boundaries and jealousies of national sovereignty and tradition. A market of this size had the potential to directly compete with the U.S. economy; it certainly created a powerful vortex into which the more entrepreneurial states of Eastern Europe were likely to be drawn. Having waived the opportunity to participate in the Marshall Plan on account of the cold war atmospherics dominant at the time, the Soviet Union would be loath to forbid its Warsaw Pact partners some measure of participation in Western Europe's economic miracle again. The implication of Gorbachev's repeal of the Brezhnev doctrine was that there were many legitimate roads to socialism, including market socialism, provided threats to Soviet national security were neither created nor exacerbated.

Military strategy would have to change for the Americans and for their NATO European allies in the 1990s—and perhaps very far from the baseline established at the end of the period of phenomenal growth in U.S. defense expenditures that occurred in fiscal years 1981–1989 during the Reagan administration. The Soviet predicament, it seemed, was that it could no longer police the contiguous empire at an acceptable cost. The U.S. dilemma was that, without an adventurous Soviet Union, the U.S. Congress and its NATO European allies could not see benefits resulting from defense buildups, but several could be derived from reductions in security spending. Most obvious for the Americans, approximately 60 percent of their total defense expenditures went, in one form or another, to the defense of Europe. Absent a tangible threat to Europe, domestic pressures, including budgetary ones, would recast U.S. priorities in the direction of light, flexible military forces for proactive use in third world conflicts that were as much political as they were military.

The apparent lapse of a security requirement for the United States and NATO to maintain conventional forces of the size and character previously deemed necessary was only the beginning. The Soviet Union pressed in all public fora for the removal of nuclear weapons from the European continent and for the eventual destruction of all superpower and other nuclear weapons. Although obviously designed to exploit the divisions within NATO over nuclear force modernization, this anti-nuclear public diplomacy of the USSR contributed to the delegitimation of the use of military force generally. After all, the threat to use nuclear weapons had been the sine qua non by which the United States and the Soviet Union regulated their military competition once both sides had developed and deployed significant nuclear arsenals. The stability of the "balance of terror," according to orthodox reasoning about the arms race, created a benign condition of military stasis. Neither side could initiate a war since any war might become nuclear, and no one could fight a nuclear war at an acceptable political cost. On the other hand, official U.S. and NATO policy was that the option of nuclear first-use remained necessary in order to deter Soviet attack on Western Europe with conventional forces.

In the final analysis, all of the foregoing social, political, and military realignments meant that the status quo in strategy would no longer suffice. Western strategy ran the risk of being cryogenically frozen in an older mode when new ideas were needed. However, previously hard-won compromises on defense issues, within NATO and within the U.S. military establishment, could not be ignored or forgotten. The United States had allegedly extended its nuclear umbrella for the protection of Western Europe for several decades, under the assumption that Americans and Europeans together could not muster the conventional forces for European defense. This reliance upon extended nuclear deterrence came at a price for both sides. For the European members of NATO, it imposed a U.S. *droit de regard* over their security decisions. For the Americans, it tied their military and political choices in security and foreign policy to the behavior of their fifteen independent-minded alliance partners. That NATO endured for forty years in approximately the same form was a tribute to perseverance on both sides of the Atlantic in the face of significant differences in political priorities and in military strategy.

A reconstituted NATO or its eventual replacement will have to deal most fundamentally with the problem set forth in this study: What strategy should come after deterrence? This problem demands further explanation, the bulk of which is presented in the following chapters. Here, a short statement of the problem and its aspects is appropriate.

Deterrence is only one kind—and a particular kind—of negative persuasion, or dissuasion. Not every military force held by one state in order to dissuade a prospective attacker is a *deterrent* force. There are basically two ways in which states can dissuade prospective attackers: (1) by creating the plausible threat of losing in battle, and (2) by threatening credibly an unacceptable level of destruction to the opponent's social value and/or to its political regime. Although these two kinds of threats can overlap at the margin, their different centers of gravity are very important for those who would call upon the threat to use force in order to prevent war.

Given the preceding assumptions, whether a threat is deterrent or of some other nature does not depend only upon the type of weapons to be used to carry out the threat. It also depends upon what is being threatened. A deterrent threat is a threat to inflict unacceptable *punishment* to the society or government of the opponent, *regardless* of whether or not his forces prevail in battle. Nuclear weapons can be ideal for making deterrent threats, although the term "deterrence" should not be used synonymously with "nuclear." Under very special conditions, conventional forces can fulfill the requirements of deterrence. When State *A*'s conventional forces can threaten to inflict unacceptable levels of societal damage on State *B*, even before the forces of State *B* have been disarmed, State *A* possesses a conventional deterrent. This has happened frequently in history when a smaller state has been confronted by a larger state. Among other significant changes they have caused in world politics, nuclear weapons make possible the infliction of unacceptable levels of destruction by smaller states against larger ones. All the smaller side needs is a counter-city deterrent for which no defenses exist.

Conventional forces are mostly used for dissuasion other than deterrence. Dissuasion is the credible threat to prevail in battle or to deny the opponent a military victory at an acceptable price. Prior to the nuclear age, it was assumed that the same military forces provided the basis for both deterrence and dissuasion. However, the missions remained distinct and strategists sometimes recognized that the enemy's capital city was a prominent jugular, the threat to which might obviate the need for further battle. Hitler assumed, as did Napoleon, that the fall of Moscow would bring about the disintegration of the rest of the Soviet or Russian armies. Napoleon was not proved right in this judgment, and Hitler drew up even shorter of his prize. The capture of NATO political capitals prior to the eventual destruction of its armed forces in battle is certainly plausible, and it can be arguably part of any sensible Soviet war plan. Successful revolutions have begun with the seizure of capital cities by revolutionary forces, as in Russia in 1917, but in others the capital cities have fallen last, as in China in 1949. Although the Soviets controlled Kabul during their military intervention in Afghanistan during the period 1979–89, they and their puppet regime did not control much else, and ultimately the Soviets were forced out. The Americans in Vietnam suffered a symbolic and decisive political defeat, if not a military one, during the Tet Offensive of 1968 when the major cities of South Vietnam were no longer proof against a coordinated uprising.

Thus, the conceptual refinement of future strategy cannot entirely omit the category "conventional deterrence." But it will have to be delimited more strictly than it has been, in order to understand what distinguishes it from nuclear deterrence and from dissuasion, conventional or nuclear. For nuclear deterrence partakes of special kinds of threats against society and government. Nuclear deterrent threats *hold hostage* the *noncombatants* of a society and the officials of its government as personal victims of terrorism, on behalf of the policy of war prevention. This is, as many ethicists have pointed out, a case of calling upon evil in order to do good. But unlike conventional deterrence, in which the risk to cities and governments might be moderated according to the finite lethalities of conventional weapons, nuclear deterrence draws strength from the unrestrained power of fission and fusion weapons. The weapons cannot be used in large numbers and in a discriminating way—or so it is argued here. Thus, the idea of *nuclear dissuasion*, of using nuclear weapons as "force multipliers" to prevail in battle, is as limited as the idea of conventional deterrence. In most cases, only overwhelming superiority in conventional forces can allow for the *deterrent* threat, as opposed to the dissuasive threat, to use those forces. And, in most instances, the use of nuclear *dissuasion*, as opposed to deterrence, can only be attempted by a nuclear-armed state against one *without* either a nuclear force of its own *or* a nuclear protector.

If the genotypes of nuclear dissuasion and conventional deterrence are atypical cases, usually operative only in asymmetrical force balances between potential opponents, it follows that conventional dissuasion and nuclear deterrence are more reliable. Keeping these distinctions straight is not just an exercise in taxonomy. It has important implications for the preservation of peace in post-Cold War Europe. The detailed pursuit of these implications is undertaken in the following chapters. Chapter 1 reviews the political context for the development of military strategy in Europe. Chapter 2 considers the relationship between military stability and the likelihood of winning wars in their initial period. Chapter 3 reviews the issue of deterrence during war, and Chapter 4 considers "atypical" wars, which in the future might be all too typical. Chapter 5 investigates the relationship between deception and deterrence. Chapter 6 considers the attempt to substitute non-nuclear dissuasion for nuclear deterrence, in the form of anti-nuclear strategic defenses that could defeat nuclear offenses. Chapter 7 summarizes conclusions and makes additional observations.

Strategy after Deterrence

1

REMOVING THE NUCLEAR SHADOW: THE POLITICAL CONTEXT

Technology and politics are taking the superpowers into the postnuclear era.[1] This is not an era in which nuclear weapons will be irrelevant. But the shadow cast by U.S. and Soviet nuclear weapons over the rest of international relations will be diminished. The result is a situation that is less likely to lead to a war totally destructive of civilization, should deterrence fail. However, deterrence may be less secure as complexity replaces simplicity and as the instinct of nuclear dread no longer suffices to keep superpowers and their allies from being at swords' points.

The downside of a less dreadful, and perhaps less secure, deterrence has at least four aspects with regard to U.S., Soviet, and NATO European force structures and war plans. These include (1) the possibility of high-technology conventional warfare, including war in Europe, (2) the challenge of preserving stable deterrence and attaining arms control with a potpourri of nuclear and improved conventional forces, (3) the replacement of a single political divide between the East and the West with a plural set of controversies, and (4) the "ACI factor" of accidental, catalytic, or inadvertent war, which can never be ruled out of war plans or arms-control negotiations.

MODERN CONVENTIONAL WARFARE

The paradox of nuclear weapons is that they may purchase superpower strategic stability at the cost of more instability in areas outside U.S. and Soviet core security zones or obviously vital interests. Although no war has been fought in Europe for more than four decades, the possibility of conventional war looms larger in the minds of NATO military planners as NATO and Warsaw Pact nuclear forces are either withdrawn from the theater of operations or dismantled. The INF agreement of December 1987 eliminated two entire categories of U.S. and Soviet nuclear weapons intended for use in regional Eurasian conflicts. As a result, the issue of NATO nuclear modernization in Europe was left hostage to two forces largely beyond U.S. control: West German domestic politics and Soviet use of preventive diplomacy to forestall U.S. and NATO modernization initiatives.

Absent nuclear modernization, NATO becomes more dependent on its ability to deny the Soviet Union any plausible war plan for victory in Europe without nuclear escalation. It is conceded by many members of the Western alliance that this tasking makes for long odds.[2] The point is not that a Soviet *blitzkrieg* will break through to the English Channel before NATO or the individual nuclear members can make a decision to grant nuclear release. This worst case scenario is far from likely. Instead, the problem is that war growing from a political crisis of ambiguous origins could provide military opportunities to a Soviet leadership that saw NATO as being politically divided.[3] Among the military realities that will impact upon NATO's cohesion at the brink of war is the fact that Soviet forces may attack NATO territory, thereby inhibiting nuclear release orders that would strike commingled Western and Eastern forces.

NATO has been given a breathing space by Gorbachev's conventional force reduction initiatives, most notably his December 7, 1988 United Nations speech announcing large unilateral reductions in Soviet ground forces.[4] That this is an exercise in Soviet public diplomacy designed to put NATO and the United States on the defensive cannot be denied. But it is a great deal more. Underlying the Soviet move is the recognition that neither superpower can depend in the future upon nuclear weapons to join together what crisis perceptions have torn asunder. First, neither side can assume that its own nuclear modernization program will provide a significant qualitative edge relative to the mission capabilities of its opponent's forces. Second, the costs of deterrence failure when deterrence rests mainly on nuclear weapons are unacceptably high. Third, the Soviet Union has shifted its doctrinal emphasis in escalation control with regard to war in Europe. Until 1963, the Soviet expectation was that any war in Europe would begin with nuclear weapons or would promptly escalate into theater, and then strategic, nuclear exchanges. During the mid-1960s, the Soviet view began to shift toward a recognition of the debate within NATO over flexible response, although Soviet commentators remained skeptical of flexible nuclear response. Following major doctrinal decisions in 1966 and the official adoption by NATO of flexible response in 1967 (MC 14/3), Soviet military writers acknowledged that the conventional phase of a war in Europe might be extensive and, under some conditions, might remain below the nuclear threshold altogether.[5]

Although Gorbachev's initiatives put some pressure on the Americans and their NATO European allies to respond, the initiatives also provide breathing room for the reconsideration of prevailing NATO military strategy. While public attention is focussed on arms control, military planners may need to take harder looks at how a war in Europe might actually have to be fought. The investigation is, from the NATO standpoint, temporarily reassuring. Trends in Soviet military doctrine and force structure seem incontestably to NATO's advantage. However, modern conventional warfare would stress the prevailing NATO defense doctrines at several levels. First, the doctrine of flexible response calls for NATO to respond to any provocation with a symmetrical response that is tailored to stop the attack without provoking undue fear of escalation. Yet—and in contrast to this declaratory doctrine—the uncertainty about nuclear escalation was held to be the real deterrent to any aggression by the Pact. Second, the forward defense strategy (to be revised, in favor of reduced NATO and U.S. active duty forces in Europe supported by increasing reliance on reserves) positioned national corps defenders as close to the inter-German border as possible in order to preclude the gratuitous yielding of West German territory. This deployment scheme made easier some variations of the Soviet encirclement operation likely to be conducted against NATO's central front.[6] Third, the NATO defense plan without the participation of the French, which was reserved to national decision based on national interests, allowed no space to trade for time. This precluded innovative approaches to defense in depth, maneuver-oriented defense, protracted civil-military resistance, and other schemes that might otherwise provide options for extended war fighting without nuclear escalation.[7]

This is not to belittle NATO's considerable forces in place and potential reserves once mobilized, which obviously contribute to deterrence. In the past these were underlays beneath a nuclear overlay, which was the *ultima ratio* on which everyone depended when the uncertainties of conventional defense were tabulated. It was expected that, however dangerous high-technology conventional warfare might be, it could not go on for very long until one side or the other chose to escalate. Absent strategic and theater-nuclear forces superior to those of the Pact in survivability, diversity, and firepower, NATO could not assume that any level of nuclear escalation would be more forbidding to its adversaries than to its members.

Furthermore, conventional deterrence cannot be equated with conventional defense. A given force structure or set of war plans can provide for one without the other. Deterrence by dint of conventional forces is described as deterrence by "denial" instead of the deterrence by punishment that is thought characteristic of nuclear retaliation. The assumption is that deterrence by denial is surer to be invoked once the attacker has struck, whereas deterrence by retaliation, especially by nuclear retaliation, may be withheld at the brink.[8] This is one reason for the proposal made by Professor Samuel P. Huntington that NATO consider adopting a strategy of conventional retaliation, which might be more credible than nuclear under the exigent circumstances.[9]

However, we know precious little about the relationship between deterrence and operational art, or the art of war applicable to the conduct of strategic campaigns in a theater of operations. Wars that should have been deterred in the past by defender forces that ultimately prevailed were not deterred at the moment of truth.[10] In addition to the problem of a low batting average, deterrence based on conventional denial forces may cost the defender as much of its valued resources and territory as the attacker. This is especially so in densely populated and highly industrialized Western Europe. The more it "succeeds," any plan for fighting a defensive conventional war in Western Europe extracts a higher price from the surrounding population in the West than in the East. The Soviet Union, which would be considered in many situations to have been the instigator of attack, would escape significant destruction within its own territory.

Deterrence based on conventional denial also has this drawback: The costs of deterrence failure can be estimated with greater certainty than the costs of nuclear deterrence failure. Prospective attackers may be willing to run bold risks, and history provides illustrative evidence that attackers' estimates often fall short of reality. Paradoxically, this risk-taking propensity on the part of attackers can pay large dividends if the element of surprise is sufficiently great. Surprise can act as a logarithmic transformation of attacker combat power so that the nominal force balances are less relevant to outcomes than standard models would predict.[11] Hitler's attack on the Soviet Union of June 22, 1941 and the Japanese attack on Pearl Harbor of December 7, 1941 provide two well-known examples of the power of surprise to transform a potential standoff or defeat for the attacker into a disaster for the defender.

Of course, Hitler and the Japanese leadership were ultimately defeated, but under conditions of protracted global warfare that are unlikely to characterize any major coalition war of the future. In World War II, the Western allies had approximately two years to plan for Operation Overlord, the invasion of Normandy, with the luxury of homeland sanctuary for the United States, the principal partner.[12] The Soviets pushed the Wehrmacht back on the Eastern Front from Stalingrad to Berlin at a cost that is still beyond reckoning, but that by any measure of social or military losses is beyond any in U.S. experience.[13] Moreover, it took the Soviets several years to sufficiently develop their skills in operational maneuver before the decisive battles against the Germans on the Eastern Front could be fought. Soviet forces had to be restructured after the disasters of summer 1941 and their command system had to be overhauled, including the replacement of many leading field commanders and the development of an oversight system from Headquarters, Supreme High Command (STAVKA, VGK) to the relevant fronts and theaters of operation.[14]

Western Europe will not have this much time or opportunity to recover from future war. The war plans of the Soviet Union would almost certainly require that a rapid and decisive outcome be obtained before NATO had the opportunity and could make the decision for nuclear escalation.[15] If nuclear weapons were used in battle, the destruction would be that much worse. The notion that very selective use of short-range nuclear weapons in Western Europe could somehow stop the Pact offensive without encouraging equal or greater nuclear retaliation is overly optimistic as a basis for serious planning. Fighting on Western European soil, the armed forces of the Warsaw Pact would have no incentive to withhold a nuclear response within the theater of strategic military action (TSMA) once NATO had used nuclear weapons. In fact, the Soviet nuclear release to front commanders might be given even sooner, if NATO authorized nuclear release and the fact soon became known to Soviet intelligence.[16]

The last point brings out the relationship between command and control arrangements for the withholding or release of nuclear weapons and the stability of deterrence once a crisis has begun to slide toward war. In addition, command, control, and communications (C^3) systems have much to do with the control of escalation below the nuclear threshold and, with more uncertainty, above it. The mix of conventional and nuclear weapons that is likely to characterize the era of postnuclear deterrence creates additional imponderables with regard to peacetime arms control and wartime escalation control. The first section of this chapter argued that conventional defense is an insufficient guarantee against failure of conventional deterrence. The next section will show that the unique identities of conventional and nuclear weapons, strategic and substrategic weapons will be blurred over the technology horizon, with political and military complications for deterrence in Europe.

A MIXED BAG OF FORCES AND DETERRENCE STABILITY

In the 1990s and beyond, the superpowers and their European allies will be substituting conventional ordnance for nuclear for several reasons. First, for theater missions, the use of any nuclear weapons risks escalation to uncontrolled U.S.-Soviet homeland exchanges, with their catastrophic consequences. Second, "technology push" has already made available non-nuclear weapons with accuracies sufficient to destroy hard military targets, including those that were formerly targeted by their theater-based or strategic nuclear forces.[17] Third, the widespread availability of cruise missiles launched from various land-based, sea-based, or airborne platforms provides a versatile alternative to weapons that are easier to detect, identify, and destroy preemptively.[18] Two cautions must be offered with regard to this roseate picture of conventional substitution for nuclear. First, accuracy alone does not a successful weapons system make: The combination of accuracy, yield, and target characteristics determines whether the proposed systems have marginal cost efficiency or wartime effectiveness. Second, with regard to the cost side of the equation, the rising unit costs of some conventional high-technology weapons could price them out of purchase in quantities sufficient to be of interest.

Future U.S. and allied NATO land, sea, and airborne general-purpose forces will be more dependent than now on satellites for reconnaissance and surveillance, communications, navigation, and targeting. Systems such as NAVSTAR/GPS (Global Positioning Systems) will make possible accuracies in aiming of conventional weapons that allow for more precise and discriminating attacks against highly defended military targets.[19] Communications satellites and proliferated ground terminals, including portable ones, will permit rapid and secure communication within and across theaters of operations in "real time." Sensors based in space and airborne will complement terrestrial sniffers and snoopers, allowing for envelopes of reconnaissance and surveillance exceeding even those now provided for U.S. carrier task force fleet air defense. For example, the United States plans to deploy wide-area surveillance systems with infrared and radar detectors aboard satellites. These aids to strategic surveillance will be complemented by tactical warning and attack assessment sensors and processors also based in space. A satellite such as the BSTS (Boost Surveillance and Tracking System) under development for the U.S. Strategic Defense Initiative (SDI) could carry packages for strategic and for tactical warning and attack assessment.[20] Users could identify their needs with regard to range and degree of detail and be provided with responses pertinent to their problems, virtually without delay in digital format for enhancement of particular features.

Improved wide-area and focussed surveillance will limit the opportunities for surprise attack preceded by massive mobilization. But it is not so clear that the defense will necessarily come out ahead, since the offense benefits from improved reconnaissance, target identification, and precision aiming.[21] Nor is the possibility of strategic military deception removed by the improvement in remote sensing and data processing that might be thought to favor the defensive. Strategic military deception depends more upon the exploitation of defender vulnerabilities, including perceptions and expectations on the part of policymakers that prove to be mistaken.[22] Only some kinds of military deceptions require that the prospective attacker deceive the intended victim by creating false expectations that the defender would not otherwise entertain. Other deceptions, and equally successful ones, simply allow the defender to continue along the lines of self-deception until time has passed for any meaningful course correction.[23] The implications for crisis stability and war in Europe, the Middle East/Southwest Asia, and Korea are that a large mobilization by either side would not go undetected, but a partial and more ambiguous mobilization might be less obvious in its intent, and more amenable to use in deception planning for prospective attackers.

The substitution of improved conventional for nuclear firepower is not without its problems for arms control. The cruise missile offers the potential for a severe trade-off at the margin between arms control and deterrence stability. Conventionally armed cruise missiles cannot be distinguished from nuclear without intrusive on-site inspections. But conventional cruise missiles offer survivable, comparatively inexpensive, and nonprovocative-of-first-strike attributes that offset many of their arms-control drawbacks. Nuclear-armed cruise missiles do threaten crisis stability in addition to the obvious issues that they raise for superpower arms control. Under the provisional START guidelines negotiated by President Reagan and taken up by President Bush, for example, sea-launched cruise missiles were left off the menu for later discussion. Counting rules for air-launched cruise missiles were more easily determined within the overall ceilings of 6,000 strategic nuclear reentry vehicles, of which 4,900 would be based on ballistic missiles.[24] Nuclear-armed, sea-launched cruise missiles have dual roles in U.S. defense planning. They augment theater-nuclear capabilities in order to deter any Soviet use of nuclear weapons in support of a strategic-theater operation in Europe or Asia. And they provide prospectively usable military power, although with extreme risk, against a Soviet conventional offensive into Western Europe. Conventionally armed, sea-launched cruise missiles (SLCMs) would be preferred by NATO for the destruction of many targets without the risks of collateral damage and nuclear escalation attendant to nuclear detonations. But nuclear-armed SLCMs might be the weapons of first choice by NATO for first-use if it was felt necessary to demonstrate resolve in addition to causing the destruction of discrete targets.[25]

A noisy debate took place in NATO during the period 1979–1983 over the issue of INF deployments and, thus, over the related question of "no first-use." Soviet declaratory policy began to resolve this even under Brezhnev, when it became official declaratory policy that the USSR renounced nuclear superiority with the objective of making a strategic first strike.[26] Andropov subsequently moved to exclude the possibility of any nuclear first-use, and his successors have upheld him. The Soviet general staff has also signed on.[27] The reasons for this are not entirely altruistic. Studies conducted at the Voroshilov Military Academy during the 1970s and Soviet military exercises then and since have identified many problems attendant even to relatively selective use of nuclear weapons in a contemporary or future theater offensive.[28] The paradox in Soviet military development with regard to selective nuclear options is that, although capabilities have improved in recent decades, confidence in the effective use of these capabilities to support general purpose forces has declined.[29] The Soviets would obviously prefer to avoid first-use, or any use, of nuclear weapons in the Western TVD (Theatre of Military Actions, originally a Russian term), and only part of the reluctance is explained by the fear of escalation that might escape control.

The fear of escalation is real enough. The Soviet Union has never expected that limited nuclear wars could be fought successfully, and this assumption has not been part of their military planning for war in Europe. U.S. and NATO analyses that offer a nuclear-expedient view of the Soviet war-planning process draw inferences from Soviet discussions that, taken in context, are based on contingencies outside of Europe. The Soviet general staff might plan for contingent use of nuclear weapons in the Far East or for expedient use of nuclear charges to support allies outside of

Europe—say, the Syrians—who were on the threshold of losing control of their state. In the latter case, it is doubtful that the control of nuclear weapons would be handed over to the Soviet ally or client; the precedent set during the October 1962 Cuban missile crisis argues against Politburo interest in devolution.

It is sometimes supposed that, in response to a demonstrative nuclear first-use by NATO, the USSR would blanket the European theater of operations with massive retaliatory strikes in order to paralyze NATO's will to resist or to remove those remaining NATO weapons that could reply in kind. No one can exclude this option from the Soviet repertoire, but it is equally likely that any response to demonstrative NATO first-use would be more discriminating than that. And it might not have to be nuclear. The key indicator for deciding how optimistic the Soviets might be about war in Europe—although optimism would always be guarded with nuclear weapons over the horizon—is the aggregate *vulnerability of NATO delivery systems and nuclear charges* (together with the C^3 essential to support them) that can be *destroyed preemptively by Soviet conventional means*. Thus, conventional force reductions can contribute to nuclear stability if the reductions are accompanied by other measures that NATO should take anyway. These measures include reduction of the vulnerability of nuclear delivery systems and charges through hardening and dispersal programs. The problem of Lance nuclear missile modernization can be seen from many perspectives, but this is surely one of the more important ones. It is not so much the numbers of Soviet or Pact short-range nuclear missiles relative to the number of U.S./NATO ones that is significant for deterrence or crisis stability. The more important question is whether the overall complement of NATO nuclear charges deployed in Europe can be destroyed or degraded by conventional preemption to a degree sufficient to make *other than massive nuclear retaliation* futile. If the Soviets can place NATO into this dilemma, they will not have removed all risks but they will have exercised escalation control and intrawar deterrence to the extent that prevailing force balances and war plans matter at all.[30]

The foregoing analysis suggests that, notwithstanding arms control and deterrence complications, the two superpowers and their allies in Europe will be more instead of less inclined to substitute conventional for nuclear firepower. This projection does not do away with nuclear weapons in the background as last-resort destroyers of civilization and, thus, residual supports for the overall thralldom on which deterrence depends. But with regard to the specifics of war planning by the Americans, the Soviets, and their European allies, the drawing away from nuclear dependency for war fighting, if need be, is a trend that will not be reversed. Better conventional weaponry and increased political momentum for nuclear arms limitation come together in favor of limiting the destruction attendant to wars that must be fought. This probably means wars outside of Europe. For the superpowers are now facing an environment in Europe that, at the level of high politics in defense and security, all but excludes resorting to war as a deliberate policy choice.

POST-BELLICIST EUROPE

The coming together of nuclear and conventional force reductions in Europe poses the distinction between deterrence stability and first-strike stability. Until now, the preoccupation of governments and military planners has been to treat deterrence and first-strike stability as two faces of the same problem.[31] If one reduced first-strike incentives, then one automatically reduced the probability of war. This was thought to apply at two levels: at the level of strategic and theater-nuclear forces, especially the former; and at the level of conventional force balances.

The problem of first-strike stability was substituted for the larger problem of deterrence stability for several reasons. First, before both superpowers acquired survivable strategic nuclear arsenals, the problem of nuclear surprise attack loomed large in planners' near-term agendas.[32] Second, estimation of force balances and prevailing wartime attrition rates were difficult enough, even without nuclear escalation, given all the uncertainties attendant to war in Europe.[33] Third, it seemed plausible to assume that the large superpower nuclear arsenals, absent significant force reductions, might themselves become the proximate causes of war rather than the deterrents of it. This was the familiar problem of crisis instability. Crisis instability was not eliminated by having survivable superpower strategic nuclear forces, although second-strike capability was thought to be a necessary condition for crisis stability. Crisis management was also bedeviled by the fallible decision-making processes characteristic of leaders under stress, who might opt for preemption in the mistaken supposition that they were cornered by an adversary who had already launched an attack or had decided to.[34]

The reduction of U.S. and Soviet strategic nuclear inventories seems plausible in the aftermath of the INF treaty and in view of Gorbachev's perspective on superpower arms control. The Soviet general secretary has already made unprecedented proposals with regard to conventional force reductions in Europe and elsewhere. His perspective departs from precedent most fundamentally in its assertion that security can no longer be attained unilaterally.[35] Stable deterrence, beyond the accomplishment of nuclear peace per se, requires superpower cooperation to transform the political landscape. This means several things. It means, first, that the condition of stasis in European politics in which a dividing line between "East" and "West" marks the dimensions of tolerable security policies must now change. Second, the reach of military power projection from Moscow or Washington into the center of Europe is attenuated compared to cold war expectations in both capitals. Third, the Soviets and the Americans, in order to move from the dead center of cold war politics toward something else, need an equally significant movement in their politico-military and military-technical doctrines.

The first problem is to break the stasis of bloc politics without permitting the spectre of German political reunification to escape superpower control. Soviet agreement in July 1990 to the incorporation of a reunified Germany into NATO was a success for U.S. and NATO tenacity, and an important marker for a new superpower security relationship in Europe. A further implication is that, since the Warsaw Pact has now effectively dissolved as an offensive military threat, NATO will eventually evolve into more political than military alliances.

Another issue in breaking cold war stasis is accommodating the economic aspirations of the united European Community (after 1992) to the expedient solutions within Eastern Europe to economic development. The present economic topography of Eastern Europe permits many variations, from the comatose Rumanian to the assertive Hungarian systems. Then, too, the East and West German economies need one another just to maintain the status quo in growth and development, to say nothing of future progress in human rights and cultural exchange. The economic takeoff that could attend the unification of EEC markets carries the downside risk of leaving Eastern Europe so far behind as to direct EEC entrepreneurs outside of Europe for new customers. Economic détente, prompted by *Ostpolitik* and military détente in the 1970s, requires rethinking in the 1990s and beyond, in order to prevent the EEC and *Comecon* communities from becoming more dissimilar instead of less.

The second aspect to breaking the connection between first-strike stability and the larger problem of political deterrence is the military reach of the superpowers into Central Europe. The present extended reach of the Soviets and the Americans into the center of Europe is based on two sources, one military and the other political. The military source is the unique character of Soviet and U.S. nuclear arsenals compared to others.

The superpowers can, with more or less plausibility, extend deterrence via their nuclear umbrellas where others, including the British and French with their own national nuclear forces, fear to tread.[36] The political source of extended reach is the shared vulnerability and risk between Washington and Western Europe, on one hand, and Moscow and Eastern Europe, on the other. Conversely, weaker superpower nuclear forces less capable of providing "extended" deterrence, or perceptions by European members of NATO or the Warsaw Pact that risks are unequal, result in shorter reach and more divided alliances.

Superpower strategic nuclear arms control threatens both the political and the military dimensions of this relationship of extended reach. That is why it becomes so controversial in Europe, regardless of the lay of the land in Moscow and in Washington. Especially in NATO, the United States must engage in arms-control negotiations with the USSR without stepping out of bounds on either side of a narrow zone. One side of the zone is labelled "coupling" and the other, "firebreaks." Coupling implies indivisible fate; firebreaks allow for graduated deterrence, which is thought to be more convincing—and therefore more deterring—than massive retaliation. Too much coupling provides for too little in the way of firebreaks; too many firebreaks erode the perception of coupling. Without firebreaks, deterrence is all of a piece; it can fail only catastrophically. Without coupling, the Soviets may not be persuaded that NATO is indivisible at the level of shared political objectives, although it would be no surprise to Moscow if NATO national doctrines for operational war fighting remained distinct.[37]

A third aspect to transcending European stasis is adjustment of prevailing or recent military doctrines. The Soviet Union under Gorbachev has stolen a march in this regard. The doctrine of reasonable sufficiency (*razumnoye dostatochnosti*)—or in its less expansive variant, defensive sufficiency—was first articulated as applicable to the politico-military level of Soviet military doctrine. This meant the level at which it is decided who the likely adversaries are, what kinds of wars the Soviet Union might have to fight, and other scope and domain issues connecting Marxist-Leninist models of reality to the international security system.[38] The military-technical level of Soviet military doctrine is more specific with regard to the preparedness measures and investment priorities the USSR must choose. At this level, Soviet planners must take into account the finite nature of economic resources, the process of weapons development and innovation, and the qualities of command, training, logistics, and other functions that support military strategy, operational art, and tactics (i.e., the conduct of wars, campaigns, and battles).[39]

Defensive sufficiency has, according to Col. Gen. Makhmut Gareyev and other Soviet political and military leaders, moved beyond the politico-military level and into the military-technical realm.[40] This means that the Soviet military leadership is adjusting to the possibility of a defensively oriented conventional force establishment in Eastern Europe and in the western USSR. This would be in keeping with the declarations by the Warsaw Pact and by Soviet defense minister D. T. Yazov that Soviet and Pact military doctrine exclude surprise attack and aggression by the USSR with either conventional or nuclear weapons.[41] Gorbachev's announcement on December 7, 1988 at the United Nations of his plans for unilateral reductions in Soviet general purpose forces seemed to follow the train of previous politico-military pronouncements into the military-technical realm of force preparedness, structure, and training.[42]

Defensive sufficiency has created debate within Soviet military and political circles, but it has also sparked disagreement within the Western alliance. If defensive sufficiency is fully implemented as advertised, and if the Soviet ground forces are divested of any capacity for surprise attack, then the politics as well as the strategy of deterrence will have changed. Instead of nuclear first strike or conventional blitzkrieg, the weakening of the blocs creates the potential for a return to the traditional unilateralism of the European state system in which plural risks of war replace a singular one.

The first challenge to superpower military reach in the aftermath of defensive sufficiency, political disagreement that is beyond deterrence, might grow out of mishandling the German problem. The freedom from tight bipolarity means that West Germans are free to seek political consanguinity and markets eastward, and East Germans, to exercise more assertiveness in developing economic competency despite attitudes in Pankow. This benign future is at the mercy of a Soviet *droit de regard* over the NATO nuclear modernization and conventional disarmament questions. The Soviets will obviously exploit any division between West Germany and the United States over the modernization of short-range, ground-launched missiles. Conventional arms control or disarmament pursuant to the CFE (Conventional Forces in Europe) talks is hostage to the Soviet assurance that, in giving up fast attack capabilities now deployed in East Germany and Czechoslovakia, it is not allowing for a repeat of Operation Barbarossa at the hands of an emboldened NATO, a reunited Germany, or both.

A second challenge could come from the revival of intra-European political disagreements that cross the East-West border in elliptical orbits.

Economic, energy, and human rights issues all have this potential, as do issues of arms control and force modernization, which are poorly handled by the blocs. Appeals to an "Atlantic to the Urals" zone of demilitarization between NATO and the Warsaw Pact call forth a solution that makes the blocs seem obsolete. If bloc obsolescence is in train, then what is to preclude Greeks from fighting with Turks, or Rumanians with Hungarians? As U.S. and Soviet nuclear arsenals are reduced and NATO and Pact general purpose forces restructured to preclude offensive operations, the ties that bind East and West Europeans within an alliance-based security system will be loosened. Self-help and the management of nationalism will become more important as components of a new security roadmap in Europe.

Stable political deterrence in Europe, especially under conditions of force drawdowns and superpower political withdrawal, requires that the expectation of conflict be replaced by something else. That something else must include the presumption that a single more inclusive security zone would replace two hostile ones. A demilitarized Europe from the Atlantic to the Urals has been an evocative theme for discussion from De Gaulle's time to Gorbachev's. Building such an expanded security zone would require more than dismantling and carting away nuclear weapons, and even more than divesting conventional forces of blitzkrieg capabilities. Several political steps would be necessary beyond these military ones.

First, neither the Soviets nor the Americans must harbor extended security ambitions beyond the territories they or their major allies now control. Second, neither superpower must aspire to acquiring a first-strike capability in strategic nuclear forces. Third, both NATO and the Warsaw Pact must somehow accommodate the twin pressures for deterrence and détente, which NATO has acknowledged in its declaratory policy since the Harmel Report.[43] These objectives are not beyond the reach of military and political possibility even now, but they require a consistency of pursuit that is uncharacteristic of the West in general and of the USSR from the late Brezhnev years until Gorbachev's time.[44]

THE ACI FACTOR

Having fulfilled these political conditions, deterrence is not guaranteed to work, but is only favorable disposed. It can still be rocked by the "ACI factor": accidental, catalytic, or inadvertent war. These are conflicts that can start in a fashion that neither side quite expected, or, having started in the expected fashion, rapidly escape policymakers' control over military

events. However, there are important differences among accidental, catalytic, and inadvertent wars, that are pertinent to future deterrence stability
in Europe under fast-moving political conditions.

Strictly speaking, accidental war is a contradiction in terms. Some
leaders must decide for war as opposed to peace, and some battles must
be fought.[45] Accidental war is more properly seen as a technological
malfunction that spills over into a crisis, and the crisis then deteriorates
into war. In the early years of the nuclear age, it was thought that false
radar warnings, caused by natural phenomena (e.g., geese) or other stimuli,
could provoke a mistaken launch of bomber forces. Accidental war also
includes the possibility of a deranged general or policymaker ordering a
nuclear attack on false premises, as in popular literature and films, or a
computer system breaking down and causing missile launches.[46] Expert
analysts feel that the problem of purely accidental war, at least nuclear,
has been mitigated by electronic locks on nuclear weapons, elaborate
institutional safeguards against unauthorized individual initiative, and
other safeguards that cannot easily be overturned. Moreover, during
nuclear crises policymakers become more sensitive to the possibility of
accidental outbreak of war and, therefore, are presumably more vigilant
against it.[47] The U.S. experience during the Cuban missile crisis of 1962
bears this out.

Catalytic war, in the case of the superpowers, would be a conflict that
begins between their allies or protectorates, probably outside of Europe,
and spreads to Europe through a process of escalation. The possibilities
are numerous, such as expansion of an Arab-Israeli war, war between India
and Pakistan, or war between China and India. Analysts have many
favorite scenarios.[48] Catalytic war is certainly possible, but so far the
Americans and Soviets have shown remarkable restraint with regard to
this risk. Perhaps the most serious incident was the U.S.-Soviet confrontation during the October War of 1973. Soviet General Secretary Leonid
Brezhnev is alleged to have threatened unilateral Soviet intervention in
Egypt, presumably to rescue its beleagured Third Army from the Israelis,
as a cease-fire agreed upon by Kissinger and the Soviets seemed to be
crumbling.[49]

The possibility of direct U.S.-Soviet military conflict was never as
serious in 1973 as it was in 1962. Nevertheless, U.S. policymakers took
precautions in response to apparent Soviet military preparations for intervention, including the readying of airborne divisions in the southern
USSR. The United States ordered a DefCon 3 (Defense Condition 3)
worldwide alert for all military forces, in order to send a message to the

Soviet Union that its use of military force without U.S. blessing would constitute a serious provocation. U.S. and Soviet fleets kept close company in the Mediterranean, and operations were tasked on the assumption that actual shooting war was not beyond the realm of possibility.[50] In 1967, the Americans and the Soviets exchanged verbal brickbats with regard to the outcome of the Six Day War, and on June 10 Soviet Premier Aleksei Kosygin is reported to have told U.S. President Lyndon B. Johnson in essence that "If you want war, you will get war."[51] Kosygin may have been reacting to the earlier U.S. move ordering the Sixth Fleet in the Mediterranean to move eastward toward a better position from which to defend Israel. This may have appeared to the USSR as part of the necessary preparation for an attack on Egypt. In response to Kosygin's threat, Johnson told Secretary of Defense Robert S. McNamara to move the Sixth Fleet closer to the Syrian coast, in order to signal even more clearly the U.S. intent to support Israel.[52]

Inadvertent war or escalation, the third aspect of the ACI triad, occurs when the outbreak or the intensity of fighting exceeds policymakers' expectations, although fighting itself is no surprise.[53] Wars can be started deliberately by policymakers who expect that they will be of short duration or of limited consequences. Leaders are all too frequently disabused of this optimism about the shortness, or the limited destructiveness, of wars.[54] World War I provides a textbook case. Policymakers and military planners in the autocracies and democracies alike expected a short war lasting months instead of years. None foresaw the four-year stalemate that toppled the autocratic regimes of Germany, Russia, and Austria-Hungary and denuded the democracies of Britain and France of a generation of manpower.

In the nuclear age, inadvertent escalation could come about as a result of "rules of engagement," which allow room for ambiguous interpretation of standing orders. Such a situation is not inconceivable at sea, or in the aftermath of dispersal of NATO nuclear weapons from their storage sites in Central Europe.[55] Rules of engagement must of necessity leave some discretion to commanders on the spot. Once engaged in combat, those commanders must accomplish their missions within political constraints. The political constraints are rarely without some ambiguity. Political leaders cannot always resolve the tension between two equally important, but contradictory, objectives: avoiding unnecessary or misguided attacks, on one hand, and preventing surprise at the hands of an enemy attacker, on the other. The captain of the USS *Stark* chose one solution, and the captain of the *Vincennes* another. But neither could have it both ways.

In the nuclear age, the practice of brinkmanship borrows something from each side of the avoidance-prevention dilemma.[56] Leaders want to demonstrate resolve but remain aware that too much resolution can suggest desperation. Moreover, the operational level of warfare can confound crisis management in ways that leaders do not always anticipate. Thus, in the Cuban missile crisis, President Kennedy wanted very much to maintain control over events. But within a very short time during a critical point in the crisis, three confounding incidents made crisis management seem insecure. First, a Soviet surface-to-air missile (SAM) based in Cuba shot down a U.S. U-2 reconnaissance aircraft, killing its pilot. Second, another U-2 strayed off course and entered Soviet air space, causing Soviet air defense fighters to scramble. Khrushchev later noted that the Soviet Union could easily have taken this reconnaissance flight as a deliberate provocation, or as a necessary prelude to a preemptive strike against the Soviet Union by the United States. Third, a second letter from Khrushchev arrived a day after an earlier letter had indicated readiness to settle the crisis on U.S. terms. The second letter was more harsh and demanded additional concessions the Americans were not prepared to make.[57]

Soviet military writers have expressed awareness that modern combat operations even without nuclear weapons will be more difficult to manage than formerly, in terms of the relationship between operations and objectives. According to M. M. Kir'yan, the changed nature of combat operations demands "new methods of managing troops" and new "technical means of exercising command and control."[58] As the enemy has increased active electronic countermeasures, commanders must rely on complex automated systems that provide for operativeness, stability, covertness, and continuity of command and control over troops and means of combat. The preservation of "stability of command and control" under the conditions of modern, combined arms operations takes on new urgency for Soviet planners.[59] There are at least two reasons for this. First, the collapse of battlefield command and control systems may disrupt the plan of battle and bring about military defeat at the tactical or operational level. Second, the danger of inadvertent escalation grows larger as the destruction of command systems proceeds more rapidly, since Soviet (and NATO) communications, warning, and assessment systems for nuclear conflict are vulnerable to imminent destruction during the initial phases of a conventional war in Europe.

The ACI factor acts as a caution against excessive optimism about the ability of "high politics" to determine strategy or crisis and wartime outcomes. Politics does set the context, but the devil is still in the details of crisis management and military operations. Carl Von Clausewitz explained why in his classical discussion of "friction" in warfare, which he explained as the force that distinguished real war from war on paper.[60] The best designed plans must allow for things to go wrong when actual fighting or nuclear crisis management begins. In addition, things will almost certainly go wrong in ways that cannot be foreseen by even the greatest genius; nor can redundancy alone compensate for the effects of friction in all cases. Finally, whereas friction acted in Clausewitz's day to slow down the pace of wartime operations, in nuclear crisis management it may speed up the deterioration of crisis control by policymakers.[61]

CONCLUSION

The problem of political deterrence is more difficult and multifaceted than that of nuclear or conventional military deterrence per se. Deterrence of military aggression in Europe is a necessary, but not sufficient, condition for peace there. What is also required are changed political expectations on the parts of both East and West about the meanings of politics in Europe and the objectives that parliaments and politburos define for their warriors and diplomats. Prevention of nuclear first strike or conventional military aggression can be made very likely by adjusting force balances, while leaving intact contextually inappropriate political perceptions. If the character of Europe is to change without a war developing during the transition from two security zones to one, U.S., European, and Soviet leaders must spell out a transition strategy whose essence they have agreed on. Even this agreement does not preclude war as a last resort, nor does it sweep nuclear weapons into the dustbin of history.

One possible role for nuclear weapons in a relatively denuclearized world is to serve as nuclear "residuals" that hedge against the day when conventional deterrence fails and self-defense forces prove to be inadequate. Chapter 2 explores this possibility through the prism of a very useful Soviet military planning construct, the "initial period of war." Mostly conventional deterrence in Europe, compared to that which is nuclear dependent, opens the door to surprise attack and decisive war-winning strategies on the heels of war's outbreak. Questions of mobilization, deployment, and coalition management, which have seemed irrelevant due to the apparent omnipotence of nuclear weapons, now require prompt attention from U.S., NATO, and Soviet planners.

NOTES

The author gratefully acknowledges comments on an earlier draft of this chapter by Andrew Goldberg and references to Soviet sources suggested by Jacob W. Kipp, John G. Hines, and Phillip A. Petersen.

1. The concept of postnuclear era is explained in Edward N. Luttwak, "An Emerging Postnuclear Era," *The Washington Quarterly* 11, no. 1 (Winter 1988): 5–18.

2. See John J. Mearsheimer, *Conventional Deterrence* (Ithaca, N.Y.: Cornell University Press, 1984), Ch. 6. The issue of conventional force balances in Europe and the likelihood of successful conventional defense for NATO is obviously contentious among analysts. See, for example: John J. Mearsheimer, "Why the Soviets Can't Win Quickly in Central Europe," *International Security* 7, no. 1 (Summer 1982): 3–39; Barry R. Posen, "Measuring the European Conventional Balance: Coping with Complexity in Threat Assessment," *International Security* 9, no. 3 (Winter 1984/85): 47–88; Joshua M. Epstein, Dynamic Analysis and the Conventional Balance in Europe," *International Security* 12, no. 4 (Spring 1988): 154–65; and Eliot A. Cohen, "Toward Better Net Assessment: Rethinking the European Conventional Balance," *International Security* 13, no. 1 (Summer 1988): 50–89. Each of these articles contains numerous references, and the authors carry on the debate in a series of exchanges in the Spring 1989 issue of *International Security*, passim.

3. See Christopher N. Donnelly, "Soviet Operational Concepts in the 1980s," *Strengthening Conventional Deterrence in Europe: Proposals for the 1980s: Report of the European Security Study* (New York: St Martin's Press, 1983), 105–36, and William E. Odom, "Soviet Military Doctrine," *Foreign Affairs* 67, no. 2 (Winter 1988/89): 114–34 on Soviet doctrine pertinent to war in Europe. Donnelly's article is especially useful on the preparatory phase of Soviet contingency planning. Odom distinguishes among Soviet military-technical preparedness for three generic missions: stability of the rear; contiguous theater war; and noncontiguous war, which may occur in several theaters simultaneously.

4. On May 11, 1989, Gorbachev offered to negotiate bilateral NATO-Pact reductions in forces, allowing each side some 1.3 million personnel and 20,000 main battle tanks, along with other reductions in main equipments. See Atlantic Council of the U.S., *Indicators of Change in Soviet Security Policies*, 25 Feb., 1990, 2.

5. I am indebted to Michael MccGwire for helping to put this in context. See Michael MccGwire, *Military Objectives in Soviet Foreign Policy* (Washington, D.C.: Brookings Institution, 1987). However, the expectation that global war will soon disappear as a serious Soviet planning contingency is partly dependent upon Soviet reading of Western intentions. See Marshal N. V. Ogarkov, *Vsegda v gotovnosti k zashchite Otechestva* (Always in Readiness to Defend the Fatherland)(Moskow: Voyenizdat, 1982), 16 and M. A. Gareyev; *M. V. Frunze: Military Theorist* [Original ed.: Voyenny teoretik (Moscow: Voyenizdat, 1985)] (New York: Pergamon Brassey's 1988), 213–14. For the Soviet approach to threat assessment in historical perspective, see John Erickson, "Threat Identification and Strategic Appraisal by the Soviet Union, 1930–1941," in Ernest R. May, ed., *Knowing One's Enemies: Intelligence Assessment before the Two World Wars* (Princeton: Princeton University Press, 1984), 375–423. A discussion of the Soviet view of NATO escalation doctrines is contained in Andrew C. Goldberg, *New Developments in Soviet Military Strategy*, Significant Issues Series 9, no. 7 (Washington,

D.C.: Center for Strategic and International Studies, 1989). See also Stephen J. Cimbala, *Nuclear Endings* (New York: Praeger Publishers, 1989), 21–24 and Ch. 5.

6. Soviet experience with encirclement operations in the Great Patriotic War is analyzed in V. A. Matsulenko, *Operatsii i boi na okruzheniye* (Encirclement operations and combat) (Moskow: Voyenizdat, 1983). I am grateful to John G. Hines and Col. Robert L. Stockwell for calling this to my attention, and to Hines for the opportunity to read a draft paper on the subject of Soviet encirclement operations under modern conditions.

7. For a resume and critique of conventional deterrence proposals, see Josef Joffe, *The Limited Partnership: Europe, the United States and the Burdens of Alliance* (Cambridge, Mass.: Ballinger Publishing Co., 1987), pp. 131–72.

8. See Glenn H. Snyder, *Deterrence and Defense: Toward a Theory of National Security* (Princeton: Princeton University Press, 1961), 3–16, 31, 33–40, 50; and Robert J. Art and Kenneth N. Waltz, eds., *The Use of Force: International Politics and Foreign Policy* (Boston: Little, Brown, 1971), 56–76.

9. Samuel P. Huntington, "The Renewal of Strategy," in Samuel P. Huntington, ed., *The Strategic Imperative* (Cambridge, Mass.: Ballinger Publishing Co., 1982), 1–52.

10. On this, see Mearsheimer, *Conventional Deterrence*, passim and Geoffrey Blainey, *The Causes of War* (New York: The Free Press, 1973).

11. Ariel Levite, *Intelligence and Strategic Surprises* (New York: Columbia University Press, 1987); Richard K. Betts, *Surprise Attack: Lessons for Defense Planning* (Washington, D.C.: Brookings Institution, 1982); Klaus Knorr and Patrick M. Morgan, eds., *Strategic Military Surprise: Incentives and Opportunities* (New Brunswick, N.J.: Transaction Books, 1983); Michael I. Handel, *Perception, Deception and Surprise: The Case of the Yom Kippur War*, Jerusalem Papers on Peace Problems 19 (Jerusalem: Leonard Davis Institute, Hebrew University, 1976).

12. Martin Van Creveld, *Supplying War: Logistics from Wallenstein to Patton* (London: Cambridge University Press, 1977), Ch. 7.

13. John Erickson, *The Road to Berlin* (Boulder, Colo.: Westview Press, 1983). See also B. V. Panov, V. N. Kiselev, L. I. Kartavtsev, et al., *Istoriya voyennogo iskusstva* (The history of military art) (Moskow: Voyenizdat, 1984).

14. Col. David M. Glantz, *Deep Attack: The Soviet Conduct of Operational Maneuver* (Fort Leavenworth, Kan.: Soviet Army Studies Office, 1987).

15. C. N. Donnelly et al., *Sustainability of the Soviet Army in Battle* (The Hague: SHAPE Technical Center, 1986).

16. In spring 1989, NATO's Wintex/Simex exercise sharpened German and U.S. differences over the issue of short-range nuclear weapons detonated on German territory. See *Der Spiegel*, no. 18 (May 1, 1989): 23–27. Soviet nuclear release procedures remain obscure. See Stephen M. Meyer, "Soviet Nuclear Operations," in Ashton B. Carter, John D. Steinbruner, and Charles A. Zraket, eds., *Managing Nuclear Operations* (Washington, D.C.: Brookings Institution, 1987), 470–534.

17. Carl H. Builder, "The Impact of New Weapons Technologies," in Stephen J. Cimbala, ed., *Strategic War Termination* (New York: Praeger Publishers, 1986), 157–73.

18. On the implications of cruise missile technology see Richard E. Thomas, "High Speed Cruise Missile Technology in the USSR," in Jacob W. Kipp et al., eds. *Soviet Views on Military Operations in Space*, STRATECH Studies SS86–1, (College Station, Tex: Center for Strategic Technology, July 1986), 191–220, and David S. Sorenson, "Defending against the Advanced Cruise Missile: The Ultimate Defense Nightmare?" in

Stephen J. Cimbala, ed., *Strategic Air Defense* (Wilmington, Del.: SR Books, 1989), 139–60.

19. Paul B. Stares, *Space and National Security* (Washington, D.C.: Brookings Institution, 1987), Ch. 3, esp. pp. 53–65.

20. See Gen. John L. Piotrowski, "Space Based Wide Area Surveillance," *Signal* 43, no. 9 (May 1989): 30–36 for background on U.S. planning. I am grateful to Neil Munro of *Defense News* for sharing perspective on this topic.

21. Albert Wohlstetter, "The Political and Military Aims of Offense and Defense Innovation," in Fred S. Hoffman, Albert Wohlstetter and David S. Yost, eds., *Swords and Shields: NATO, the USSR, and New Choices for Long-Range Offense and Defense* (Lexington, Mass.: Lexington Books, 1987), 3–36.

22. Patrick M. Morgan, "The Opportunity for a Strategic Surprise," in Knorr and Morgan, eds., *Strategic Military Surprise*, 195–246.

23. Donald C. Daniel and Katherine L. Herbig, "Propositions on Military Deception," in Donald C. Daniel and Katherine L. Herbig, eds., *Strategic Military Deception* (New York: Pergamon Press, 1981), 3–30.

24. Robert Einhorn, "The Emerging START Agreement," *Survival* 30, no. 5 (September/October 1988): 387–401.

25. Gregory F. Treverton, "Theater Nuclear Forces: Military Logic and Political Purpose," in Jeffrey D. Boutwell, Paul Doty, and Gregory F. Treverton, eds., *The Nuclear Confrontation in Europe* (London: Croom, Helm, 1985), 87–112.

26. Raymond L. Garthoff, *Detente and Confrontation* (Washington, D.C.: Brookings Institution, 1985), 771.

27. Col. Gen. Makhmut Gareev, "Soviet Military Doctrine: Current and Future Developments," *RUSI Journal* (Winter 1988): 5–10.

28. John G. Hines, Phillip A. Petersen, and Notra Trulock III, "Soviet Military Theory from 1945–2000: Implications for NATO," *The Washington Quarterly* 9, no. 4 (Fall 1986): 117–37. See also Army Gen. I. V. Shav'rov, "Osnovy i soderzhanie voennoi strategii" (Principles and content of military strategy), *Journal of Soviet Military Studies* 1, no. 1 (April 1988): 30–53.

29. Notra Trulock III, "Soviet Perspectives on Limited Nuclear Warfare," in Hoffman, Wohlstetter and Yost, eds., *Swords and Shields*, 53–86.

30. Components of the Soviet non-nuclear theater offensive in Europe are outlined in Goldberg, *New Developments in Soviet Military Strategy*, 20–23, and MccGwire, *Military Objectives in Soviet Foreign Policy*, 79–89. See also V. G. Reznichenko, I. N. Vorob'yev, and N. F. Miroshnichenko, *Taktika* (Tactics) (Moskow: Voyenizdat, 1987), Ch. I, Part 2:

> But no matter how mighty nuclear weapons may be, it would be impossible and, moreover, unsuitable to use them to achieve all objectives in battle. The fire of conventional weapons, the power and effectiveness of which have risen dramatically, is an important means of completing the enemy's defeat, if battle involves nuclear weapons, and the principal means of destroying the enemy in combat operations in which nuclear weapons are not used.

31. The problem of first-strike stability is quite complicated in itself. See Paul K. Davis, *Studying First-Strike Stability with Knowledge-Based Models of Human Decisionmaking* (Santa Monica, Calif.: RAND Corporation, 1989) (R–3689–CC). I am grateful to Daniel Goure for helpful suggestions pertinent to this issue.

32. Richard K. Betts, "Nuclear Surprise," in Betts, *Surprise Attack*, 228–54.

33. In addition to the references in Note 2, see James J. Schneider, *The Exponential Decay of Armies in Battle* (Fort Leavenworth, Kan.: School of Advanced Military Studies, 1985).

34. For a discussion, see Richard Ned Lebow, *Nuclear Crisis Management* (Ithaca, N.Y.: Cornell University Press, 1987), Ch. 2.

35. Mikhail Gorbachev, *Perestroika: New Thinking for Our Country and the World* (New York: Harper and Row, 1987).

36. Joffe, *The Limited Partnership*, Ch. 5.

37. For more on this, see Robert Jervis, *The Illogic of American Nuclear Strategy* (Ithaca, N.Y.: Cornell University Press, 1984), Ch. 2.

38. Raymond L. Garthoff, "New Thinking in Soviet Military Doctrine," *The Washington Quarterly* 11, no. 3 (Summer 1988): 131–58.

39. Harriet Fast Scott and William F. Scott, *Soviet Military Doctrine: Continuity, Formulation and Dissemination* (Boulder, Colo.: Westview Press, 1988) esp. Ch. 1. See also Gareev, *M. V. Frunze*, pp. 378–79. According to Gareev, the political bases of military doctrine "disclose the sociopolitical essence of modern wars, the nature of the political goals and strategic missions of a state in a war, the basic requirements on strengthening national defense and the organizational development and training of the armed forces." The military-technical bases of doctrine determine:

> what the strategic nature of a future war can be like and for what sort of war and against what enemy one must be prepared to fight; what Armed Forces are needed for such a war (their effective strength, organization and technical equipping); what the methods could be for carrying out strategic and operational-tactical missions in a future war; what forms and methods can be used to train an army and navy (to carry out military training and indoctrination) considering the nature of a future war.

40. Gareev, "Soviet Military Doctrine: Current and Future Developments."

41. Minister of Defense of the USSR and General of the Army D. T. Yazov, "Voennaya doktrina Varshavskogo Dogovora–doktrina zashchity mira i sotsialisma" (Military doctrine of the Warsaw Pact: A doctrine for the defence of peace and socialism), Krasnaya zvezda, 28 July 1987: 2; D. T. Yazov, "O Voennoi Doktrine gosudarstv-uchastnikov Varshavskogo Dogovora" (On the military doctrine of the Warsaw Pact), *Krasnaya zvezda*, 30 May 1987: 1–2 (Official policy statement released by Warsaw Pact).

42. Jack Mendelsohn, "Gorbachev's Preemptive Concession," *Arms Control Today*, March 1989: 10–15.

43. The text of the Harmel Report appears in Stanley R. Sloan, *NATO's Future: Toward a New Transatlantic Bargain* (Washington, D.C.: National Defense University Press, 1985) 219–22.

44. Seweryn Bialer, *The Soviet Paradox: External Expansion, Internal Decline* (New York: Alfred A. Knopf, 1986), esp. Ch. 1, pp. 41–108.

45. For an elaboration of this point, see Geoffrey Blainey, *The Causes of War* (New York: The Free Press, 1973), Ch. 9.

46. The concept of accidental war is explained in Paul Bracken, "Accidental Nuclear War," in Graham T. Allison, Albert Carnesale, and Joseph S. Nye, Jr., eds., *Hawks, Doves and Owls: An Agenda for Avoiding Nuclear War* (New York: W. W. Norton, 1985), 25–53.

47. Lebow, Nuclear Crisis Management, passim.

48. An informative discussion is provided in Henry S. Rowen, "Catalytic Nuclear War," in Allison, Carnesale and Nye, eds., *Hawks, Doves and Owls*, 148–166.

49. See Barry M. Blechman and Douglas M. Hart, "The Political Utility of Nuclear Weapons: The 1973 Middle East Crisis," *International Security* 7, no. 1 (Summer 1982), reprinted in Steven E. Miller, ed., *Strategy and Nuclear Deterrence* (Princeton: Princeton University Press, 1984), 273–97.

50. Bruce G. Blair, "Alerting in Crisis and Conventional War," in Carter, Steinbruner, and Zraket, eds., *Managing Nuclear Operations*, 75–120, esp. 95.

51. Robert S. McNamara, *Blundering into Disaster: Surviving the First Century of the Nuclear Age* (New York: Pantheon Books, 1986), 13.

52. McNamara, *Blundering into Disaster*, 13.

53. On inadvertent war and escalation, see Bracken, "Accidental Nuclear War," and also Barry R. Rosen, "Inadvertent Nuclear War? Escalation and NATO's Northern Flank," *International Security* 7, no. 2 (Fall 1982), reprinted in Miller, ed., *Strategy and Nuclear Deterrence*, 85–112.

54. Blainey, *The Causes of War*, 35–56, 206–27.

55. See Paul Bracken, *The Command and Control of Nuclear Forces* (New Haven: Yale University Press, 1983), Ch. 5.

56. Brinkmanship is analyzed in Thomas C. Schelling, *Arms and Influence* (New Haven: Yale University Press, 1966), 99–105.

57. Graham T. Allison, *Essence of Decision: Explaining the Cuban Missile Crisis* (Boston: Little, Brown, 1971).

58. Doctor of Military Science and Professor Lt.-Gen. M. M. Kir'yan, *Voenno-tekhnicheskiy progress i vooruzhennye sily SSSR* (Military-technical progress and the named forces of the USSR) (Moskow: Voyenizdat, 1982), 280–81.

59. Ibid., p. 282. According to Kir'yan, the problem of improving effectiveness of command and control (*effektivnosti upravleniya*) while maintaining "unity of administrative and combat breakdown" (*edinstva organizatsionnago i boevogo deleniya*) is resolved by various methods, including the skillful reorganization of forces into new operational configurations (299–300).

60. Carl Von Clausewitz, *On War*, ed. and trans. Michael Howard and Peter Paret (Princeton: Princeton University Press, 1976), 119–22.

61. See Richard Ned Lebow, "Clausewitz and Crisis Stability," *Political Science Quarterly* 103, no. 1 (Spring 1988): 81–110.

2

THE TEMPTATION TO ATTACK:
THE INITIAL PERIOD OF WAR

Whether wars can be won in their earliest stages or "initial period" is important to political and military stability in modern Europe. History shows that prospective attackers who anticipate a favorable outcome frequently assume as well that the war will be short. A longer war introduces more uncertainties and shakes up the odds of success. States that seek to deter war, or to defend successfully against surprise, must also pay special attention to the initial period of war. It is the time in which an opponent is likely to maximize success based on deception, surprise, and stratagems. Knowledge of the attacker's potential weaknesses is never more valid to a defender than in the first few weeks or months of war, after which those weaknesses may no longer exist to be exploited. In this chapter, I question how the superpowers and their allies have adapted contemporary forces and doctrines to these conditions, and what future prospects there are for improved stability and deterrence.

Modern war in Europe, should it occur, would almost certainly involve a level of destruction that would preclude protracted fighting on a global scale of the kind that took place in World War II. Much more likely, if any war is at all likely, is a short war in which nuclear escalation is precluded, limited territorial gains are made, and negotiations are conducted between the adversaries while fighting continues. More than several weeks or months of war without nuclear escalation or conventional stalemate seems highly improbable. However, if the political correlation of forces is such that war no longer seems improbable, policymakers and military planners will seek recipes to avoid either stalemated and prolonged conventional military operations or nuclear escalation. Efforts to do so are prudent hedges on the part of professional planners against the uncertainty of deterrence. But viewed from abroad, possible recipes for success may contribute to crisis instability and reduce the chances of avoiding war.

THE INITIAL PERIOD OF WAR

The Soviets have carefully studied the period of time from the commencement of hostilities until friendly forces are within grasp of their initial operational and strategic military objectives. They refer to this as the "initial period of war."[1] The authoritative study by S. P. Ivanov on this subject published in 1974 was part of a broader interest within the Soviet military establishment in the problems of operational art on a theater scale.[2] Having turned away from the one variant war model of the Khrushchev years, Soviet military planners reviewed their World War II experience with regard to strategic operations conducted by several fronts in a continental theater of operations on a strategic scale.[3] Those studies revealed the strengths and weaknesses of the Soviet conduct of operational and operational-strategic campaigns in the early period of war and subsequently. The Soviets would have to apply these lessons in the context of contemporary military theory and postwar experience. Account would also have to be taken of the nuclear "revolution in military affairs," which could not be repudiated as a technological fact, although it could perhaps be circumvented by the proper selection of menu items from policy and strategy.[4]

Deployment of nuclear weapons in the NATO theater and in U.S. strategic arsenals meant that war carried to its extreme would end the Soviet regime and society. Therefore, by the sensible reckoning of any Soviet planner, this expansion of war had to be deterred. The good will of NATO could not be counted on to do this, nor could NATO's preferred doctrine of prompt nuclear escalation within the context of "flexible response" strategy be reassuring in this regard. The Soviets did not draw the conclusion that operational art on a theater-strategic scale was without merit in contemporary conditions. Instead, they sought to adapt their force structure, planning guidance, and strategy to the realities of combat under modern conditions, should war be forced upon them by NATO.[5] The wording of the last phrase is intentional. It was also the Soviet view that their forces would be fighting on the political defensive, whether they were forced into a militarily defensive posture or were able to organize a rapid and decisive counteroffensive against their adversaries.[6] Therefore, substantial changes in the political aspects of Soviet doctrine leave in place many military-technical constraints based on geography and the finite resources for force modernization in the 1990s.

A question, then, for Soviet planners in the 1970s and 1980s was how to win or avoid losing wars in the initial period against an adversary that (1) possessed nuclear weapons and (2) might preempt at least the political offensive if not the military. Operations designed to defeat NATO partially or totally in the Western TVD [Teatr Voyennykh Deystviy (Theater of Military Action)] would have to be fast moving, destroying the main bodies of resisting NATO forces, occupying significant portions of territory, and precluding to the extent possible NATO's resort to theater or other nuclear weapons.[7] Soviet military planners drew from their World War II experiences, with obvious adjustments for the presence of nuclear and high-technology conventional weapons deployed by both coalitions in Europe, the components of a possibly successful theater-strategic military offensive. These included the employment of forward detachments at the operational level, the use of mobile groups for effecting penetrations into the depth of the opponent's defenses, and the prompt launch of a strategic air operation covering the entirety of the theater of operations. These were not the only, but arguably the primary, components of the 1980s vintage recipe for winning wars in their initial period against an opponent as well armed as NATO.

Major General I. N. Vorob'yev, instructor at the Frunze Military Academy and a frequent contributor to Soviet military journals, noted that forward detachments were widely used during the Great Patriotic War (World War II), but only after Hitler's initial thrusts had been stalemated and Soviet forces had the necessary wherewithal to turn to decisive offensive operations.[8] The use of forward detachments during the latter two periods of the Great Patriotic War has obvious implications for wars fought under contemporary conditions, according to Vorob'yev. In the concluding period of the war (by which Vorob'yev presumably means 1944 and 1945, during which the major Soviet multifront offensives against the Wehrmacht were conducted), "decisive" missions were assigned to operational forward detachments, "which had a substantial influence on the development of army and front offensive operations as a whole." Soviet forward detachments during this period seized important objectives at operational depth, disrupted the enemy's system of operational troop control and the cooperation between enemy troops and their rear support, and partially prevented the German maneuvering of operational reserves.[9]

Under contemporary conditions, operational forward detachments might be tasked for missions other than the seizing and holding of areas and objectives. Vorob'yev was writing in 1965, when Soviet doctrine was just beginning to emerge from the chrysalis of a more comprehensive view of combined arms operations. According to that view, nuclear and conventional operations would be regarded (by the 1970s) as mutually supportive in a continental TVD, not mutually exclusive.[10] Forward detachments could now accomplish essentially new missions, including the following: destruction of the enemy's nuclear systems, especially tactical nuclear weapons and delivery vehicles; destruction of small, advancing enemy reserve groupings; elimination of enemy communication centers and control points; destruction of enemy air defense (PVO) groupings, including surface-to-air (SAM) missiles and launchers, tactical aircraft at their bases, antiaircraft artillery and control and guidance facilities; and enemy rear objectives "from the march," including nuclear weapons storage and missile assembly bases.[11]

Forward detachments would not work alone to accomplish these missions. Soviet military studies emphasize that forward detachments accomplish objectives that prepare the way for the work of the main force units but do not substitute for those units. Sometimes, as in the Soviet strategic operation against Japan's Kwantung Army in Manchuria in 1945, forward detachments move faster than their corresponding main bodies of forces. Provided this has no deleterious effect on the progression of Soviet forces toward their ultimate objectives, the acceleration of forward detachments is acceptable and, in some circumstances, eminently desirable. However, it remains the case under most foreseeable conditions that forward detachments, especially those tasked for objectives in the operational depth of the opposing forces, must be accompanied by other force components that are also specially tasked and designed.

These other components are the operational maneuver groups (OMGs)—or mobile groups, as they were called during World War II—and the strategic air operation. Mobile groups are deep raiding forces that are tasked to exploit tactical breakthroughs into operational, and then strategic, success.[12] (During recent arms control negotiations, Soviet representatives have indicated that their proposed force restructuring in Europe may disband OMGs. This might be reassuring to NATO, although OMGs have no permanent, fixed structure anyway.) A strategic air operation is designed for preemptive suppression of the opponent's airpower in the theater of operations. Primary targets in the Western TVD will include NATO nuclear weapons, air defense installations, airfields for interceptors and fighter-bombers, and command and control centers.[13] In addition to this independent air operation tasked to support the objectives of front and TVD commanders, the Soviets can also be expected to employ selective airborne or airmobile (heliborne) force landings in order to neutralize or seize targets in the opponent's tactical or operational depth.[14] Rotary wing aviation deployed in larger numbers and capable of carrying larger complements of air-to-air and air-to-ground munitions allows for the rapid removal of forces from one area and their insertion into another in good time. Helicopters also provide the option of airlifting regular ground troops that have not been trained in airborne landing. Parachute forces also require special equipment, secure landing areas, and favorable weather conditions; heliborne landings allow for the carrying of larger numbers of men and quantities of equipment and for more flexibility in operations.[15]

During the 1970s and 1980s, as Col. David M. Glantz has noted, Soviet airborne forces matured into "a full-fledged vertical dimension of deep battle" and a significant component of Soviet combined arms warfare.[16] Strategic, operational, and tactical landing forces, in addition to special landing forces as probable components of strategic airborne operations, provide a full menu of options for Soviet planners. Strategic airborne forces of the present day would be composed of aircraft-delivered units up to a division in size and tasked for very deep operations in the opponent's rear. They might be saved for the later stages of war when the enemy's forces have been weakened, when they would be tasked against administrative, logistical and communications targets.[17] Strategic airborne forces can also be used to establish a presence in a particular part of a theater of operations, and their accompanying diversionary operations could be tasked to attack nuclear weapons and weapons storage sites, transportation centers, command and control systems, and other targets of opportunity designed to disrupt NATO's reinforcements and combat stability.[18] Operational airborne forces would operate at depths of 100 to 300 kilometers in assistance to front operations and against nuclear delivery means, command and control, reserves, logistics, and against part of NATO army group forward defenses.[19] At the tactical level, reinforced motor rifle battalion-size helicopter assault forces will support division and army forward detachments. Forces landed by helicopter could be assigned to destroy enemy covering forces, to preempt or disrupt the establishment of forward defenses, and to block movement of enemy reserves. Platoon- and company-size helicopter assault units could also be used against nuclear delivery means and command and control installations at mission depths from 20 to 100 kilometers.[20]

The question is whether the additive combination of these components and others will ensure victory in the initial period of war. Prudent Soviet planners must doubt this. They must doubt this on account of the capabilities of NATO's defenses if properly warned and mobilized to delay any Pact offensive. And they must also doubt this on account of NATO's nuclear weapons deployed in Europe and elsewhere. If the Soviets are to have any hope of achieving their war aims during the initial period of war, then they must somehow circumvent these obstacles. In addition, assuming that the doctrine of defensive sufficiency takes hold at the military-technical level in addition to the politico-military, changes in Soviet force structure and subsequently in the operative concepts of front and theater commanders are inevitable. The next three sections discuss each of these factors: the dynamics of offense and defense, the role of nuclear weapons, and the force structure and operational implications of defensive sufficiency at the military-technical level.

THE DYNAMICS OF OFFENSE AND DEFENSE

Western analysts were so bemused by improvements in the Soviet force structure during the 1970s and early 1980s that they failed to notice the impact of NATO's improvements on Soviet planning. Beginning during the Carter administration and continuing into Reagan's, NATO undertook a comprehensive reformulation of its understanding of the role of high technology in conventional war strategy. This could not be found in a single document or in the consensual policy pronouncements by which NATO must paper over its intramural disagreements. But the reformulated understanding of high-technology conventional defense could be inferred from NATO's Long Term Defense Program guidelines on force modernization, from U.S. Army AirLand Battle doctrine and other U.S. writings about conventional deep strike, and from then SACEUR Gen. Bernard Rogers's explanations of the Follow-on Forces Attack (FOFA) NATO subconcept.[21]

The acquisition of hardware and its diffusion into U.S. and allied NATO forces obviously would not take place overnight. In addition, the U.S. and NATO air-land battle and FOFA concepts would be implemented according to the various operational and tactical idiosyncrasies of the national corps commanders who would fight the forward battle in its early stages. The Soviets clearly understood all of this. Nonetheless, they took seriously the refinements in U.S. and NATO doctrine and the projected improvements in capabilities. As early as 1982, N. V. Ogarkov had noted that "the previous forms of employment of combined units and formations have in large measure ceased to correspond to present-day conditions."[22] A new U.S. military strategy, according to Ogarkov, called for "preparing the armed forces to wage a war with the employment of solely conventional weaponry."[23] This contention is repeated by Ogarkov in a 1985 publication. After discussing the nuclear strategy of the Reagan administration as being offensively oriented and designed to make possible a preemptive first strike, Ogarkov notes that the U.S. military strategy "also envisions training its armed forces to wage a war with the use of only conventional means of destruction."[24] What this might imply for the concept of the offensive engagement was noted in the authoritative study of tactics (*Taktika*) published in 1984 under the editorship of Lt. Gen. V. G. Reznichenko and his colleagues:

> The offensive engagement today is more dynamic than in the last war. Being fully motorized and amply equipped with tanks, forces can attack with smaller densities of personnel and equipment than before, and yet in considerably greater depth and with greater momentum.[25]

In an offensive engagement using conventional weapons only, the enemy's first and second echelons and reserves are to be attacked sequentially while moving motor rifle and tank subunits into the depth of his defense. The employment of modern weaponry "increases the decisiveness of an offensive engagement."[26] Decisiveness results from the continuous increase in troop capabilities and their ability to defeat the enemy even without having overall superiority over him in forces and equipment.[27] Although decisiveness was important in offensive operations in past wars, in modern conditions offensive operations are even more decisive still. Motor rifle and tank subunits are capable of (1) quickly breaching a deeply echeloned enemy defense that combats offensive nuclear weapons and armored vehicles, and (2) conducting aggressive combat operations in any season, on any terrain, at any time of day or night.[28]

Note that this assessment concerns Soviet capabilities for conducting offensive engagements using conventional weapons only. Its apparent optimism masks a concern on the part of Soviet authors that these desiderata may not be met successfully in the event of actual war, as opposed to the conduct of military exercises. The issue is even more complicated for Soviet planners now that the Warsaw Pact has virtually disbanded. Much depends on the correct timing and coordination of efforts. This has several implications. First, the Soviets and their allies must achieve some measure of surprise, although total surprise in the sense of catching NATO completely off guard would be difficult to impossible.[29] However, and very significantly for NATO, the improved conventional defense brought about by the NATO Long Term Defense Program launched in the late 1970s and related measures does not, in the Soviet estimate, preclude partial surprise. And partial surprise is necessary if the USSR is to have any hope of breaching a fully prepared defense in depth, which NATO is now capable of mounting.

Second, in addition to achieving at least partial surprise, a successful offensive must rapidly destroy the defender's principal assets standing in the way of operational and tactical success. These are, in the case of NATO, its nuclear and chemical weapons; tanks, infantry-fighting vehicles, and self-propelled artillery; antiaircraft weapons, fixed-wing aircraft, helicopters, and airborne assault forces; and NATO's command, control, and communications system for theater war.[30] The last item, command and control, will not only be targeted for destruction but also for deception, jamming, and other nondestructive measures of neutralization.[31] NATO's political control and decision-making cohesion are included here, although at a higher level and somewhat before operations commence for maximum effect. The objective will be to get Soviet and allied forces into NATO's operational depth early, to disrupt the combat cohesion and stability (zhivuchest') of NATO's defending forces, and to prevent or dissuade the Americans and NATO from undertaking nuclear escalation.[32]

The Soviets assume that they will be opposed by a defense that is resistant to breakthrough and encirclement. Modern defenses, according to Soviet military studies, are established to greater depths and are more echeloned compared to their World War II predecessors. The defensive side has extensive means for preventing a breakthrough. NATO exercises, according to Soviet authors, establish a tactical defensive zone of three to four times the depth of defenses it had during World War II.[33] In order to break through such defenses during the first twenty-four hours of an operation, attacking forces must establish great momentum. Soviet military exercise ZAPAD–81 is judged to have established that these requirements are not unrealistic under present conditions.[34] However, the defender must not be underestimated. The experience of NATO exercises shows Soviet planners that in order to disrupt an offensive, fire strikes must be delivered on the entire depth of the enemy's combat formations. Fire barriers are set up where appropriate, and combined thrusts are carried out against attacking troops that have penetrated deeply into the defense.[35]

Therefore, two important considerations for Soviet planners are (1) the massing of required force superiorities on the decisive sectors of attack and (2) the preservation of control and combat stability throughout the duration of the operation. As to the first, John Hines has noted that the contemporary Soviet planner may be prepared to settle for overall equality or less in the TVD (TSMA), provided the requisite force superiorities can be mustered at the axis or axes of the main thrust.[36] The second aspect, control and combat stability, grows from a greater appreciation of the relevancy of cohesion and sustainability under the assumption of a theater-strategic operation in which nuclear weapons would not be used.[37]

Assessments are complicated by the potential for the defensive side to overtake the planned offensive in mobilization, concentration, and deployment of its forces prior to war.[38] The capabilities of modern reconnaissance systems, weapons, and control make possible as never before the seizure of the initiative by the defense. This is explained in a Polish military journal in an article that is thought to reflect aspects of Soviet thinking:

Now the defender, being able to reach the enemy at distant pre-battle positions, on march routes, and in assembly regions, does not have to only wait for the blow, i.e., for the strike. He himself can make the decision about the beginning of the battle. The choice of the time of encounter has ceased to be an exclusive attribute of the attacker. The use by both opposing sides of powerful strike means can, in a short period of time, lead to sudden changes in the situation, a reevaluation of the correlation of forces and the capabilities of the sides, and, as a result, their intentions. The weaker can suddenly become the stronger.[39]

The author goes on to note that the formation of the theory and practice of air-land combat operations is the most significant trend in contemporary warfare.[40] In short, current and future conventional weapons technology may make it possible to overturn the enemy's plans, to attack enemy forces at great depth, and to inflict decisive losses, whether one is fighting *from the offensive or the defensive*.

Control and combat stability are separate but related considerations for Soviet planners and commanders in their assessment of what can be accomplished under modern conditions when fighting from offensive or defensive strategic deployments. The operational configuration of tailored ground and air units must be carefully thought out, and the coordination (*vzaimodestviye*) among the various headquarters and force components thoroughly rehearsed.[41] Control, according to authoritative Soviet military discussions, must be stable, continuous, efficient, and covert.[42] "Stable" means that command and control must be conducted successfully regardless of enemy pressure, and "continuous" signifies that this must occur without interruption. Efficiency (*operativnost'*) of command and control is the rapid implementation of all troop command and control measures before and during battle, in order to forestall the enemy in operations.[43] Covertness is the requirement to disguise plans and implementing measures in ways as diverse as limiting the number of persons privy to plans, maintaining proper communications security, camouflage, and deception (*maskirovka*).[44]

It is very significant that the Soviets judge that NATO views disruption of the opponent's stability of command and control as one of the primary conditions for success in battle. NATO is also judged to have developed the appropriate means for carrying out this mission, including long-range precision weapons, mobile ground troops, and airmobile forces. The U.S. Army AirLand Battle concept is described in one authoritative Soviet source as a "three-dimensional" approach to operations, with implications for the conduct of the defensive as well as for the offensive. Defensive combat in an air-land operation, according to this Soviet source, is a combination of static and dynamic actions by combined-arms formations and units. It assumes integrated applications of the principles of positional and mobile defense with the purposes of halting an offensive and seizing the initiative. Defense is conducted no less decisively than offense.[45]

Decisiveness implies in this context that the attacker must maintain a tempo of operations that moves faster than the reactions of the defender and that the offensive must not let up. The uninterrupted conduct of battle at high tempo creates unfavorable conditions for the enemy's use of nuclear weapons. He cannot accurately determine targets for nuclear strikes; moreover, he must frequently move his nuclear attack systems.[46] Surprise in operations, which is described as "the most important principle of military art," is not a one-time event but is to be imposed on the enemy repeatedly. Surprise lies at the basis of all the combat operations of the troops.[47] Surprise during the initial period of the war must be followed up and repeated or the success of the entire operation may be jeopardized. Follow-up is important because surprise attained at the beginning of a battle may exhaust itself rapidly. Commanders must capitalize on previously attained surprise and introduce new elements of surprise into the operations of all troops.

Thus, it is imperative, from the standpoint of expert Soviet military analysts, that command and control organs react to the development of events faster than those of the opponent. The operational loop of collection, analysis, decision, and implementation must be closed before "critical time"—the time within which a mission can be accomplished successfully (taking into account the anticipated reactions of the opponent)—is exceeded by control time required by friendly forces to decide and act.[48] If command and control organs are slow to react to events, orders may be obsolete and inconsistent with battlefield events. Delayed solution of problems related to the possible use of nuclear and high-technology conventional weapons can mean a loss of initiative and even defeat.[49]

We will see later that the problem of command and control is by no means limited to the tactical or operational-tactical level (involving divisions and corps), at least from the Soviet perspective. Assuming that nuclear weapons can be kept out of the conflict or that the side prevailing in a mainly conventional war can absorb limited nuclear attacks and retaliate in kind, the question of superior control in a theater-strategic operation becomes very significant. The Soviets and NATO have approached this problem with different philosophies and Soviet re-thinking of the problem will be mandated by the reunification of Germany and its incorporation into NATO.

NATO STRATEGY AND SURPRISE

NATO's flexible response strategy assumes that resistance to conventional attack on the alliance will take place in three stages: direct defense; deliberate but limited nuclear escalation; and, all else having failed, strategic nuclear forces of the United States and perhaps those of Britain and France used against targets in the Soviet homeland.[50] Clearly, this strategy is designed as mainly one of deterrence; critics would say, deterrence only. Henry Kissinger's now-notorious statement in Brussels in 1979 worded the dilemmas of flexible response in an age of superpower strategic parity cruelly, but effectively. Kissinger noted that the United States should not make threats that it cannot mean, or, if it does mean them, whose execution would destroy civilization. He also noted that the "secret dream" of all Europeans is to have a nuclear war, if it comes to that, fought over their heads directly between the superpowers.[51] Intentionally tactless, the statements were designed to galvanize support for a rethinking of the role of nuclear weapons in NATO military strategy. Kissinger's deliberate exaggeration and distortion were designed to make a point.

The point that Kissinger was attempting to make concerned NATO deficiencies in force structure. It had neither the strategic nuclear superiority nor the equivalent conventional forces to dissuade attack or to enforce escalation discipline once the attack had been set in motion. In this judgment Kissinger was not alone; NATO commanders had called in the 1970s and 1980s for improved conventional forces, and NATO committed itself to modernization and force structure improvements under the Long Term Defense Program. However successful these initiatives proved to be with regard to conventional force improvements, they could not remove nuclear weapons from the picture. To diminish the role of nuclear weapons in NATO military strategy, NATO would have to achieve arms limitation and reduction agreements with the Soviet Union. Thus, the Carter administration and NATO embarked in 1979 on the "two-track" solution of planning to begin deployments of Pershing II and ground-launched cruise missiles (GLCM) in 1983, pending superpower arms-control agreements that would make the deployments unnecessary. As a result of the INF Treaty of December 1987, all ground-launched missiles of the superpowers deployed in Europe or elsewhere with ranges of 500 to 5,500 kilometers were designated for destruction.[52]

The elimination of the long- and shorter-range ground-launched nuclear weapons from the Eurasian theaters of operations did not end NATO's dilemmas of strategy and politics with regard to the deployment of nuclear weapons. Nuclear weapons are dissimilar from conventional weapons not only in the amount of destruction they can cause in a short time. They also create powerful political symbolism within NATO of succor or abandonment, of dominance and submission, of shared decision making versus unilateral demarches.[53] In short, the politics of NATO nuclear weapons, including U.S. nuclear weapons deployed in Europe, cannot be separated from delicate issues of sovereignty. He who has nuclear weapons has the finger on the trigger of absolute war, and, as the French have correctly seen to the annoyance of the Americans, a deterrent force sufficient to trigger total war need not be self-sufficient against the strategic retaliatory forces of a superpower adversary.

Because the politics of NATO nuclear weapons are so sensitive, any departure from a sense of shared fate imposes blockage in the arteries of consensual nuclear strategy and doctrine. The more nuclear weapons are eliminated from the European theater, the more acute this problem becomes. Reliance on short-range nuclear forces threatens to "singularize" the West Germans with regard to vulnerability during the early stages of any war. Removal of all nuclear weapons from Eastern and Western

Europe (a "third zero") separates the retaliatory-punishment aspect of the NATO deterrent from the denial aspect, unless the alliance is ready to invoke U.S. strategic forces immediately upon the event of conventional aggression. Moreover, it might necessitate increases in U.S. or NATO standing-ground and tactical air forces during a period of time in which demographic and economic factors do not augur favorably for increases in either. Ingenious ideas for improving NATO's conventional defenses have come forth from members of the U.S. Congress and their staffs, from U.S. and European research centers, and, by mirror imaging, from the Soviets themselves.[54] All have the objective of lengthening the fuse between initial military engagements and strategic nuclear war. Unfortunately, all have the deficiency of depending upon the preservation of some NATO "nuclear residuals" in the event that deterrence fails.[55]

The probability that deterrence will hold in Europe depends upon the dissuasion of deliberate aggression, but not entirely. It also depends upon the avoidance of accidental or inadvertent war through unintended deterioration of a crisis. The period of threat preceding war, as the Soviets describe it, is one in which their armed forces are in great danger of being caught by surprise. In a nuclear war, the ability to seize the strategic initiative "in the first minutes" will have a "decisive" impact on the development of military action and on the duration and outcome of the conflict. Soviet forces must be prepared for the transition from conventional to nuclear operations at any moment. The first volume of 1970s lecture materials from the Soviet Academy of the General Staff declassified by the U.S. government (Voroshilov lectures) discussed the "forms of initiation of war by the aggressor" and, with regard to NATO, specified the following possibilities:

—surprise strikes with unlimited use of nuclear weapons;
—a strike with initially limited use of nuclear weapons and subsequently going over to full use of the complete nuclear arsenal;
—strikes by groupings of armed forces deployed in the TSMAs (TVDs) without the use of nuclear weapons;
—initiation of war by gradual expansion of local wars.[56]

Initiation of war by the United States and its NATO allies through a general nuclear attack was studied as "the basic form of initiating war, with respect to American doctrine."[57] This form of initiating war is the most dangerous and can have the greatest consequences if unexpected and not reacted to promptly. The Soviet authors describe at some length how the United States would orchestrate a nuclear surprise attack.[58] Although the most dangerous from the Soviet standpoint, this course of action is not judged to be the most likely, according to the Voroshilov lecture materials. More likely is the limited use of nuclear weapons, followed by the unlimited use of complete U.S. and NATO arsenals.[59] Of course, it will be the objective of Soviet policy to prevent NATO from taking this decision by dissuasive diplomacy or coercive military demonstrations, or both. The Soviet political leadership probably judges that their chances for doing so are better under conditions of nuclear parity than previously.

Crisis stability in Europe thus depends in part on preserving credible deterrence while, at the same time, avoiding unnecessary provocation. Whether the strategic nuclear and general purpose forces of the two sides can be generated simultaneously to high alert levels without running immoderate risks of war is unknown. Apparently, NATO forces have never been fully alerted; Soviet strategic nuclear forces have been maintained at alert levels considerably lower than the U.S. forces, with the exception of ICBMs, which are in both cases launch-ready within several minutes. The Soviets distinguish among three levels of combat readiness: constant, or routine, combat readiness; increased ("higher") combat readiness; and full readiness.[60] They also attribute to U.S. forces variable levels of combat readiness. For U.S. strategic nuclear forces, the ICBMs are assumed to be ready within one to two minutes. Submarines on patrol are said to require fifteen minutes to initiate combat, and other submarines (ballistic missiles, or SSBNs, are the issue here), one to two days. According to Soviet estimates of U.S. combat readiness, 40 percent of the U.S. strategic bomber force is kept at a level of readiness such that flight operations can begin in fifteen minutes, with six hours required for the remainder of the bomber force.[61] Soviet planners attribute to U.S. ICBMs flight times to target of twenty-five to thirty minutes; for submarine-launched ballistic missiles launched from stations in the North, Mediterranean, and Norwegian seas, ten to twelve minutes; and for operational-tactical rockets, three to five minutes.[62] U.S. forward-land and carrier-based strategic aircraft, according to Soviet estimates, can launch attacks against their territory within two to three hours; tactical aircraft can strike targets in the USSR within thirty to thirty-five minutes; and ground forces can launch an invasion within twenty-four hours after having received an order.[63] In sum, "as a result of progress and development in the means of war and the methods of conducting war, the possibilities of surprise attack by the enemy have increased significantly."[64]

The possibility of a surprise attack on the Soviet Union by NATO is frequently dismissed by Western analysts as a case of Soviet disinformation or projection of their own intentions onto hypothetical Western forces. However, there is some clear evidence that the Soviet concern with victimization by surprise attack is genuine, apart from the obvious historical shadow cast by the impact of Operation Barbarossa in 1941. The combination of sensing and aiming technologies for conventional forces or for nuclear weapons used against discrete targets increases the probability of counterforce preemption. Soviet sensitivity to this possibility was apparently acute in the early 1980s. During NATO command-post exercise "Able Archer" conducted in November 1983, Warsaw Pact intelligence monitored the flow of events according to the tasking laid down by experience and precedent. The exercise included practice with NATO nuclear release procedures. British and U.S. listening posts detected unusual Soviet sensitivity to unfolding events, with a significant increase in the volume and sense of urgency in Warsaw Pact message traffic.[65] On November 8 and 9, according to Soviet defector Oleg Gordievsky, an "Operation Ryan" message was sent from Moscow Center to KGB residencies abroad. Operation Ryan (for *raketno yadernoye napadeniye*, or nuclear missile attack) had been established in 1981 for intelligence-gathering and strategic warning with regard to the possibility of nuclear surprise against the Soviet Union and its East European allies.[66]

Under this operation, the KGB and GRU (the military intelligence directorate of the Soviet General Staff) were tasked to cooperate in gathering strategic warning indicators. KGB members were to concentrate on the political side of the equation; GRU on the military. The KGB in Britain were tasked to observe work patterns at the foreign and defense ministries and in the prime minister's office; to maintain watches over the U.S. embassy and of the precincts of MI5 and MI6; to note any unusual troop movements and increased activity at bases and airports; and to observe any signs of food stockpiling and other civil defense measures being set in motion. Regular reports were demanded every fortnight.[67] The head of the First Chief Directorate of the KGB instructed his senior officers that the Politburo had demanded a special assessment because "belligerent imperialist circles in the U.S.A." were "getting ready for war and are preparing new weapons systems which could render a sudden attack feasible."[68]

Gordievsky's testimony on these points will undoubtedly be dismissed by some as disinformation or exaggeration. Nevertheless, it underscores a Soviet interest in carefully tracking those developments in technology and policy that create potential vulnerability to surprise. In this instance, it was probably the impending NATO deployments of Pershing II ballistic missiles with estimated six minutes flight time to important targets in the western Soviet Union that produced the immediate anxiety. However, pessimists in Moscow perhaps underestimated the difficulty that NATO would have in taking such a momentous decision, even after having been attacked. NATO has never developed consensual doctrine for the follow-on use of tactical or battlefield nuclear weapons in Europe if and after the first and limited demonstrative uses have failed to halt a Soviet conventional offensive.[69] In addition, serious political release and operational problems complicate the issue of initial or subsequent NATO nuclear use. The bottom-up release procedure begins with a request from a corps commander who foresees that, within the next twenty-four to thirty-six hours, his conventional defense will be unable to hold. The request passes through intervening headquarters (CENTAG, Central Army Group, for example) to the Supreme Allied Commander (SACEUR), and then to the U.S. National Command Authority and the NATO Nuclear Planning Group (on behalf of the Defense Planning Committee).[70] Approval is then transmitted back down through intervening levels to corps, and appropriate information is sent to the launch unit. The process is designed, according to Jeffrey McCausland, to produce a decision within twelve hours and to convey appropriate release authority and targeting information down the chain to launch units in another twelve hours.[71] According to McCausland:

The designed planning time from initial request to use nuclear weapons until actual firing is twenty-four hours. In actual exercises, this time has sometimes ballooned to over sixty hours *with no involvement by national command authorities and little interference by electronic warfare assets*.[72] (Italics added.)

Release would not be granted unconditionally; it would be tied to specific requests for packages of weapons, anticipated targets, and so forth. However, in view of operational problems that are not unrelated to the political ones of obtaining consensus on nuclear release in good time, uncertainties mount. Target coordinates nominated by corps commanders when the request for release is initiated will undoubtedly have to be modified subsequently. Fast-moving operations will require that corps commanders nominate targets based on estimates of the future positions of the targets and of their own future positions (forward or rearward). An example of the complexity that results is provided by the problem of target planning for surface-to-surface missile strikes:

> All surface-to-surface battlefield nuclear systems are coordinated through the corps headquarters. The requirements for target analysis to ensure effective results and to avoid unnecessary collateral damage are fairly complex. Analysis therefore requires a significant period of computation time, and the necessary computations cannot be done in advance. All targets have to be analyzed just prior to attack, since both targets and delivery systems are mobile.[73]

These political and operational constraints are among the reasons why NATO has made emphatic its distinction between the U.S. Army version of deep strike incorporated into Airland Battle and the NATO subconcept of FOFA. The implications of offensive strikes beyond those necessary to restore the status quo ante and of the use of nuclear weapons early on were attributed by Europeans to the U.S. Army AirLand Battle doctrine.[74] Even without nuclear weapons, NATO and Soviet capabilities for deep strike against second echelon forces and other vital rearward targets argued for additional concern on the part of both sides' planners about the consequences of even partial surprise.

There is an apparent paradox in the development of Soviet and Western doctrine with respect to surprise under modern conditions. Surprise has more devastating consequences than ever before, and for that reason it is tempting to prospective attackers under some conditions. However, the temptation is modified when nuclear weapons have the potential (1) to be introduced into the immediate battle front and (2) if necessary, to inflict punishment all out of proportion to any assumed gains. Thus, partial surprise, which maintains war below the nuclear threshold, is prerequisite to the exploitation of surprise for attaining political objectives. The question is whether partial surprise effectively exploited can be turned into a partial victory that leaves one side's forces in control of assets representing a significant improvement in its prewar position. For this favorable outcome to come about, some notion of war limitation within mutually acceptable political and military constraints must either predate the outbreak of war or evolve during its conduct.[75] The prospect for controlling escalation once the nuclear threshold has been crossed in Europe is so foreboding that Soviet and Western military planners have all but assumed it away. Efforts to reduce the risk of strategic military surprise and the competency of offensive military operations compared to defense have emphasized conventional forces and doctrines. This opens the door to some solutions but also introduces additional complications into the relationship among stable deterrence, surprise, and war limitation.

DEFENSIVE SUFFICIENCY AND CONVENTIONAL DETERRENCE

Converging streams of military thought and policy expediency have led General Secretary Gorbachev and President Bush to the brink of nuclear disengagement and conventional arms reductions in Central Europe. Even prior to Gorbachev's announcement on December 7, 1988 that he intended to reduce unilaterally Soviet forces by 500,000 (including 50,000 reductions in active duty personnel in Eastern Europe), NATO and the Warsaw Pact were headed in complementary directions with regard to arms race and crisis stability.[76] The first motivating factor was the breakthrough at Reykjavik in 1986, where Gorbachev and Reagan found common ground on the essence of future START reductions. The second was the INF agreement of December 1987, now well on the way toward implementation. This set two noticeable precedents: asymmetrical reductions favorable to NATO, and a verification regime that allowed on-site inspection, of a rather intrusive kind, on U.S. and Soviet territory. The third was the nonagreement or tacit acknowledgment by the superpowers that the United States was not going to abandon the SDI as a research and development program (Gorbachev's concession), but that the Americans would conduct development and testing activities under SDI in a manner consistent with the "narrow" or strict interpretation of the ABM (Anti-Ballistic Missile) Treaty of 1972.

In addition to these incentives for reducing arms or stabilizing the growth of inventories of weapons, confidence- and security-building measures between the blocs moved forward with the Stockholm agreements of 1986. These seemed likely to lead to additional restrictions on the conduct of exercises and other measures to reassure national leaders against the possibility of preemption or inadvertent war. These confidence- and security-building measures (CSBMs) were designed to complement any reductions in force structure intended to make forces less capable of surprise attack or large-scale offensive operations. Along with this, the Americans and Soviets reached agreement on the creation of Nuclear Risk Reduction Centers in each country. These centers would facilitate data clearance and review for INF and serve as potential clearinghouses on other issues. The risk reduction centers had originally been envisioned by

U.S. senators Sam Nunn (D.-Ga.) and John Warner (R.-Va.) as something more ambitious, but their establishment contributed another marker to the series of agreement on accident prevention and clarification of data bases (including agreements on the notification of ballistic missile test launches with aim points beyond national territory).[77] Also contributing to crisis stability or to arms-control verification were previous agreements on the prevention of nuclear war, INF verification protocols and the possible precedent set for START verification, and the U.S.-Soviet cooperative ventures in seismic monitoring of nuclear tests.

The Bush administration inherited from the Reagan administration a framework for the reduction of superpower strategic nuclear weapons. If implemented as described by U.S. officials in 1988, it would reduce U.S. and Soviet notional nuclear charges to 6,000, with a maximum of 4,900 accountable re-entry vehicles on land- and sea-based ballistic missiles and a maximum of 1,100 on strategic bombers—on the assumption of different accountability standards for air-launched (strategic) cruise missiles (ALCMs) compared to gravity bombs and short-range attack missiles (SRAMs).[78] Sublimits had been established on numbers of heavy ICBM launchers and on the warheads allowable on those launchers by the time Bush assumed office, but other issues remained unresolved, including the counting rules for ALCMs and the status of sea-launched cruise missiles. It seemed apparent that both the Americans and the Soviets agreed on the principal objective of strategic force reductions as increased stability, so that the forces remaining after reductions occurred should be more surviv-able and diversified than those prior to agreement. The Soviet force structure would be more affected in the near term by a START regime of this kind, since the balance among warheads on ICBMs, SLBMs, and bombers would be changed dramatically, should the USSR desire to take maximum advantage of counting rules for bomber weapons compared to others.

Even strategic force reductions below 6,000 on each side could hardly change the essential condition of second-strike capability and first-strike incapacity shared by the superpowers.[79] The U.S. SDI program was for the foreseeable future in pre-deployment status, and the Soviet treaty-limited BMD around Moscow, although upgraded in the 1980s, was far from having territorial defense capability.[80] Military planners, therefore, faced the likelihood of strategic stasis, but the uncertainties over surprise attack and offensive operations remained at the conventional level. Soviet capabilities for offensive operations on a strategic-theater scale were judged to have grown considerably since the mid-1960s, both absolutely and relative to those of NATO, and despite the fact that NATO had not been standing still.[81] Moreover, the Soviets had begun in the 1970s to develop a command and control system for theater war that provided for greater prewar readiness, improved operational-strategic coordination at the theater level, and a conceptual framework for military planning designed to put into place the technology for militarily decisive operations in the Western TVD without the use of nuclear weapons.[82]

Soviet military authorities judged by 1985 that the problem of instability growing out of competitive prewar mobilization was going to have to be faced in their planning guidance. In a noteworthy departure from the precedent set by V. D. Sokolovskiy's *Voyennaya strategiya* (Military strategy) in the 1960s, Col. Gen. M. A. Gareyev in his prize-winning *M. V. Frunze: Military Theorist* doubted whether mobilization of all desired forces and means prior to war was either necessary or possible.[83] The Sokolovskiy volume reflected the shared conviction of the Soviet leadership in the 1960s that any war between East and West would shortly become all-out nuclear. By the time of *M. V. Frunze*, Soviet planning guidance and military theory had changed considerably, beginning in 1966 with a major shift toward a priority for the prevention of world war and the nuclear destruction of the USSR.[84] Prevention of the nuclear destruction of the Soviet Union could come about even after a Soviet first strike against U.S. strategic nuclear forces. Therefore, escalation to that level would have to be forestalled (*sderzhivaniye*) and the Soviet ground and tactical air forces in Europe would have to fight below the nuclear threshold. Soviet theater-nuclear and strategic nuclear forces would assume the roles of counterdeterrents to NATO's theater-nuclear and strategic nuclear deterrents.[85]

Even without nuclear escalation, the problem of military stability and the possibility of first-strike fears leading to war demanded further attention. In *M. V. Frunze*, Gareyev refers to mobilization as "tantamount to war" in the sense that mobilization sends signals to the other side, raising its level of awareness and probably heightening its sensitivity to any putative indicators of planning for surprise attack.[86] The Soviet armed forces would prefer to have authorization for prewar mobilization that was proof even against worst-case surprises, but most likely the post-1985 political leadership will deny them this.[87] Therefore, the Soviet armed forces may have to undertake war under disadvantageous conditions and allowing for the possibility of enemy preemption with conventional deep strike. In the view of the Soviet military leadership, contemporary Soviet doctrine emphasizes the prevention (*predotvrashchat'*) of war. For this purpose, the political leadership must be permitted to avoid provocative mobilizations inviting NATO preemption.[88]

The issue of alternate conventional defense postures and their relationship to strategic stability has been taken up by both Soviet and Western analysts. According to the schematic developed by Josef Joffe, Western analysts can be divided into "forwardists" or "rearwardists."[89] Forwardists are those on both sides of the Atlantic who argue that new technologies and strategies for deep strike will disconnect the spearheads of the Soviet offensive from its tail, thus bringing it to a halt. Forwardists rely heavily upon new technologies for sensing, aiming, and electronic support measures, countermeasures, and counter-countermeasures.[90] They are also strategically inclined to take the battle into the opponent's territory by using combined-arms forces for conventional retaliatory offensives.[91] Rearwardists prefer to devise innovative methods for deflecting or absorbing an opponent's attack through the improved use of terrain features; better coordination of the use of standby reserve (territorial), ready reserve, and active duty forces; improved opportunities for operational maneuver on the part of the defender; or a variety of absorption-sponge strategies that soak up the attacker's forward thrusts, pinch off his flanks, and exhaust the impetus of his attack.[92]

The proposals of Western forwardists and rearwardists have been criticized by other writers on several grounds.[93] The most common criticism is that they conflate conventional defense and conventional deterrence; methods to improve the denial capabilities of NATO or Pact ground and tactical air forces are assumed to contribute to improved deterrence. But deterrence in Europe does not rest only—on even mainly—on denial capabilities as long as nuclear weapons remain in the arsenals of the superpowers and their allies.[94] This is so for at least three different reasons. First, if employed against European targets, the superpowers' nuclear arsenals (even at lower levels) can drastically modify battlefield outcomes. Beyond the expenditure of a few of these strategic weapons, the conflict will almost certainly escalate beyond either side's control. Second, nuclear and conventional weapons are commingled in NATO and Soviet general purpose ground, air, and naval forces. Isolation of the conventional battlefield from the nuclear one would tax the Pact and NATO command systems beyond their present or foreseeable capabilities.[95] Third, the independent strategic nuclear forces of Britain and France, the latter not subject to NATO command, further diminish the likelihood that a conventional war in Europe not confined to Germany could be fought without nuclear escalation.

None of this suggests that the status quo in Europe from the standpoint of political stability is the most desirable condition from the standpoint of military stability. If this were so, the Americans, the Soviets, and their allies would not be seeking alternatives to the present situation. The issue is how to make the transition from a condition of conventionalized nuclear stability to one of nuclearized conventional stability, and, within a future political environment more permissive of progress, conventional stability alone.[96]

Andrey Kokoshin, deputy director of the Institute for the Study of the U.S.A. and Canada of the USSR Academy of Sciences, and Major General Valentin Larionov, professor in the General Staff Academy, have developed a typology of possible approaches to making this transition to greater conventional stability in Europe.[97] Their typology includes four variations of strategic orientation with the appropriate force posture and doctrines in support. In each case, it is assumed that NATO and the Warsaw Pact have assumed a politically defensive stance and have developed a preferred orientation, force posture, and military doctrine for response. The first option is that each side is prepared upon attack to launch an immediate retaliatory offensive, with the goal to "transfer combat operations to enemy territory and air-space as rapidly as possible" through military operations of a "decisive" and uncompromising nature.[98] This conforms in some respects to Huntington's notion of the conventional retaliatory offensive and is distinguished by the Soviet authors from a counteroffensive in virtually the same way that Huntington makes the distinction between the two.[99] This posture prepares forces of the two sides for meeting engagements, or fast-moving encounter battles, and necessitates constantly high levels of readiness. Force capabilities suitable for a decisive retaliatory offensive have many similarities with those appropriate for preemption. Therefore, a two-sided capability for decisive conventional retaliation may not be the most crisis-stable posture, although it would theoretically remove first-strike capabilities.

A second posture combines the capabilities for a strong positional defense with those for a decisive counteroffensive.[100] The battle of Kursk is used to illustrate the system of distributing forces and weapons for the positional defense–counteroffensive posture, allowing for the differences in peacetime and wartime operations.[101] The distinction between capabilities and plans for a retaliatory offensive compared to a positional defense-counteroffensive is that the counteroffensive takes place later, after the defender has stalled the attacker's offensive and seized the initiative. The retaliatory offensive, on the other hand, commences simultaneously with the attack. Thus, the defense counteroffensive posture is not as dependent upon the promptness of deep strikes as is the retaliatory offensive. Therefore, it is judged to be more crisis stable. It can be inferred that the counteroffensive, although less given to preemption-proneness, nonetheless represents an ambitious strategy according to which the defender inflicts decisive defeat on the attacker. The defender's counter-strokes would be of operational-strategic (theater) depth and comprehensiveness and would be pursued until the enemy was totally defeated on his own territory.

A third option, according to the schematic of Kokoshin and Larionov, would provide for both sides the capability to rout an invading force on their own territory, without resorting to the offensive outside of their borders.[102] The defender's objective is to restore the status quo ante, and the capacity for counterstrikes is limited to the operational (army group or army) level. An example given by the authors is the defeat of the sixth Japanese Army in the Mongolian desert in August 1939, by the First Army Group of Soviet-Mongolian troops under the command of G. K. Zhukov (later marshal of the Soviet Union and defense minister). The Japanese invaders of Mongolian territory had superior numbers of troops (75,000 versus 57,000) but the Soviet-Mongolian defenders were favored by superiority in armor and other equipment. Although they routed the Japanese incursion into Manchuria, Soviet forces did not counterattack Chinese territory occupied by Japan. Military operations, having begun on August 20, ceased on September 16 following negotiations between the Soviet Union and Japan. Both sides had political incentives to settle this conflict in a limited manner. Soviet attention was focussed on Europe, where the fruits of the Ribbentrop-Molotov Pact would shortly be harvested in Poland and in the Baltic states. The Japanese were not prepared for a major land war against the Soviet Union. Thus, the Khalkin-Gol operation, as it is now known in Soviet military-historical writing, ended one phase of military operations between the USSR and Japan during World War II.

A fourth option reviewed by Kokoshin and Larionov assumes that both sides choose strategically and operationally defensive force postures. Neither the decisive strategic counteroffensive nor the operational counteroffensive is admissible in this option; counterattacks would be possible at the tactical level (e.g., division or lower). Forces and doctrines appropriate for this option would correspond to some Western proposals for "non-offensive defense," according to the Soviet authors. Strike aviation, reconnaissance-strike complexes, tank and air assault divisions, and other

accoutrements of surprise attack and offensive operations would be pro-
scribed according to this option. As a result of these limitations on force
capability and operational concept, victory is possible only at the tactical
level, not at the operational or strategic.[103]

This resume of conventional defense options shows considerable sophis-
tication in the thinking of Soviet defense analysts and an awareness of
predominant trends in Western studies of nonoffensive defense, conventional retaliation, and other aspects of operational art. This "think piece"
is not the equivalent of Soviet military doctrine, either at the politico-
military or military-technical level. But it does outline many of the generic
strengths and weaknesses of points along the conventional deterrence
risk-payoff spectrum.

Several points with regard to conventional stability are brought to mind
after reviewing the generic options of conventional retaliation, strategic
counteroffensive, operational counteroffensive, and tactical defense with
limited counterattack. First, within a given policy guidance and force
structure, there are many possible dynamics with regard to operational
readiness, interest in surprise, capacity for deception, and so on. Readiness
is as much a qualitative as a quantitative matter. Thus, the significant and
unilateral reductions announced by Gorbachev on December 7, 1988—if
fully implemented—are consistent with a more assertive tactical doctrine
or a less assertive one, and new force structures may place greater reliance
upon rapid mobilization, which may cause the opponent to react and so
contribute to the syndrome noted by Gareyev in which mobilization might
be tantamount to war.

In an analysis of the implications of Gorbachev's reductions, Phillip A.
Karber notes that Gorbachev's initiative of December 1988 was carefully
prepared diplomatically and places the West on the arms-control defensive.[104] In addition, the cuts in numbers of personnel and equipment are
meaningful. If we consider the relevant equipments that Gorbachev has
proposed to remove from Soviet forces deployed in the German Democratic Republic, Poland, Czechoslovakia, and Hungary, Table 1 results.

The pertinent question is the impact of these reductions on the Soviet
prospect for deterring attack or for winning wars in their initial period
while forestalling nuclear escalation. With regard to the outcomes of CFE
negotiations and related agreements on confidence building, Soviet military planners have several choices of emphasis. They can argue for a
smaller, more modernized force that is trained and equipped for rapid,
fast-moving offensive operations, a sort of mini-blitz force. Such a force
would offer hedges against surprise, which the Soviet armed forces have

Table 1
Gorbachev's Proposed Central European Force Reductions

Current WTO Assets		Gorbachev Cut	Per Cent Reduction
Tanks	19,650	5,000	25% to 14,650
IFVs	10,688	1,440	13% to 9,228
APCs	13,330	252	2% to 13,078
Tube Arty	8,195	792	10% to 7,403
Heavy Mortar and MRLs	3,980	324	8% to 3,656
Air Defense Guns	3,876	96	2% to 3,780
SAMs	3,227	216	7% to 3,011
Attack Helos	906	36	4% to 870
Combat Aircraft	1,050	uncertain	uncertain

Adapted from Phillip A. Karber, "The Military Impact of Gorbachev Reductions," Armed Forces Journal International, January 1989, p. 58.

historically regarded as necessary. Second, if modernization lags, they may argue for retention of a larger-than-efficient force structure in order to compensate for NATO's technological advantages (which are presumed to be temporary). This force would, however, be smaller than the present force, especially in Eastern Europe and in the western military districts of the Soviet Union. Reductions would be made from baseline 1988 levels in order to keep the pressure on NATO for arms control, which is necessary to provide a breathing space for the Soviet economy. If the Soviet reductions emphasized the elimination of tanks, artillery, armored infantry-fighting vehicles, assault-crossing units, and other components of large offensive operations, the post-reduction Pact force would be putatively incapable of meaningful surprise on the Central Front.

A third option is to restructure the Soviet armed forces by redefining the relationship between regular and reserve or militia forces. This was a matter of some contention within the Soviet leadership during the 1920s. Debates between Mikhail Frunze and Leon Trotsky involved, among other issues, the appropriate relationship between professional cadre armies and territorial-militia forces.[105] The discussion of manpower policy has once again become a contentious issue in Soviet military and other journals, and members of the Soviet military leadership have entered into the controversy. For the most part, the Soviet military leadership remains skeptical of any program that would rely upon militia forces to provide the balance of fighting power in the early stages of war. Modern war would seem to demand of units and subunits great cohesion under the pressure of unprecedented destruction and confusion. This could hardly be expected of forces that had not trained together repeatedly and were not kept at high peacetime levels of readiness.[106] On the other hand, the proponents of a more territorial-militia force can point to quotations from Engels, Trotsky, and Lenin in support of the notion that a truly socialist society requires a people's army in the most literal sense. A reduced cadre–militia mobilization force would be organized for the defense of the Soviet Union against foreign invasion and would have little practical application to global power projection or surprise attack in Europe.

Of course, one cannot look only at the ground forces for evidence of Soviet or NATO capability with regard to surprise and forestalling surprise. As Admiral Chernavin reminded his interlocutors from the U.S. Naval Institute *Proceedings*, the Soviet Union perceives the U.S. "maritime strategy" to be operationally aggressive at the very outset of war.[107] The U.S. maritime strategy under Reagan called for prompt forward operations against the Soviet surface and submarine fleets, and against bases for Soviet naval air, in order to pressure the USSR on its flanks while land forces held the ring in Western Europe.[108] Future U.S. naval operations will almost certainly exploit stealth technology for land-attack bombers and cruise missiles, improved space-based sensors for detection and tracking of targets, and more lethal weapons suites for the prompt destruction of surface ships and submarines.[109] The Soviets will be hard pressed to maintain the present "bastions" that protect their SSBNs and other contiguous maritime assets against U.S. and allied efforts to place those assets into prompt jeopardy. Therefore, Western negotiators should expect Soviet requests to trade off reductions in their ground forces for comparable restrictions on U.S. and NATO maritime forces, including sea-based tactical air forces that might be used to support ground operations in Europe.

CONCLUSION

The relationship between political and military stability, deterrence, and the initial period of war in Europe has been explored. Prevailing superpower and allied forces and doctrines seem to preclude confidence in short wars, favorable outcomes, and conflict maintained below the nuclear threshold. Beneath this appearance that all is well, waters of technology and military-planning guidance roll, and potential maelstroms lurk. Conventional deep-strike systems with the potential for inflicting massive and militarily decisive losses on the opponent raise one set of cautionary flags. So, too, do superpower and allied cuts in the sizes of forces, if they are not accompanied by equal emphasis on confidence- and security-building measures to make more transparent the intentions of the two blocs. The role of nuclear weapons in NATO's defense policy now more than ever requires clarification. The gyration between "weapons for combat attrition" and "weapons for deterrence," with regard to NATO theater-nuclear forces, needs a more careful calibration, since both the modernization and the reduction in size of these forces is surely on the way. Although at lower levels, "nuclear residuals" in U.S. strategic and NATO theater-nuclear forces will be needed by NATO policymakers and military planners to hedge against conventional defeat, to reinforce deterrence, and to maintain military establishments that are inexpensive relative to the cost of switching to conventional forces entirely.

NOTES

1. S. P. Ivanov, *Nachal'nyy period voyny* (The initial period of war) (Moskva: Voyenizdat, 1974) is an important reference and is available in the U.S. Air Force Soviet Military Thought Series (Washington, D.C.: U.S. Government Printing Office). I have profited immensely from the opportunity to read a draft manuscript on this subject by Dr. John Yurechko and from suggestions with regard to sources by Dr. Graham H. Turbiville, Jr. The Soviet journal *Voyenno-istoricheskiy zhurnal* covers this topic extensively; in 1985, it published an especially interesting series of articles. See, for example, Lt. Gen. A. I. Yevseyev, "O nekotorykh tendentsiyakh izmenenii soderzhaniya i kharaktem nachal'nogo perioda voyny" ("On certain tendencies in the changing contents and character of the initial period of war"), *Voyenno-istoricheskiy zhurnal*, 11 (November 1985): 10–20. According to Lt. Gen. M. M. Kir'yan, the initial period of a war is "the time during which the belligerents fought with previously deployed groupings of armed forces to achieve the immediate tactical goals or to create advantageous conditoins for commiting the main forces to battle and for conducting subsequent operations." Kir'yan, "The Initial Period of the Great Patroitic War," *Vizh* 6 (June 1988): 11–17. See also the references in Yevseyev's article.

2. Col. David M. Glantz, *Deep Attack: The Soviet Conduct of Operational Maneuver* (Fort Leavenworth, Kan.: Soviet Army Studies Office, 1987).

3. According to Soviet historical analysis of the Great Patriotic War, during its early and middle stages Soviet forces were forced to fight on the strategic defensive or to limit their strategic offensive operations to counteroffensives on the main sectors. In the third

period of the war (essentially 1944–1945), when the Soviets had the initiative and requisite force groupings, an offensive began with several strategic operations conducted successively on different sectors. The scale of strategic operations increased accordingly. Depth of operations increased from 100–250 km in the first period to 250–600 km in the third; the average daily rate of advance, from 4–5 km to 15–20 km or more; the scope of a frontal operation, from 250–1,000 km to 450–1,400 km. See B. V. Panov, V. N. Kiselev, I. I. Kartavtsev, et al., *Istoriya voyennogo iskusstva* (Moskow: Voyenizdat, 1984), Chapter 10.

 4. See Jacob W. Kipp, *Barbarossa, Soviet Covering Forces and the Initial Period of War: Military History and AirLand Battle* (Fort Leavenworth, Kan.: Soviet Army Studies Office, n.d.).

 5. John Erickson, Lynn Hansen, and William Schneider, *Soviet Ground Forces: An Operational Assessment* (Boulder, Colo.: Westview Press, 1986).

 6. See M. A. Gareyev, *M. V. Frunze: Voyennyy teoretik* (Moskow: Voyenizdat, 1985), published in English as *M. V. Frunze: Military Theorist* (New York: Pergamon Brassey's, 1988), and N. V. Ogarkov, *Vsegda v gotovnosti k zashchite Otechestva* (Always in readiness to defend the fatherland) (Moskow: Voyenizdat, 1982).

 7. Christopher N. Donnelly, "Soviet Operational Concepts in the 1980s," *Strengthening Conventional Deterrence in Europe: Proposals for the 1980s*, Report of the European Security Study (New York: St Martin's Press, 1983), 105–36.

 8. Maj. Gen. I. N. Vorob'yev, "Forward Detachments in Offensive Operations and Battles," *Voyennaya mysl'* no. 4 (April 1965), in Joseph D. Douglass, Jr. and Amoretta M. Hoeber, eds., *Selected Readings from Military Thought, 1963–73*, Vol. 5, pt. 1 (Washington, D.C.: U.S. Government Printing Office, n.d.), 96–105.

 9. Vorob'yev, "Forward Detachments in Offensive Operations and Battles," p. 97.

 10. "Strategic Operations in a Continental Theater of Military Action" in Ghulam Dastagir Wardak, comp., and Graham Hall Turbiville, Jr., gen. ed., *The Voroshilov Lectures: Materials from the Soviet General Staff Academy*, Vol. I: *Issues of Soviet Military Strategy* (Washington, D.C.: National Defense University Press, 1989), 257–314. See also Ogarkov, *Vsegda*, 34–35 for a discussion of the "strategic operation in a theater of military action."

 11. Vorob'yev, "Forward Detachments in Offensive Operations and Battles," 99.

 12. On the application of the mobile group concept to contemporary Soviet strategy, see Donnelly, *Red Banner: The Soviet Military System in Peace and War* (Alexandria, VA: Jane's Publishing, 1988), 254, and John G. Hines and Phillip A. Petersen, "The Warsaw Pact Strategic Offensive: The OMG in Context," *International Defense Review* (October 1983): 1391–95.

 13. "Air Operations to Destroy Enemy Aviation Groupings," in Wardik and Turbiville, *Voroshilov Lectures, I*, pp. 315–40. See also Phillip A. Petersen and Maj. John R. Clark, "Soviet Air and Antiair Operations," *Air University Review* (March-April 1985): 36–54.

 14. James F. Holcomb and Graham H. Turbiville, Jr., "Soviet DESANT Forces, Part I: Soviet Airborne and Air-Assault Capabilities," *International Defense Review* 9 (1988): 1077–82; Graham H. Turbiville, "Soviet Airborne Operations in Theatre War," *Foreign Policy* 13, nos. 1 and 2 (1986): 160–83. The ground component of the 1980s version of the Soviet theater-strategic offensive was heavily dependent on air mastery, including Soviet air and antiair operations that neutralize or destroy NATO C^3, airfields, air defenses, nuclear weapons storage sites, and nuclear capable launchers. Tactical and

operational-tactical desants would have been undertaken by regular motor rifle troops as well as by specialized airborne or airmobile forces, if necessary.

15. David M. Glantz, *The Soviet Airborne Experience* (Fort Leavenworth, Kan.: Combat Studies Institute, 1984), 150.

16. Ibid., 157 and passim.

17. Ibid., 156.

18. *Spetsnaz* missions may be strategic, operational, or tactical. Strategic missions are intended to disrupt the political cohesion of the opponent by creating chaos and demoralization and by reducing his ability or will to prosecute the war. Operational spetsnaz missions in most cases are assigned to front and subordinate commands (350–1,000 km) and would involve GRU, airborne, and army-level units in intelligence (razvedka) and sabotage of a more directly military nature, compared to strategic. Tactical missions would be conducted at shorter range, within 100 km or so, at a lower level of organizational support (division). Spetsnaz operations are carefully coordinated with those of other forces, they prepare troops for operation in conventional or nuclear environments, and—in the case of strategic spetsnaz operations—they require the collaboration of the GRU, KGB, General Staff, and Supreme High Command (VGK). See John J. Dziak, "Special Operations in Soviet Strategy," in Frank R. Barnett, B. Hugh Tovar, and Richard H. Shultz, eds., *Special Operations in U.S. Strategy* (Washington, D.C.: National Defense University Press/National Strategy Information Center, 1984), 95–134, esp. 104–05.

19. Glantz, *Soviet Airborne Experience*, 156.

20. Ibid., 157.

21. For an evaluation, see Boyd Sutton et al., "Strategic and Operational Implications of Deep Attack Concepts for the Defense of Central Europe," in Keith A. Dunn and William O. Staudenmaier, eds., *Military Strategy in Transition: Defense and Deterrence in the 1980s* (Boulder, Colo.: Westview Press, 1984), 60–83.

22. Ogarkov, *Vsegda*, 34.

23. Ibid., 16.

24. N. V. Ogarkov, *Istoriya uchit bditel' nost' i*(History teaches vigilance) (Moskow: Voyenizdat, 1985), 68–69.

25. V. G. Reznichenko, I. N. Vorob'yev, N. F. Miroshnichenko, and Yu. S. Nadirov, "The Essence and Features of an Offensive Engagement," *Taktika* (Tactics) (Moskow: Voyenizdat, 1984), Ch. 2, part 1.

26. Ibid.

27. Ibid.

28. Ibid.

29. See P. H. Vigor, *Soviet Blitzkrieg Theory* (New York: St Martin's Press, 1983).

30. John G. Hines and Phillip A. Petersen, "The Changing Soviet System of Control for Theater War," *International Defense Review* 3 (March 1986), revised in Stephen J. Cimbala, ed., *Soviet C3* (Washington, D.C.: AFCEA International Press, 1987), 191–219. An updated and revised version will appear in Stephen J. Cimbala, ed., *The Soviet Challenge in the 1990s* (New York: Praeger Publishers, forthcoming).

31. On Soviet deception, see Richard J. Heuer, Jr., "Soviet Organization and Doctrine for Strategic Deception," in Brian D. Dailey and Patrick J. Parker, eds., *Soviet Strategic Deception* (Lexington, Mass.: Lexington Books, 1987), 21–54, and William R. Harris, "Soviet *Maskirovka* and Arms Control Verification," 185–224, in the same volume. Also useful are Russel H. S. Stolfi, "*Barbarossa*: German Grand Deception and

the Achievement of Strategic and Tactical Surprise against the Soviet Union, 1940–1941," in Donald C. Daniel and Katherine L. Herbig, eds., *Strategic Military Deception* (New York: Pergamon Press, 1981), Ch. 9, and David M. Glantz, "Surprise and *Maskirovka* in Contemporary War," *Military Review* 68 (December 1988): 50–58.

32. See John G. Hines, Phillip A. Petersen, and Notra Trulock III, "Soviet Military Theory from 1945–2000: Implications for NATO," *The Washington Quarterly* 9, no. 4 (Fall 1986): 117–37, and Donnelly, "Soviet Operational Concepts."

33. Reznichenko et al., "Combat Tasks," *Taktika* (Moscow: Voyenizdat, 1984), Part 3, Ch. 2.

34. Ibid.

35. Ibid.

36. John G. Hines, "How Much Is Enough for Theater War? The Soviet Military Approach to Sufficiency of Conventional Forces in Europe," Appendix X in U.S. Congress, General Accounting Office, *NATO-Warsaw Pact Conventional Force Balance: Papers for U.S. and Soviet Perspectives Workshops*, Supplement B to Report to Chairmen, Committees on Armed Services, U.S. Senate and House of Representatives. (Washington, D.C.: General Accounting Office, 1988) 35–47.

37. Christopher N. Donnelly, et al., *The Sustainability of the Soviet Army in Battle* (The Hague: SHAPE Technical Center, 1986).

38. "Strategic Deployment of the Armed Forces," in Wardak and Turbiville *Voroshihlov Lectures, I*, 205–32.

39. Col. Stanislaw Koziej, "Anticipated Directions for Change in Tactics of Ground Troops," *Przeglad Wojsk Ladowych* (Ground forces review), September 1986, 5–9. Dr. Harry Orenstein, trans.

40. Ibid.

41. On the concept of *vzaimodeistviye*, see Wardak and Turbiville, *Voroshilov Lectures, I*, Glossary, 365, 380, for operational and strategic coordination, respectively.

42. V. G. Reznichenko, et al., "Principles of Command and Control of Troops," *Taktika* (Moskow: Voyenizdat, 1987), Ch. 2, part 1.

43. Ibid.

44. Ibid.

45. V. G. Reznichenko, et al., "Basic Factors Determining the Nature and Methods of Combined Arms Combat," *Taktika* (Moscow: Voyenizdat, 1987), Ch. 1, Part 1.

46. V. G. Reznichenko, et al., "Basic Principles of Modern Combined Arms Combat," *Taktika* (Moscow: Voyenizdat, 1987), Ch. 2, Part 4.

47. Ibid.

48. Unfortunately, there is no Soviet equivalent to the copious outpouring of U.S. academic social science literature on military command and control. In addition, the Soviet frame of reference with regard to the theory of military art and strategy, relative to command and control, is entirely different from the U.S. or Western. See A. S. Milovidov and V. G. Kozlov, *Filosofskoye nastrediye V. I. Lenin i problemy sovremennoy voyny* (Philosophical heritage of V. I. Lenin and the problems of contemporary war) (Moskow: Voyenizdat, 1972); U.S. Air Force Soviet Military Thought Series (Washington, D.C.: U.S. Government Printing Office, undated, 45–47, 106–07, 110–16, and 126–27; P. K. Altukhov, ed., *Osnovy teorii upravleniya voyskami* (Fundamentals of the theory of troop control) (Moskow: Voyenizdat, 1984); D. A. Ivanov, V. P. Savel'yev, and P. V. Shemanskiy, *Osnovy upravleniya voyskami v boyu* (Fundamentals of troop control in battle) (Moskow: Voyenizdat, 1977); Stephen M. Meyer, "Soviet Nuclear Operations,"

in Ashton B. Carter, John D. Steinbruner, and Charles A. Zraket, eds., *Managing Nuclear Operations* (Washington, D.C.: Brookings Institution, 1987), 470–531; Hines and Petersen, "Changing Soviet System of Control"; Jacob W. Kipp, "The Role of Staff Culture in the Development of Soviet Military Theory," *Signal* (December 1985), reprinted in Stephen J. Cimbala, ed., *Soviet C3* (Washington, D.C.: AFCEA International Press, 1987), 47–55.

49. Reznichenko et al., "Principles of Command and Control of Troops."

50. On flexible response, see David N. Schwartz, *NATO's Nuclear Dilemmas* (Washington, D.C.: Brookings Institution, 1987), Ch. 6.

51. Kissinger is cited in Schwartz, ibid., 234–35.

52. Strobe Talbott, *The Master of the Game: Paul Nitze and the Nuclear Peace* (New York: Alfred A. Knopf, 1988).

53. On this, a very useful discussion is in Josef Joffe, *The Limited Partnership: Europe, the United States and the Burdens of Alliance* (Cambridge, Mass.: Ballinger Publishing Co., 1987).

54. On nonoffensive defense, see Horst Afheldt, "New Policies, Old Fears," *Bulletin of the Atomic Scientists* (September 1988): 24–28, and John Grin and Lutz Unterseher, "The Spider Web Defense," *Bulletin of the Atomic Scientists* (September 1988); 28–30. For a critique of conventional defense proposals in Europe, see Joffe, *Limited Partnership*, 148–165.

55. "Principles of Strategic Action of the Armed Forces," in Wardak and Turbiville, *Voroshilov Lectures, I*, 233–56.

56. Ibid., 244–245.

57. Ibid., 245.

58. Ibid., 245–246.

59. Ibid., 247.

60. "Combat Readiness of the Armed Forces," in Wardak and Turbiville, *Voroshilov Lectures I*, 177–204.

61. Ibid., 182.

62. Ibid., 184.

63. Ibid.

64. Ibid.

65. Gordon Brook-Sheppard, *The Storm Birds: Soviet Postwar Defectors* (New York: Wiedenfeld and Nicolson, 1989) 329. I am grateful to Gretchen Campbell and Bruce Blair for calling this source to my attention.

66. Ibid., 330–331.

67. Ibid., 331.

68. Ibid., 332.

69. Jeffrey D. McCausland, "Battlefield Nuclear Weapons and NATO Defense: Doctrines and Technologies," in James R. Golden, Asa A. Clark and Bruce E. Arlinghaus, eds., *Conventional Deterrence: Alternatives for European Defense* (Lexington, Mass.: Lexington Books, 1984), 117–88.

70. Ibid., 180. See also Catherine McArdle Kelleher, "NATO Nuclear Operations," in Carter, Steinbruner and Zraket, eds., *Managing Nuclear Operations*, 457–465.

71. McCausland, "Battlefield Nuclear Weapons."

72. Ibid., 181.

73. Ibid., 183.

74. See Boyd Sutton, et al., "Strategic and Doctrinal Implications of Deep Attack Concepts for the Defense of Central Europe," in Keith A. Dunn and William O.

Staudenmaier, eds., *Military Strategy in Transition: Defense and Deterrence in the 1980s* (Boulder, Colo.: Westview Press, 1984), 60–83.

75. For an expansion, see Paul Bracken, "War Termination," in Carter, Steinbruner and Zraket, eds., *Managing Nuclear Operations*, 197–216.

76. Jack Mendelsohn, "Gorbachev's Preemptive Concession," *Arms Control Today*, March 1989, 10–15.

77. Arms Control Association, *Arms Control and National Security: An Introduction* (Washington, D.C.: Arms Control Association, 1989), 99.

78. Michele A. Flournoy, "START Thinking about a New U.S. Force Structure," *Arms Control Today* July/August 1988: 8–14.

79. See Michael M. May, George F. Bing, and John D. Steinbruner, *Strategic Arms Reductions* (Washington, D.C.: Brookings Institution, 1988).

80. Sayre Stevens, "The Soviet BMD Program," in Ashton B. Carter and David N. Schwawrtz, eds., *Ballistic Missile Defense* (Washington: Brookings Institution, 1984), 182–220.

81. For various perspectives on this issue, see the Spring 1989 issue of *International Security*, articles by Eliot Cohen, Joshua Epstein, John Mearsheimer, and Barry Posen. See also Congress of the U.S., Congressional Budget Office, *U.S. Ground Forces and the Conventional Balance in Europe* (Washington, D.C.: CBO, 1988).

82. John J. Yurechko, "Command and Control for Coalitional Warfare: The Soviet Approach," *Signal* 40 (December 1985), reprinted in Cimbala, ed., *Soviet C3*, 17–34.

83. M. A. Gareyev, *M. V. Frunze: Military Theorist*, 216. Gareyev cites V. D. Sokolovskiy, *Voyennaya strategiya* (Military strategy) 2nd ed. (Moscow: Voyenizdat 1963), 22.

84. Michael MccGwire, *Military Objectives in Soviet Foreign Policy* (Washington, D.C.: Brookings Institution, 1987), Ch. 2 and 3.

85. Hines, Petersen, and Trulock, "Soviet Military Theory," and Raymond L. Garthoff, "Mutual Deterrence, Parity and Strategic Arms Limitation in Soviet Policy," in Derek Leebaert, ed., *Soviet Military Thinking* (London: Allen and Unwin, 1981), 92–124.

86. Gareyev, *M. V. Frunze: Military Theorist*, 216.

87. I am grateful to John Hines for this suggestion.

88. See Marshal of the Soviet Union and Minister of Defense Sergei Akhromeyev, "Doktrina Predotvrashcheniya voyny, zashchity mira i sotsializma," (A doctrine for the prevention of war, the defense of peace and socialism), *Problemy mira i sotsializma* (Problems of peace and socialism) 12 (December 1987): 23–28.

89. Joffe, *Limited Partnership*, 148–64.

90. Chris Bellamy, *The Future of Land Warfare* (New York: St Martin's Press, 1987), 243–73.

91. Samuel P. Huntington, "The Renewal of Strategy," Ch. 1 in Huntington, ed., *The Strategic Imperative: New Policies for American Security* (Cambridge, Mass.: Ballinger Publishing Co., 1982), 1–52.

92. Andreas von Bulow, "Defensive Entanglement: An Alternative Strategy for NATO," in Andrew J. Pierre, ed., *The Conventional Defense of Europe: New Technologies and New Strategies* (New York: Council on Foreign Relations, 1986), 112–52.

93. See Francois L. Heisbourg, "Conventional Defense: Europe's Constraints and Opportunities," in Pierre, ed., *The Conventional Defense of Europe*, 71–111, esp. 106–7.

94. An excellent discussion of this appears in Joffe, *Limited Partnership*, passim, esp. 132–33.

95. Paul Bracken, *The Command and Control of Nuclear Forces* (New Haven: Yale University Press, 1983), Ch. 5.

96. For an expansion of this point, see Stephen J. Cimbala, *Strategic Impasse: Offense, Defense and Deterrence Theory and Practice* (Westport, Conn.: Greenwood Press, 1989).

97. Andrey Kokoshin and Maj. Gen. Valentin Larionov, "Protivostoyaniya sil obshchego naznacheniya v kontekste obespecheniya strategicheskoye stabil' nosti" (The Counterpositioning of Conventional Forces in the Context of Ensuring Strategic Stability), *Mirovaya ekonomika i mezhdunarodnye otnosheniya* 6 (1988): 23–31.

98. Ibid.

99. The distinction between conventional retaliation and counteroffensive is explained in Huntington, "Renewal of Strategy."

100. Kokoshin and Larionov, "Confrontation of Conventional Forces."

101. Andrey Kokoshin and Maj. Gen. Valentin Larionov, "The Battle of Kursk in Light of Contemporary Defensive Doctrine," *Mirovaya ekonomika i mezhdunarodnye otnosheniya*, 8 (1987): 32–40. Translated by Kent D. Lee. I am grateful to Peter Adams for calling this source to my attention.

102. Kokoshin and Larionov, "Confrontation of Conventional Forces."

103. Ibid.

104. Phillip A. Karber, "The Military Impact of the Gorbachev Reductions," *Armed Forces Journal International* January, 1989: 54–64.

105. See Gareyev's discussion in *M. V. Frunze: Military Theorist*, 108–9.

106. Martin Van Creveld, *Fighting Power: German and U.S. Army Performance, 1939–45* (Westport, Conn.: Greenwood Press, 1982).

107. See the interview with Admiral Chernavin in *Proceedings* of the U.S. Naval Institute, February 1989, 75–79.

108. There is now a large volume of material on U.S. maritime strategy. Capt. Peter N. Swartz, USN, has published several editions of his article, "Contemporary U.S. Naval Strategy: A Bibliography," which appeared in the January 1986 issue of Naval Institute *Proceedings*. This issue also contained the authoritative public exposition of the Reagan administration maritime strategy by Adm. James D. Watkins, USN, then chief of naval operations. For an assessment of U.S. maritime strategy beyond the Reagan years, see Rear Adm. William A. Owens, USN, and Comdr. James A. Moseman, USN, "The Maritime Strategy: Looking Ahead," *Proceedings* of the U.S. Naval Institute, February 1989, 24–33.

109. Owens and Moseman, "The Maritime Strategy: Looking Ahead," 24–33.

3

LIMITING WAR: ON THE EXTENSION OF DETERRENCE INTO MILITARY CONFLICT

"CONVENTIONAL" DETERRENCE?

Chapter 2 considered the prospects for the outbreak of war in a period of transition from primarily nuclear to primarily conventional deterrence in Europe. This chapter supposes that efforts to prevent war may not always succeed, and it asks what the implications are for present and future superpower strategy. Can war under present or future conditions of technology and policy, and between superpowers and their allies, be limited? No question is more difficult to answer than this. The mere posing of the question creates intellectual perturbations among those who are dedicated to the proposition that deterrence simply must not fail in Europe, or in any direct U.S.-Soviet confrontation elsewhere.

This may be well and good, but when one extends the notion of deterrence into conventional war, and especially into general coalition war between NATO and the Warsaw Pact, one borrows from a bank with dwindling assets. The curiosity of the 1980s was the fascination of European and U.S. strategists (who often were of different ideological persuasions) with "conventional deterrence," as if concepts developed from nuclear strategy could be easily adapted to conventional. The assumption was that the logic of deterrence could explain historical outbreaks of

This chapter includes material that first appeared in my monograph, *Nuclear War Termination*, published by the Strategic and Defence Studies Centre, Research School of Pacific Studies, The Australian National University, in 1989. I am grateful to Professor Desmond Ball for his encouragement of my research on this topic.

conventional war, regardless of time and place, since deterrence was in essence a psychological process. The psychology of deterrence was thought to be a useful explanatory paradigm for small and larger wars, old and new wars, and wars in all types of international systems.

This movement to import the concepts of nuclear deterrence strategy into the analysis of conventional war began with John Mearsheimer's highly regarded work *Conventional Deterrence*.[1] This study focussed the attention of scholars on the historical record of futile efforts to prevent war and asked whether there were any consistent patterns of explanations for these failures. It turned out that there were important strategic patterns. Mearsheimer found that a prospective attacker who could contemplate with high probability of success a rapid and decisive victory, or blitzkrieg, was more likely to start a war than one who faced an extended war of attrition with uncertain outcome.[2]

Mearsheimer's careful analysis, like that of many academic scholars, then trickled down to a larger academic and pubic audience. The term "conventional deterrence" became *au courant* among many users who had their own policy or bureaucratic agendas. What many of these second-generation proponents of conventional deterrence did not realize was how dependent the logic of deterrence was on the conceptual frameworks developed for the analysis of nuclear strategy. For the logic of nuclear strategy is fundamentally different from the logic of conventional strategy. This is not only because nuclear weapons can destroy more things within a short time, compared to non-nuclear weapons.

The major reason why nuclear strategy must be different from conventional strategy is that nuclear weapons carry symbolism that other weapons do not. Robert Jervis has identified a phenomenon that he calls "conventionalization" of nuclear strategy, of which he is rightly critical.[3] Conventionalization of nuclear strategy leads to arguments that wars can be fought and won with nuclear weapons in the same way that they once were fought with conventional weapons. It is important to understand that the conventionalization of nuclear strategy is only one-half of this problem. The other half is the nuclearization of conventional strategy.[4]

The nuclearization of conventional strategy begins with the labelling of all forms of dissuasion as "deterrent" situations. Strategic dissuasion of prospective attackers by well-prepared defenders certainly preceded the nuclear age.[5] Attackers who backed up from the brink prior to the advent of nuclear weapons did so for the most basic of reasons: They could not write a scenario in which the armed forces of the opponent could be defeated in battle. Before nuclear weapons, defeat of the opponent's armed forces in battle was *prerequisite* to fulfilling the political objective of causing the opponent's government to capitulate to your policy demands. The strongest effort was made by proponents of strategic airpower between World War I and World War II to deny this axiom. The records of World War II settled the issue decisively: Strategic air bombardment prior to the nuclear age could not by itself win wars involving major powers on opposite sides. In the war against Germany and Japan, almost the opposite was the case: Air bombardment became significant only after U.S., Soviet, and Allied ground forces had punished the German war machine significantly and had rolled back its glacis from two directions.[6]

After nuclear weapons this dependency on defeating the enemy's armed forces in battle, as a necessary prelude to imposing one's political demands upon his government and society, no longer existed. Now the governments and societies of prospective opponents could be coerced "over the heads" of their general purpose armies and fleets. This not only made war quicker and deadlier in a technical sense. It also changed the relationship between force and policy in a simple, yet profound, way. Nuclear weapons were weapons of coercion, not weapons for actual combat. This fact was not at first appreciated among scholars and government officials, and it is still widely disputed. A profound gulf exists at present (in the later 1980s) between the military technologists in weapons laboratories, who promise "cleaner" and more "surgical" nuclear weapons for the future, and the political leaderships in Western societies, who have all but abandoned the idea of nuclear first-use despite its residual character in NATO declaratory doctrine.[7]

The dissuasion provided by conventional forces derives from what Glenn Snyder termed "deterrence by denial," as opposed to "deterrence by punishment," which was thought to be characteristic of nuclear forces.[8] This very important distinction nevertheless contributed to linguistic confusion: The term "deterrence by denial" is almost self-contradictory. A better term would have been "dissuasion by threat of successful defense," since "defense" in this context means defeating the invader's armies and holding territory. A *deterrent* force by definition includes a *punishment* component, above and beyond that inherent in the defender's resistance to the attacker's invading forces. Without the notion of punishment inflicted above and beyond the immediate costs to attacking forces, the concept of deterrence loses its center of gravity. Deterrence can operate *whether or not the attacker expects to succeed in battle*, if the defender can nevertheless inflict politically unacceptable damage to the attacker's forces and society in return.

Therefore, successful deterrence has more to do with coercion than with war. This is the most important insight to be derived from Thomas Schelling's work on nuclear strategy.[9] Nuclear weapons lend themselves to making ugly threats for the purpose of avoiding war, not prevailing in it. The despicable character of nuclear weapons is what makes them politically useful, both in peacetime and during crises. However, nuclear weapons also carry as coercive instruments the potential to become sorcerer's apprentices. If they are believed to be actually useful in war, as opposed to being credible deterrents of war, then they may become the proximate causes of war. This is the familiar problem of preemption, in which one side attacks another for fear of being subject to attack first.[10] Notice how different this is from the relationship between force and policy in the prenuclear age. At that time, it made less sense to argue that the weapons for war could also be the proximate causes of it because there was more time to reconsider a decision even after war had broken out. Unlike conventional forces, nuclear weapons—especially plentiful strategic nuclear weapons deployed in diversified ways—must be operated on hair triggers. This is because of the speed with which they can destroy one another and, thus, make preemption seem feasible to desperate attackers.

It has been argued that there is nothing new about this situation of time urgency in the relationship between force and policy based on weapons' characteristics. The situation preceding World War I during the July crisis of 1914, for example, is often compared to the temptation for preemption that might be characteristic of a superpower nuclear crisis. There is an important similarity in the two situations, having to do with the command and control systems for the use of military forces. In 1914, as in the present age, command systems did not provide for the flexible mobilization of forces and means in order to send deliberate signals prior to war, or to keep war restrained after it began. This might also be true of nuclear command and control systems during a future superpower crisis.[11] I will say more about this in a later section of this chapter.

However, it is important not to overtax the analogy between the mobilization systems of the great powers in July 1914 and the present relationship between nuclear weapons and U.S. or Soviet foreign policy. The analogy breaks down with respect to the awareness of contemporary political leaders of the consequences of having even a small number of nuclear weapons strike their societies. As a result of scientific facts revealed in open publications and other sources, U.S. and Soviet leaders can have no doubt that general nuclear war would be catastrophic. And even "limited" nuclear war has no necessary absolution from escalation into a world war destructive of U.S., Soviet, and other societies. It is very significant that the Soviet political and military leaderships have acknowledged this point publicly since 1977, and with greater emphasis subsequently.[12] The political leaders of World War I entered into war with entirely different expectations: They foresaw a short, victorious war that would undoubtedly result in a postwar increase in their political and military status.[13] If we judge that prewar expectations about postwar outcomes held by political leaders are important determinants of the decision for war or peace, then the Soviet general secretary and the U.S. president operate in an entirely different context from the Russian czar, German kaiser and British prime minister of 1914.

Nuclear war could still happen, even with smaller arsenals than are presently deployed by the Americans and Soviets. History provides plenty of evidence that leaders act against the presumptions of rational decision making. However, this observation, supported by much of the research on decision making related to international crisis and war, cuts against the assumption that there is such a thing as conventional deterrence comparable to nuclear deterrence.[14] The literature on psychology of deterrence only reinforces the conclusion that conventional deterrence is highly failure prone, and for very good reasons. The possibility of surprise and initiative leading to victory in a short war, coupled with suitable political antagonism, has proved an irresistible temptation to many heads of state. The temptation existed because the possible outcomes of battlefield encounters, however unfavorable they might be, did not include the destruction of the attacker's society regardless of the performance of his armed forces. My argument in this is disputed by fashionable schools of nuclear strategy, which contend that the performance of U.S. nuclear weapons relative to Soviet would matter greatly, and that a suitable margin of superiority would provide victory for one side or the other.[15] I do not agree with this position and will let the issue stand for the moment; I will return to it later.

The immediate point is that "irrational" leaders (whether deemed so by the calculus of Bentham, Freud, or Rousseau is rarely specified) abound, and so deterrence might fail despite the dread of nuclear punishment and the widespread deployment of nuclear weapons. And so it might; the issue is one of likelihoods and uncertainties, sprinkled with a healthy dose of common sense. And common sense suggests that there is a worst case to be avoided at all costs: a failure of conventional deterrence followed by a nuclear war born of escalation. This is precisely the scenario for which NATO and the Warsaw Pact may be headed with conventional emphasis deterrents that are still backed up by nuclear weapons, but by fewer and only the most destructive. The point that nuclear weapons exist for coercion, not fighting, should be underscored here. Various technology and policy studies have suggested that smaller and more discriminating nuclear weapons, with improved accuracies and terminal homing, could re-conventionalize nuclear war. Policy planners would no longer be so fearful of nuclear escalation if the first blows involved smaller detonations precisely targeted and having lesser degrees of collateral damage.

However, this effort to de-fang nuclear weapons by the application of technology for precision aiming and reduced collateral damage may remove the most important benefit that nuclear weapons convey. This is the inappropriateness of those weapons for any use other than to destroy the social values of the opponent in retaliation for aggression—despite the opponent's ability to prevail on the battlefield. For, by making the opponent's calculus of military victory irrelevant to the social outcome, nuclear weapons separate the existential defeat of civilization from the sovereign control of the state. Superpower nuclear weapons transfer sovereignty to a nuclear social contract that demands that Leviathan (nuclear deterrence) be acknowledged as decisive for total war *and* for limited war also. It is for this reason that the feared "stability-instability paradox," that superpower nuclear stalemate made it easier to engage in war below the nuclear threshold, did not come about.[16] Superpower conflicts below the nuclear threshold did not break out as compensation for strategic nuclear stalemate because NATO and Warsaw Pact conventional defense forces are connected by strategy and policy to nuclear Leviathans that promise to obliterate the distinction between state and society.

It also follows that, if Leviathan is dethroned and nuclear Lilliputians are in place, then fightable wars for statist purposes may seem reasonable again. NATO's dissuasion would reside in "usable" nuclear and conventional forces, but not in the threat of absolutely unacceptable punishment. There are two schools of thought about this eventuality: One fears that usable nuclear weapons will fail to deter and will bring on the very war they are designed to help prevent; the other, that usable nuclear weapons are a necessary component for credible deterrence. The second school cannot have it both ways, though. If nuclear weapons are for battlefield use as "force multipliers," then they are being used in the same way as conventional weapons; that is, they are *not* being used as deterrents. It might be objected that this is not so: Battlefield nuclear weapons are connected by the Great Chain of Deterrence to theater and strategic nuclear forces. This is the NATO rhetoric, not a political or strategic fact. Nuclear weapons are only connected to the Great Chain of Deterrence if they are part of a punishment capability, not a denial one; otherwise, they are performing the same function as conventional forces, although at higher risk and with more inadvertent destruction.

Aspects of this mostly theoretical discussion must be deferred until the concluding chapter. Until these issues are resolved in policy and in strategic planning, little closure can be obtained on the matter of controlling escalation in Europe. I will spell out the reasons for this in the sections of this chapter that follow.

NATO STRATEGY

NATO has long presumed—and embodied in its declaratory "flexible response" strategy dating from 1967—that escalation in Europe can be graduated into increments of conventional defense, deliberate but controlled escalation, and strategic nuclear war involving superpower homelands.[17] This bonding between conventional denial capabilities and nuclear retaliation was judged necessary on account of the alleged disparity between NATO and the Warsaw Pact in conventional forces forward deployed, or capable of being rapidly mobilized, for war on the Central Front. The U.S. forces forward deployed in the Federal Republic of Germany, however, carried another message. They would become involved in "conventional" war immediately, and with highly symbolic consequences. The Russians could not attack "NATO Europe" without attacking North America, in the sense that U.S. forces under U.S. commanders (although under the command of "NATO" SACEUR, who is a U.S. general) would be fighting and dying immediately. The impact on U.S. public opinion could be easily imagined; those soldiers forward deployed on the East-West border were a "Lusitania force" designed to invoke U.S. public wrath for revenge. Notwithstanding their contribution to NATO denial capabilities, the U.S. corps in West Germany had additional—and more symbolic—functions, which the Soviet war planner could not overlook.

This symbolism of U.S. general purpose forces deployed in Western Europe was complemented by the administrative and organizational arrangements by which NATO would operate. In theory and according to the dictates of NATO and U.S. policy, nuclear weapons will not be used in wartime without the most careful policy review and the most extensive administrative deliberations. The time it would supposedly take a corps commander's request to work its way up the NATO chain of command, to receive the appropriate approvals, and to find its way back down again might take as many as sixty hours.[18] Were this the only chain of command by which the nuclear release could be granted, it is doubtful that the threat to employ short-range nuclear weapons promptly, once war had begun, would remain credible.

The nominal procedure for "bottom up" release is a clue that in wartime, NATO is not fully dependent upon this mechanism. It has other procedures by which the time from perceived need to nuclear release can be accelerated. In addition, the various national nuclear forces of Britain, France, and the United States can receive authorization to launch their respective weapons regardless of judgments by the higher political and military authorities in NATO. This arguably reinforces deterrence, since the Soviets' calculations become more complicated, but after war has begun it may play havoc with the control of escalation. Then, too, NATO has less to say about the British or French decisions to invoke their strategic retaliatory forces but perhaps more influence (certainly in the British case) over the use of tactical nuclear weapons of sub-INF ranges. The tactical nuclear weapons that remain after the INF treaty eliminations must be of ranges less than 500 kilometers; these include air-delivered and ground-launched weapons, while additional nuclear weapons assigned to targets in Western or Eastern Europe are presumably based at sea.

As Paul Bracken has noted, the organizational difficulties in controlling escalation with force structures and doctrines now prevailing in Europe are immense.[19] U.S. and other NATO general purpose forces have nuclear capable launchers distributed among armies, fleets, and tactical air forces. The U.S. weapons not based at sea are safeguarded against accidental or unauthorized use by electronic locks, which can be unlocked only by appropriate codes, released at the direction of the president of the United States or a lawful successor.[20] Under normal peacetime conditions this procedure raises few questions. The main concern is to prevent terrorists from getting hold of warheads from nuclear weapons storage sites in which they are kept under guard.

During an intense superpower or NATO–PACT crisis, however, the simple problem of protection is compounded by the corollary concern over vulnerability. If the weapons are not dispersed from the small number of storage sites in which they are concentrated, they can be destroyed easily by Soviet attackers, even without using nuclear weapons. Thus, dispersal becomes prerequisite for prelaunch survivability once the Soviets have given evidence of serious preparation for war. Dispersal of the warheads from their storage igloos raises other issues, though. Dispersal does not mean that the warheads will be mated immediately with their intended launch vehicles. Nor is it necessary that warheads, having been dispersed, will be armed immediately. Some weapons will be available on platforms such as Quick Reaction Aircraft, which will not require dispersal for prelaunch survivability. The tendency of higher level commanders and of politicians will be to husband authority to use nuclear weapons even if the risks of having forward-deployed weapons overrun are thereby increased. As Gregory F. Treverton has noted, if the stark choice between using or losing nuclear weapons is presented to NATO political leaders as such, they will prefer to lose them.[21]

The choice is unlikely to be presented so starkly. Escalation may not be as deliberate as that. The nuclear threshold may be eased across instead of being violated with a thunderclap. This has serious consequences for the subsequent process of escalation, and for the probabilities of controlling it.

This problem of easing across the nuclear threshold is presented by the decision to disperse nuclear weapons in Europe from their storage sites to locations proximate to their intended launch vehicles. Let us assume that launchers and warheads are not yet mated, nor warheads armed. However, the movements to relocate warheads from their storage bunkers will be noted by Soviet intelligence takers using electronic and other means of gathering information. The Soviet collectors may also know whether, and when, NATO has decided to arm the warheads that have been dispersed. There is reason to be pessimistic about NATO's capabilities for concealing this decision for very long; within minutes if not sooner, Soviet commanders will learn that NATO has prepared itself for nuclear first-use or for second strike. Soviet SIGINT (Signals Intelligence) capabilities in Western Europe are impressive, and there is some evidence from previous NATO exercises that decisions to "go nuclear" were quickly and correctly understood by putative Warsaw Pact adversaries.[22]

SOVIET RESPONSES

What the Soviets might do in response to a raising of NATO nuclear alert levels, dispersal of nuclear warheads, or arming of those warheads cannot be known ahead of time, even by the Soviets themselves.[23] One can draw from the Soviet military literature statements of general principles. The effects of NATO decisions on Soviet operational procedure are harder to surmise. As to principles, one might note that Soviet military writers greatly stress the importance of surprise as a principle in military art. Marshal N. V. Ogarkov gave evidence of this in his frequently cited book published in 1982, *Vsegda v gotovnosti k zashchite Otechestva* (Always in readiness to defend the homeland):

> The situation has become sharply altered under present conditions. The element of surprise already played a determinate role in World War II. Today it is becoming a factor of the greatest strategic significance. The question of shifting the armed forces and the management of the national economy onto a war footing and their mobilization deployment in a short time period is much more critical today.[24]

This has been underscored by other Soviet military writers and has been "traditional" in Soviet military thought since the death of Stalin. It assumes special significance, according to contemporary Soviet and Warsaw Pact military writers, under present-day conditions for two reasons. First, the nuclear revolution in military affairs has created the possibility of accomplishing strategic aims in a short time period. Prior to the nuclear age, it was necessary to defeat the armed forces of the opponent by a sequence of tactical victories building into operational ones, and operational into strategic. Nuclear weapons made it possible to accomplish strategic aims at the outset of war, perhaps within the first few minutes.[25]

Second, by the 1970s Soviet military writers recognized that a second, postnuclear revolution in military affairs was beginning. It did not repudiate the nuclear revolution but set alongside it the possibility of accomplishing decisive aims at the theater-strategic scale with conventional weapons. Marshal N. V. Ogarkov noted in 1985 that the development of improved conventional weapons would have important implications for NATO strategy and, therefore, for Soviet military planners. NATO, according to Ogarkov, was prepared to exploit new technology in order to develop a new concept of combined air and ground operations for the use of its forces within the European theater of operations.[26] The NATO concept, according to Ogarkov, assumed "the sudden unleashing of combat operations simultaneously by air, naval and ground forces with the wide use of the latest conventional, highly accurate weapons and reconnaissance-strike systems to great depth to inflict maximal losses upon enemy troops, achieving an overwhelming superiority over them in a short period of time and subsequently attacking to seize their territory."[27]

The Soviet view of emerging NATO strategy was judged by Western experts to have been drawn from the Soviets' own preferred doctrine, were the technology in reconnaissance and conventional deep strike available for their commanders. Christopher Donnelly noted that the preferred

Soviet strategy for war in Europe envisioned getting fast-moving operational raiding formations into and beyond NATO's tactical depth; disrupting NATO's command, control, and cohesion at the operational and operational-strategic (or TVD) level; and thereby preventing the reinforcement of NATO's forward echelons by its rearward ones until the former have been separated from the latter.[28] This having been accomplished, the encirclement of the dying embers among NATO's forward-deployed corps in CENTAG and parts of NORTHAG (Northern Army Group) will be accomplished rapidly and their destruction ensured. The Soviets have reviewed their experiences in encirclement operations during the Great Patriotic War to draw lessons relevant to the execution of such an operation under present conditions in Europe.[29]

Col. David M. Glantz, Dr. Jacob W. Kipp, and others at the Soviet Army Studies Office (SASO), Fort Leavenworth, Kansas have noted in several publications how intensely Soviet military theorists have mined their World War II experience for operational insights applicable to contemporary and future war.[30] This interest has shown up in the Warsaw Pact military literature outside of the Soviet Union as well. Dr. Harold Orenstein of SASO has translated an important article from the Polish *Przeglad Wojsk Ladowych* (Ground forces review) by Col. Stanislaw Koziej. The author notes that a "great deal of attention is being devoted lately to the improvement of conventional weapons" leading to the "gradual obliteration of the differences between the efficiency of nuclear means and that of conventional means."[31] Precision weapons represent a "revolutionary" transformation in the means of combat because they make accuracy relatively independent of distance or meteorological conditions.

The development of air-land combat operations, according to this Polish military writer, has decisive importance for the evolution of military art. The formation of the theory and practice of air-land combat operations, according to Koziej, "must be acknowledged as the most significant developmental tendency in modern tactics of ground forces."[32] Other imminent changes in operational art made possible by the new technologies for sensing and aiming include the broadening of the role of mobility in all troop operations; the growth and significance of the "information struggle," including electronic warfare; and the further refinement of deep raiding operations, including the use of operational maneuver groups (OMGs). Of this last development, Koziej notes:

One can anticipate that, in addition to one's own strike means, various operations on the rear of the enemy, in particular the organized elements of the combat formation such as separate subunits, raid subunits and groups, desant-assault groups [parachute-landing], desant helicopters, special subunits, and envelopment subunits, will play a very large role. . . . Raids which reach the most important targets located in the depth of the enemy formation contribute to the weakening of that formation, the breakdown of its structure, and the negation of the possibility of realizing operations which had been planned earlier.[33]

THE CONSTRAINT OF TIME

Clearly, conventional operations pose some of the same dilemmas as nuclear. The time for reacting to enemy moves after they have been observed has been shortened. Failure to react rapidly and decisively has even more drastic consequences than formerly. The time cycle within which plans can be disrupted and initiative can pass to the opponent is also compressed. This did not happen all at once. Marshal Ogarkov, using the accepted theoretical paradigm of Marxism, notes in *Vsegda* that new weapons do not immediately impact upon strategy in a meaningful way. New qualities of weaponry and command systems must accumulate into a critical mass, after which they do make a difference.

Once the accumulation of sufficient quantities of new weapons and command systems is sufficient to make a qualitative transformation in warfare, the change may be drastic. Ogarkov notes with particular interest, and relevance for escalation, the "dialectical contradiction" that has characterized the development of troop control (*upravleniye voyskami*).[34] Before World War II it sometimes required years to prepare military campaigns; during World War II months were required to prepare for front operations. However:

In present day conditions, where the potential adversary possesses weapons which make it possible to launch surprise attacks [*vnezapniye udary*], and execute swift maneuver and redeployment of troops, only a few weeks or even a few days can be allocated for preparation. Therefore, in conditions of increasingly more highly dynamic combat operations and nontypicalness of combat situations, as never before greater flexibility and efficiency of leadership are demanded.[35]

The insistence upon flexibility from commanders at all levels is at variance with the popular image of Soviet armed forces as rigid and immobilized by the absence of unambiguous orders from higher authority. If this stereotypical view of Soviet operational art has ever been valid, it was valid for certain time periods only and in regard to tactical, not operational, commanders. At least since the Russian civil war and earlier, according to some historians, Soviet military writers have emphasized the indeterminacy of combat operations and the necessity for all commanders to maintain flexibility, to adapt to changed conditions, and to take advantage of opportunities to exploit success.[36]

Strategic Theater Operations

This is now more imperative than ever before. Methods of operational art and new weapons have evolved to the point at which strategic aims can be accomplished on a theaterwide scale, and without nuclear weapons. This would have been inconceivable in Europe when the superpowers and their allies were more reliant upon nuclear weapons for attacking forces in their operational and operational-strategic depth. Now, commanders and military planners have potentially feasible (although not risk avoidant) options, provided that certain favorable conditions exist.

These favorable conditions include increases in the level of troop readiness for rapid mobilization and deployment, which is now judged to be of the highest strategic importance. The difficulty is that forces cannot be maintained fully mobilized in peacetime. It would be too expensive and provocative—thus, inexpedient or inadvisable, according to Ogarkov.[37] This judgment was later confirmed by then Deputy Chief of the General Staff M. A. Gareyev in his authoritative *M. V. Frunze: military theorist.* Gareyev critiques the view offered in the seminal work on military strategy, *Voyennaya strategiya*, edited by V. D. Sokolovskiy in several editions. According to the Sokolovskiy volume, a majority of the necessary measures for strategic deployment of forces could be taken during the threatening period preceding war.[38] This reflected the then predominant view influenced by Khrushchev's version of the revolution in military affairs, emphasizing reliance on nuclear weapons instead of conventional forces (especially the ground forces).[39] Gareyev in *M. V. Frunze* pays lip service to the Sokolovskiy recommendation in theory, and then cautions that it is not always feasible in practice. According to Gareyev, it may actually be counterproductive, since mobilization along with the entire range of measures for strategic deployment of forces "has always been considered tantamount to a state of war and it is very difficult to achieve a return from it back to a peacetime status."[40]

Gareyev demonstrates awareness of the problem of crisis management and its interaction with stable deterrence. Mobilization of forces is a signal to a prospective opponent that the time for making decisions is being compressed and the field of alternatives narrowed. Richard Smoke, who has extensively studied the problem of escalation, notes that an important variable is the perceptual field of the policymaker during a crisis or wartime situation.[41] He develops this construct in an interesting way. From Schelling we have learned that escalation may occur when one opponent crosses a saliency or threshold that has previously been observed, such as nuclear first-use, important geographical boundaries, and so on.[42] Smoke notes that this is important but insufficient by itself to guarantee escalation. Escalation also depends upon the psychological impact of crossing a saliency on the policymakers and commanders of the target state. Of special importance are their perceptions of the probable future after the saliency has been crossed, compared to their perceptions without having crossed it. Perceptions of future conditions are termed "expectations" by Smoke, and he suggests that an escalation is more likely when expectations are shifted by the crossing of a saliency.[43]

Mobilizations and Alerts

This has particular relevance for the problems of mobilization and alert management in Europe. The Soviet awareness of the possibly counterproductive effects of premature mobilization is related to NATO's own problems of alert management.[44] At higher levels of alert, the wrappers that prevent accidental and unauthorized use of weapons are never officially and intentionally removed. Something more subtle happens as weapons begin to be dispersed in order to protect them. Commanders understand without explicitly being told that the emphasis is now on preserving intact the combat cohesion of their battalions, divisions, and corps, should deterrence fail. If nuclear release has not been granted, corps commanders will begin requesting authorization to use selected packages from the moment that the prospect of war is taken seriously. Organizational routines and standard operating procedures will gradually shift from a peacetime to a wartime mode. At Defense Condition 2 (in U.S. nomenclature), forces are ready for deployment into combat, with full complements of personnel and equipment. This applies to both conventional and nuclear forces. NATO has a similar cascade of alert levels from lower to higher, with the same implications of shifting from negative to positive control as alert levels are raised.[45]

Once alert levels on both sides of the NATO–Warsaw Pact divide have been raised sufficiently, the avoidance of provocation will give way in importance to the avoidance of military vulnerability to operational and tactical maneuver and fire strikes. Another subtle shift will occur. In peacetime, both the Americans and the Soviets emphasize the desire to avoid nuclear escalation and the accomplishment of strategic missions by conventional forces if at all possible. Under peacetime conditions, nuclear weapons are easily repressed far into the background of planners' concerns. They provide unpredictable denial capabilities while creating the risk of uncontrolled escalation and collateral damage to friendly forces and population. During a crisis between nuclear-armed superpowers and their allies in Europe, these peacetime expectations may undergo a change of emphasis. The policymakers' fields of expectation may change drastically as the prospect of war looms more realistically. Widely noted is the remark by John F. Kennedy during the Cuban missile crisis that the chance of nuclear war between the Americans and the Soviets was between "one out of three and even." Scholars doubt this, but what is pertinent is that Kennedy did not doubt it. Despite the fact that the United States had several options for resolving the crisis without using military force for purposes other than coercion, the president worried not just about war, but about nuclear war.[46]

And his worries were not misplaced. On Saturday, October 27, Kennedy and Khrushchev nearly lost control of events. First, a second letter from Khrushchev arrived, repudiating conditions for resolving the crisis that had been hinted at in a private letter sent by the Soviet premier the preceding day. The second letter demanded the removal of U.S. Jupiter missile bases from Turkey in exchange for Soviet removal of their missiles from Cuba. Second, Maj. Rudolph Anderson, Jr., a U.S. Air Force pilot, was shot down over Cuba in his U-2 reconnaissance plane. Khrushchev acknowledged that the downing of the plane by a Soviet-supplied surface-to-air missile (SAM) had been deliberate. This incident led to increased pressure on Kennedy from members of the ExCom (Executive Committee of the National Security Council, the top level decision making group assembled by Kennedy for the crisis) to authorize an air strike against the Soviet SAM installations in Cuba. In fact, the ExCom had previously decided upon an air strike as a necessary response should a U-2 be downed over Cuba. Now, however, Kennedy demurred.[47]

Third, a U.S. U-2 on a mission from Alaska to the North Pole overflew the Chokut Peninsula, and Soviet air defense fighters scrambled to intercept it. U.S. fighter aircraft from Alaska were sent to find the U-2 and to bring it back safely. The possibility of confrontation between Soviet air defense and U.S. escort aircraft was serious. The next day Khrushchev wrote to Kennedy, "What is this, a provocation? One of your planes violates our frontier during this anxious time we are both experiencing, when everything has been put into combat readiness. Is it not a fact that an intruding American plane could be easily taken for a nuclear bomber, which might push us to a fateful step?"[48]

Compound Fractures

Nowadays, the danger is not so much that a single incident will topple the superpowers into inadvertent war as it is that a compound fracturing of their fields of expectation will. By itself, a single incident can be evaluated and interpreted within a frame of reference that is altogether more reassuring. Thus, the failure of a 46-cent chip in the warning systems at North American Aerospace Defense Command (NORAD) in 1980, simulating a Soviet SLBM attack on the U.S. East and West coasts, did not trigger a provocative U.S. response. The operators recognized the climate of expectations as normal peacetime conditions and established through routine investigation that no real attack was in progress.[49] An optimist might argue that the incident, and many others that have occurred at NORAD for reasons of technical imperfections in the communications and automated data-processing systems, show that the system is fault tolerant. But this optimism is misplaced.

The NORAD warning system is like many complex organizations with high-risk technologies. It is able to cope easily with a single, isolated anomaly. A compound anomaly is less manageable, because it extends from a single incident into unexpected relationships among component parts of the organization. This was the finding of Charles Perrow in his study of the nuclear power plant accident at Three Mile Island near Harrisburg, Pennsylvania, in 1979.[50] One mistake led to another, as operators did things that were called for under standard operating procedures in a situation that was no longer standard. The analogy with military organizations in heightened states of alert is obvious. One has to look no farther than World War I for illustrations. The kaiser and the czar both wanted to avoid war, but neither wanted to appear intimidated by the threat of war. Each sought to use mobilization of forces as a signal of resolve that would cause the other to back off from the brink of war. Instead, the Russian and German mobilization systems sent to their prospective opponents a signal that was not fully intended. Whereas the kaiser and the czar thought they were engaged in coercive diplomacy backed by the threat of force, they had actually signalled an apparent decision to wage war. The inability of both mobilization systems to be activated in a flexible way precluded the possibility of a more subtle message of coercion, compared to the more menacing prospect of having closed off options other than fighting.[51]

The inability of mobilization systems in World War I to act as other than crude and misleading signalling devices is a harbinger of what might happen in a future superpower crisis. The distinction between coercion at the brink and the decision to resort to force is one that must be communicated to the opponent in order to maintain control over events.[52] The threatener who wishes to maintain control over events must weigh carefully the balance of deliberate and inadvertent risks. Deliberate risks are those that one side chooses to run because its calculations suggest that the costs will be worth bearing relative to the anticipated gains. In other words, deliberate risks are undertaken from the standpoint of a rational policy model, emphasizing expected payoffs attached to various alternatives and on selection criteria that provide a clear preference ordering among alternatives and their consequences.

Autonomous risks are those that are either not calculable or relatively incalculable by either side. Risks can be autonomous for various reasons. The "threat that leaves something to chance" or the "manipulation of risk" involves a deliberate choice to let some events take a "natural" course, out of control of the competing sides.[53] Another source of autonomous risks occurs when the interpretation placed on one side's move by the other is wholly at variance with the meaning intended by the first. During the U.S. escalation of the air war against North Vietnam, it was assumed by President Johnson and his advisors that the alternation of bombing pauses with intensified air attacks against North Vietnamese territory would signal the resolve not to lose, as well as the restraint not to widen the war. The signal received by Hanoi was that the United States was uncertain of its objectives, and that therefore perseverance by the North Vietnamese and their allies in South Vietnam would eventually pay dividends.

The problem of autonomous risks in nuclear crisis management, and therefore in war termination, is related to the distinction noted earlier between two kinds of decisions: the decision to use coercive threats that might call for the use of force if implemented, and the decision to use force itself. As Phil Williams nas noted, one of the key dividing lines or saliencies in superpower crisis until now has been preservation of the distinction between coercion and violence.[54] As noted earlier, the distinction was lost on the part of major powers during the crisis preceding the outbreak of World War I, so efforts to coerce were misunderstood as irrevocable decisions for war. One of the most interesting aspects of the Cuban missile crisis is how President Kennedy struggled to keep separated these two kinds of threats and decisions. The difficulty is that in order for a coercive threat to be persuasive, it must be invoked with the *credible possibility* of some punishment to follow if the threatened party does not comply. It is better if the threatener does not commit irrevocably to a certain action, but states or implies a range. Nevertheless, the party being threatened must perceive a significant probability that the threatener can, in fact, inflict some unacceptable or unpreferred costs.

Kennedy's handling of the Cuban crisis straddled this fence, but only barely. The line between the threat that left something to chance *under the control of the threatener*, versus that which took irrevocable action with less controllable consequences, was maintained in several ways. First, implementation of the blockade (quarantine) was not left to standard operating procedures. The first ship to be boarded was a Lebanese freighter under charter to the Soviets, the *Marcula*. Earlier, the Soviet tanker *Bucharest* was closely trailed by U.S. warships but allowed to proceed through the blockade to Cuba "while the ExCom discussed whether to intercept it."[55] It is possible that the original blockade line established by the navy approximately 500 miles from the eastern end of Cuba was not immediately drawn in closer, despite an order from President Kennedy to do so. This may have been one reason why the president decided to let at least one Soviet ship pass through the original line.[56]

Second, the ExCom came very close to having chosen the air strike against the Soviet medium range ballistic missile (MRBM) launcher sites both before and after the blockade was determined. Before the blockade was chosen, members of the ExCom saw an air strike as the most logical option, on the assumption that it could be "surgical" in taking out the Soviet missile complexes. The air force was asked to provide an estimate of the feasibility of such a strike, and it reported that it could not be conducted with a high probability of success.[57] The operational definition of success held by the air force was not necessarily that understood by the ExCom, but this was not immediately apparent. Revised estimates in the second week of the crisis showed that the surgical air strike could have been carried out with high confidence.[58] Air force definitions of success meant not only destruction of the missile sites but also attacks of such magnitude that the survival of the Castro regime itself would have been jeopardized. In this instance, the policymakers were fortuitously misled.

Had the surgical air strike option been implemented instead of the blockade, the United States would have been at war with Cuba, and possibly with the Soviet Union.

In a third instance, the line between coercive use of force and actual engagement in military operations was crossed by the U.S. Navy in its implementation of anti-submarine warfare (ASW). According to Admiral Anderson, the chief of naval operations at the time, "The presence of many Russian submarines in Caribbean and Atlantic waters provided perhaps the finest opportunity since World War II for U.S. Naval Anti-Submarine Warfare forces to exercise their trade, to perfect their skills and to manifest their capability to detect and follow submarines of another nation."[59] This meant that Soviet submarines, when detected, might be (and in some cases were) forced to the surface. Some of these submarines could have been armed with nuclear weapons. [The U.S. Navy view was a "correct" organizational response to operational imperatives under near-to-wartime conditions, as navy leaders undoubtedly viewed the matter.] If war should break out, the Soviet submarines would present a strategic threat that must be nullified as rapidly as possible. President Kennedy had different priorities. Aggressive ASW might suggest to the Soviets that the Americans were not just taking sensible precautions against the possible contingency of war, but provoking it.

With respect to the distinction between coercion and actual violence, the most difficult issue for Kennedy and his advisors was that the blockade, if successful, would only deter the Soviets from sending additional missiles into Cuba. It could not prevent them from bringing into a state of readiness the missiles that had already arrived. Deterrent threats and the accompanying blockade would not suffice to remove the missiles, which required a *compellent* threat. Compellent threats are required when the objective is to get the adversary to *undo* some action that has already been completed.[60] Construction of the MRBM sites proceeded until the very end of the crisis. In order to get Khrushchev to agree to dismantle and withdraw these missiles already in Cuba, Kennedy was forced to threaten very specific acts of force, tied to finite time limits for compliance. Khrushchev was informed through authoritative back-channel contacts that the president would authorize an air strike or an invasion of Cuba unless the Soviet premier complied promptly with U.S. demands:

Saturday, October 27 was the most serious time. A note was sent to Mr. Khrushchev on Saturday night saying that President Kennedy and the U.S. government would have to receive notification by the

next day that the missiles were going to be withdrawn or the consequences would be extremely grave for the Soviet Union.[61]

As Alexander L. George has noted, the threat that caused the Soviets to
remove the already assembled missiles was not one that left something to
chance, but one that was designed to leave Khrushchev with the impression that U.S. options short of force were exhausted.[62] Fortunately, Khrushchev was so persuaded. He and other members of the Politburo could
have concluded otherwise. They might have decided that the United States
was reluctant to attack the missiles in Cuba and stuck firmly to a demand
that the Americans yield missile bases in Turkey before the Soviet missiles
were withdrawn from Cuba. This inference would have been justified in
the minds of Kremlin leaders by the Americans' careful implementation
of the blockade, by Kennedy's refusal thus far to attack the SAM or
MRBM sites, and by the cards still held in Soviet hands. These cards
included the possible creation of a crisis in Berlin if the United States
moved with force against Castro.[63]

In the Cuban case, the distinction between deterrent and compellent
threats, the more passive and active kinds, is overlaid on the difference
between threats of possible violence and threats that guarantee the use of
force in certain situations. The Cuban case suggests a distinction between
threats that are tied to specific retaliatory punishment for noncompliance,
by making known the actual options that will be implemented and the time
limits for doing so, and threats that are vaguely menacing but noncommital
with regard to specific options and time limitations. Both deterrent and
compellent threats can take the form of the very specific, as to response
and time frame, or the very general, leaving the inference to the imagina-
tion of the target of deterrent threats. It might seem that all cases should
resemble the Cuban one, in which more specific and time bound threats
would be successful compared to the general and less specific ones.

But the Cuban case is exceptional in its decisional structure and frame
of reference with regard to international politics. It was a two-way contest
without the interference of third parties as meaningful players in the
bargaining. A second way in which the Cuban case was exceptional was
in the isolation of principal U.S. decision makers from the pulling and
hauling of day-to-day bureaucratic routines. This was made possible by
the enormity of the stakes as perceived by the president and by the short
duration of the crisis. A third exceptional aspect of the crisis was the
preponderance of military power, both conventional and nuclear, that
favored the United States in the Caribbean theater of military operations.

While the Soviets could engage in "horizontal" escalation in Europe in response to a U.S. invasion of Cuba, they could not prevent Castro's demise by denying an invasion force its objectives.

There is a fourth exceptional aspect to the Cuban case. It was the presence at the highest levels of policy-making of a U.S. president and advisors who saw the character of the decision making process as an important matter in itself. This has not always been the case in great power confrontations. The presence of nuclear weapons has some impact upon this, without doubt. But the personalities of leaders also matter. Robert Kennedy's influence on his brother was decisive in preventing an initial and premature resort to an air strike. John F. Kennedy's own baptism of fire in the Bay of Pigs cautioned him against assuming that military advice was sacrosanct. President Kennedy also structured the decision process so that his advisors were not the prisoners of a "groupthink" syndrome in which they competed to tell the leader what they assumed he wanted to hear. Kennedy also appreciated Khrushchev's need to save face while backing down from the extended position of political and military vulnerability into which the Soviet premier had blundered.

ORGANIZATIONAL SLIPPAGE AND ATTENUATED CONTROL

The preceding discussion reviewed some of the theory and practice of crisis management in order to draw lessons pertinent to war termination. The last lesson was that the quality of decision making is even more important in exceptional circumstances, including crisis and wartime, than it is under normal day-to-day conditions. This creates a difference in perspective, as between the top political leadership and the organizations that must carry out military and diplomatic orders. The more functionally diffuse or geographically dispersed the organization, the more slippage is possible between the intentions of leaders and the actions taken by those further down the chain of command. This operational slippage from the top to the bottom is inevitable; the objective of policymakers is to minimize it or direct it into useful channels.

Examples of this slippage can be given for nuclear command organizations and for the conduct of other U.S. military operations. As to the former, Bruce G. Blair has noted that nuclear command organizations process information and react to stimuli according to a cybernetic model first outlined by John D. Steinbruner.[64] The environment is sampled on a range of values for key variables. As long as environmental stimuli stay within the expected range, the system continues along pre-programmed routines. Thermostats and computers work on this principle. The result is that changes in environmental stimuli, as in military orders that work their way down the chain of command, must take place slowly so that organizational memory can absorb them and prepare responses. Responses that are not available in the organizational repertoire at the time they are desired by policymakers cannot be called up out of the "vasty deep." Worse, if they are called up, they will be implemented in a haphazard manner with consequences that may be far more disturbing than no response.

The major reason for this slippage is not found in the perverseness of subordinates toward leaders, although the attitude of insubordination is common enough. Undoubtedly, persons lower on the chain of command resent operational interference, of which the U.S. worldwide military command and control system (WWMCCS) provides ample opportunity. But the problems are serious enough even when subordinates are faithfully trying to carry out their assigned missions. The clogged pipeline of communications channels during the war in Vietnam was a tragicomedy that has been closely analyzed for its information "pathologies."[65] The sinking of the USS *Liberty* off the coast of Egypt during the Arab-Israeli war of 1967 resulted from a miscue in the flow of communications from headquarters to the field, and similar flaws were in evidence during the capture of the USS *Pueblo* two years later. There are multiple causes for these miscues. Communications are compartmentalized or distributed according to security classifications instead of functional need to know. One service's radio nets cannot "interoperate" with those of another. The chain of command is so top heavy that by the time orders get to the field, they are misunderstood or irrelevant. The last situation prevailed, according to Edward N. Luttwak, during the U.S. peacekeeping operation in Lebanon in 1983.[66] Luttwak's diagram of the U.S. military chain of command for the Lebanon operation suggests that correctly understood orders could only filter through it by some miracle.

Role Perceptions

One source of difficulty is that, whereas those at the top of the politico-military pyramid are working with a strategic model of preferred ends and means, those at the middle and lower levels are working to preserve their organizational ethos and professional autonomy. This difference in perspective between the putative top and middle levels of the hierarchy was embedded in the National Security Act of 1947 and the structure of the

U.S. Department of Defense. Despite several reorganization efforts, the Department of Defense remains essentially a feudal organization. The individual military services must make the detailed decisions with regard to training, budgets, and personnel without which the entire machine would come to a halt. Samuel P. Huntington has referred to this phenomenon as "servicism": international system theorists would call it sub-system dominance.[67] The Goldwater-Nichols legislation, which reorganized the U.S. Joint Chiefs of Staff (JCS) during the Reagan administration, was designed to provide a stronger voice for the chairman of the JCS as the president's principal military advisor, independent of the prevailing consensus determined by inter-service negotiation. This was a well-meant initiative on the part of Congress to strengthen the JCS as an institution, and it would be premature to evaluate it as a success or a failure.

The problem of command and control slippage is larger than the problem of JCS reform, however. The very size of the Department of Defense and the global spread of U.S. general purpose forces militate against a smoothly operating command and control system except under peacetime and low threat conditions. One reason is that the *control* is separated in the U.S. system from the *command*. Neither the office of the secretary of defense nor the secretaries of the army, navy, and air force command military forces in combat. The wartime forces are commanded on behalf of the president, the secretary of defense, and the joint chiefs of staff by the various unified and specified commanders responsible for military operations in a theater of war: commander in chief, Europe (CINCEUR); commander in chief, Pacific (CINCPAC), and so forth. The operational wartime commanders are provided with forces trained and administered in peacetime by the service departments that establish budget priorities (under nominal OSD supervision), dominate the weapons acquisition process, and provide to the U.S. Congress independent testimony about military strategy and force structure.

Thus, the United States can have a declaratory "maritime strategy," as explained by former secretary of the Navy John Lehman, Jr., which is designed for the peacetime expansion of the U.S. Navy force structure and for the corralling of the largest possible budget share from Congress. This declaratory strategy is not necessarily the actual series of maritime operations that would be conducted by U.S. naval and other commanders in a war against the Soviet Union in Europe. In fact, one can deduce from the most authoritative, public exposition of the U.S. maritime strategy, provided by James D. Watkins, the chief of naval operations in 1986, that the declaratory strategy only hints at what operational commanders might do.[68] The secretary's declaratory strategy hinted at prompt strikes against the Kola peninsula and other Soviet inland targets in order to destroy the Soviet Northern Fleet in its home waters. The operational version of the strategy, insofar as it can be inferred from public presentations, leaves this possibility open—but only under certain very limited, and favorable, conditions. In all probability, carrier admirals will be preoccupied with other missions in the earliest stages of war, including the protection of sea lanes of communication from interdiction by Soviet submarines operating in the Atlantic.[69]

Counterforce and Coercion

U.S. maritime strategy raises issues pertinent to the distinction between coercive threats that leave something to chance and actual uses of force. The strategy deliberately blurs this distinction by recommending an aggressive anti-submarine warfare campaign against the Soviet Northern Fleet, including attacks on Soviet ballistic missile submarines (SSBNs) in their "bastions" around the Kola peninsula. The argument is that the gradual sinking of Soviet SSBNs will force the Kremlin to reevaluate the nuclear correlation of forces as moving against it. This counterforce coercion is highly controversial. Critics of the strategy, including Barry R. Posen, have suggested that the prompt destruction of Soviet SSBNs may lead to inadvertent escalation.[70] John J. Mearsheimer has questioned whether the strategy can be implemented successfully, even if it were judged desirable.[71] The U.S. Navy strategy as outlined by Adm. James D. Watkins in his authoritative 1986 exposition, cited above, justifies this aspect of the strategy as contributory to war termination. So does Cap. Linton Brooks, who was one of the principal architects of the strategy.[72] The assumption is that the destruction of Soviet SSBNs will take place gradually, providing the military and political leaders of the USSR with time to reconsider their military objectives on the Central Front.

This is a coercive strategy in its intent and one that knowingly creates some risks of escalation. The effort is to influence the Soviet calculation over an extended time period, and not to provoke the USSR into nuclear retaliation. The assumption being made by U.S. planners is that the Soviets view the primary role for their ballistic missile submarines as a strategic nuclear reserve. The force would be tasked primarily for retaliation against cities in the event that the war progressed that far. It was thought by many strategic analysts that the primary tasking of the U.S. SSBN force was similar. An asymmetry would be created in which the Soviet reserve force would be threatened with destruction but the U.S. force, on account of its wider dispersion beyond its territorial waters, would not. The last queens on the nuclear chessboard would be U.S. after the bombers and land-based missiles had expended their warheads.

The U.S. maritime strategy was an interesting fusion of two streams of thought. Traditional U.S. Navy interests in protracted conventional warfare, for which maritime forces are more relevant than in short wars, were mated to theories of nuclear strategy that had begun to emerge since 1974. Previous formulations of U.S. maritime strategy had not dealt as explicitly with the issue of nuclear warfare and with the coercive—as opposed to the instrumental—uses of force. The navy drew upon trends in nuclear strategy that began with the policy reviews conducted during the Nixon administration. These culminated with the issue of National Security Decision Memorandum (NSDM) 242, the so-called Schlesinger Doctrine after the former U.S. secretary of defense who explained it publicly. NSDM 242 called for implementable options beyond those already built into the U.S. single integrated operational plan (SIOP) for nuclear war fighting.[73]

U.S. STRATEGY AND THE SEARCH FOR CONTROL

The "Schlesinger Doctrine"

James R. Schlesinger provided policy guidance toward the development of options that would allow for the control of escalation, withholding of attacks against certain targets in the earlier stages of war, and improved flexibility of targeting.[74] Schlesinger's public promulgation of this strategy was highly controversial, but its seeds were found as far back as Robert S. McNamara's pronouncements in the early 1960s, to the effect that the United States would conduct a nuclear war, to the extent feasible, according to traditional military auspices. This meant that the emphasis in the initial U.S. retaliatory strikes would be against the military forces of the attacker, especially the remaining nuclear forces.[75] McNamara outlined this logic as part of his overall development of the concept of flexible response, which he applied to the defense of Europe as well as to the deterrence of direct attack against North America.

Both McNamara and Schlesinger stirred controversy. Many audiences did not understand the difference between declaratory and action policy; in both cases the shift from previously understood U.S. strategy seemed more dramatic than it really was. Also troubling to critics was the apparent contradiction between the targeting schematics and the logic of escalation control. Counterforce targeting as explained by McNamara and Schlesinger was designed to remove the opponent's capability to continue doing damage to U.S. assets. Avoidance of cities was designed to create an incentive for him to do likewise. Although these aspects were presented as two sides of the same coin, as Schelling has noted, the assumptions on which the logics of counterforce and city avoidance are based are very different.[76] The second is a strategy of influence, relying on the credible threat to invoke a capability that is not immediately used. The first strategy is traditional in military planning: Disarm the opponent to the extent possible. The counterforce strategy became less feasible as the Soviet arsenal multiplied in numbers of delivery vehicles and in diversity of basing modes. Before leaving office, McNamara had conceded that counterforce attacks designed to disarm were not within U.S. capabilities and, therefore, were lacking in credibility as threats.

Schlesinger sought to restore credibility to counterforce threats without bringing back the spectre of large counterforce attacks. Thus, the Department of Defense sought to develop options that could allow for discriminating strikes against military and other targets. The assumption that the Soviets could be made to see that these attacks were selective and not designed to destroy their remaining forces in their entirety was central to the Schlesinger doctrine. The objective was to limit the scope of war after it broke out by using strategic nuclear forces, if necessary, in order to bring about war termination well below the level of U.S. and Soviet attacks against their respective cities. Schlesinger had taken the McNamara strategy one step further into coercion and one step away from the logic of counterforce per se. Improvements in command and control systems for the use of nuclear forces, larger and more diverse delivery systems, and the arrival in the early 1970s of acknowledged U.S.-Soviet strategic nuclear parity all pushed Schlesinger in this direction.

Schlesinger did not escape from all of the contradictions in this strategy, which were unavoidable given the destructive power of even small nuclear weapons. Even more forbidding was the dramatic symbolism of using them against a superpower or its allies. The leashing of nuclear war after it began in Europe provided little consolation to Europeans. By the time the war had been stopped, Europe would be devastated. Thus, NATO Europeans showed little interest in limited nuclear war, and they argued with some convincing logic that the prospect of limited war was less deterring than the threat of total war. The Europeans rightly suspected that the real argument was not about how best to fight a nuclear war, but how best to deter it.[77] The U.S. assumption was that more limited options represented more credible threats. The ability to execute forces in a selective and controlled manner was thought to be more deterring than the reliance upon larger, although still less than total, attacks.

Countervailing Strategy

The Carter administration sought to revise the Schlesinger doctrine after an initial flirtation with wholesale repudiation of inherited nuclear strategies. The result, "countervailing" strategy, seconded the Schlesinger emphasis upon flexible targeting and the control of escalation as desirable objectives even after deterrence had failed. The Carter doctrine, first publicly explained by then Secretary of Defense Harold Brown in 1980 during an address at the U.S. Naval War College, added other features.[78] Among these was the refinement of targeting "building blocks" to provide still more options and an attempt to clarify the objectives for which nuclear forces would be used, in addition to deterrence per se. Results of interagency policy reviews, including elaborate targeting studies, persuaded Carter administration planners that the United States had to be able to defeat Soviet strategy as it was then understood by U.S. defense planners. The Soviet strategy was judged to place emphasis upon the prompt destruction of U.S. forces and disruption of the U.S. strategic nuclear command system. Comparable threats to Soviet forces and commanders would have to be posed. Carter force modernization plans included the MX (later, Peacekeeper under Reagan) for prompt attacks on Soviet silos and command bunkers. There was significant discussion within the administration of targeting the highest political and military leadership of the USSR in order to pose the threat of personal and group demise, as well as institutional destruction, to leaders of the Soviet armed forces, state, party, and internal security organs.[79]

The Carter countervailing strategy was controversial on these last two counts especially, and the reasons why are pertinent to our discussion of escalation control and war termination. The deployment of MX signified an interest in counterforce per se as opposed to counterforce coercion. The possibility of a first strike against Soviet silos and command centers would be carefully weighed by Soviet planners, since MX seemed ideally suited for both missions. Following the NATO decision to begin deployment of Pershing II missiles in Europe (made in 1979, with deployment scheduled to begin in 1983, pending the outcome of arms-control negotiations), the Soviets could derive from U.S. and NATO force modernization an assumption of greater interest in prompt launch strategic options, including preemption. As of 1980, the U.S. ICBM force had fewer delivery vehicles and warheads, and less throw weight, than its Soviet counterpart. Some three-fourths of Soviet retaliatory capability resided in their ICBMs, whereas the comparable figure for the United States was approximately one-fourth. Therefore, although the U.S. ICBM force was not as formidable as the Soviet, the U.S. force was attacking a much more important target base, relative to the Soviets' overall deterrent. The window of vulnerability could easily have been seen from Moscow to work both ways.

Numerous force-modeling exercises in the government and in academia could capture some of the arithmetic pertinent to countersilo attacks. Therefore, despite the expressed fears of each side with regard to ICBM vulnerability, both could with some confidence arrive at reassuring calculations concerning the survivability of their deterrent forces as a whole. More difficult to extrapolate from the peacetime baseline was the vulnerability of U.S. and Soviet command systems. Therefore, the desirability and feasibility of countercommand attacks were contentious issues within, and outside, the government.[80] The feasibility of destroying the Soviet command system seemed dubious, and the desirability of it was in conflict with other aspects of countervailing strategy. The point of countervailing strategy was to continue the Schlesinger tradition of developing usable options, in the event that deterrence was failing or about to fail. The presumption was that more implementable options make more persuasive deterrents. This presumption with regard to nuclear weapons was taken over from the history of conventional warfare, through a process of transference that Robert Jervis has termed "conventionalization" of nuclear strategy.[81] McNamara had, in his remarks to a NATO ministerial meeting in May 1962, made this explicit. After acknowledging that nuclear weapons had "revolutionized warfare," he continued:

> Nevertheless, the U.S. has come to the conclusion that to the extent feasible basic military strategy in general nuclear war should be approached in much the same way that more conventional military operations have been regarded in the past. That is to say, our principal military objectives, in the event of a nuclear war stemming from a major attack on the alliance, should be the destruction of the enemy's military forces while attempting to preserve the fabric as well as the integrity of allied society.[82]

Conventionalization

There are two kinds of conventionalization with regard to the adoption of strategies for nuclear use. One recognizes the uniqueness of such strategies, and the other does not. McNamara's desire for counterforce options was not on behalf of a nuclear war winning strategy. His objective was to limit destruction in order to allow for war termination. His disinterest in nuclear superiority, or the functional equivalent of a war winning capability, was made explicit by Alain C. Enthoven and K. Wayne Smith, two of McNamara's principal advisors in the Office of Systems Analysis:

> Thus, such "nuclear superiority" as the United States maintains is of little significance, since we do not know how to use it to achieve our national security objectives. In other words, since the Soviet Union has an assured-destruction capability against the United States, "superior" U.S. nuclear forces are extremely difficult to convert into real political power.[83]

The objective once nuclear deterrence had failed was self-restraint in the hope that the other side would cooperate. Some prompt retaliation against valued Soviet assets would be required in order to convince Soviet leaders that further attacks were pointless, but the objective of these attacks was not to establish preeminent firepower ratios. They were coercive attacks designed to use selective, although still drastic, punishment in order to induce cooperation. This language sounds ironic, even oxymoronic, but McNamara did not create the irony. The irony resides in the logic of nuclear deterrence strategy, which requires options for the control of escalation even if policymakers judge the probability of escalation control to be slight. McNamara was making the best of a bad bargain between politics and technology. Nevertheless, neither he nor his successors could completely bridge the gap between the primarily demonstrative and coercive uses of nuclear force and the more traditional purpose of attrition and annihilation of the opponent's forces. Schlesinger and Brown likewise found that additional targeting options and improved command and control systems created more the illusion of control than the guarantee that it would be successful. One reason was that superpower force structures and strategies might not distinguish between first- and second-strike counterforce. Another was that there was little or no evidence of Soviet interest in reciprocal restraint. A third was the apparent lack of command and control capability on the part of either the Americans or the Soviets for protracted, general nuclear war.[84]

VIEWING NEW WINE THROUGH OLD BOTTLES: CLAUSEWITZ'S INSIGHTS INTO FRICTION AND THE CONTROL OF ESCALATION

The great Prussian military theorist Carl von Clausewitz offers profound insights into many aspects of military strategy, including insight into the factors that make war less politically and militarily controllable. War, according to Clausewitz, "is simply a continuation of political intercourse, with the addition of other means."[85] If the connection between war and politics is severed, "we are left with something pointless and devoid of sense."[86] This might seem obvious today, but it was not so to many of Clausewitz's contemporaries or to many of his successors within the higher ranks of the German armed forces.[87] As astute an observer as B. H. Liddell Hart offered the observation that Clausewitz was the "mahdi of mass" and an apostle of total war, which was exactly what Alfred Von Schlieffen and Erich Ludendorff had drawn from Clausewitz quite mistakenly.[88] This confusion arose because Clausewitz wrote of absolute war as an ideal type, a philosophical construct that showed the essence of war if unlimited by restraining forces.[89] Clausewitz derived his understanding of the essence of war from a tripartite conceptual framework, which depicted war as the product of the passions of the public at large, the policy control exercised by government, and the military excellence or lack thereof on the part of commanders.

War was kept from assuming its absolute form—that is, from escalating—by two predominant forces: the control of policy and the effects of friction. Clausewitz's discussion of friction as the force that wears down the war machine is well known but insufficiently appreciated for its subtlety.[90] Friction is "the only concept that more or less corresponds to the factors that distinguish real war from war on paper."[91] Contrary to the impression of those who have never actually fought in military campaigns, "Everything in war is very simple, but the simplest thing is difficult. The difficulties accumulate and end by producing a kind of friction that is inconceivable unless one has experienced war."[92] This is because a "military machine" is actually composed of individuals with their own will, perceptions, and motivations. Each is a potential point of friction. Action in war is likened by Clausewitz to "movement in a resistance element," like walking in water, so that "it is difficult for normal efforts to achieve even moderate results."[93]

Clausewitz saw friction primarily as a force that disrupted the cohesion of the military machine by slowing it down. In the nuclear age, the problem may be that friction acts to speed the system up.[94] Or, to extrapolate further, modern technology *reduces the amount of time for decision-making while it inundates policymakers and commanders with ever larger streams of information and data.* This creates a need for fusion and analysis centers, which, in turn, further distance the commander and policymaker from the events over which they must exercise control.

The detachment of command from control is brought about by inter-mediary processes and subalterns in the bureaucracy who are depended upon to reduce the masses of information to comprehensible and manage-able portions. As Martin Van Creveld has noted concerning the U.S. decision making in Vietnam, this detachment creates conflicting tenden-cies toward centralization and specialization. More and more specialized communications and coordination personnel are needed to keep the mes-sage traffic moving, establish and monitor protocols, and interpret the rising tide of information. This further distances senior commanders and policymakers from accurate information about what is actually going on in the field.[95]

The problem is compounded in the nuclear age by the speed with which total destruction of a society, in addition to its armed forces, can take place. Furthermore, the warning and intelligence gathering systems responsible for preventing nuclear surprise were tightly coupled to the decision making processes for threat assessment and response. This coupling of warning, threat assessment, and response in nearly real time was made necessary by the speed of ballistic missiles and the self-evident inability of either superpower to create effective defenses against them. Linking of auto-mated warning with rapid threat assessment and response was accom-plished within organizational frameworks designed specifically for nuclear command organizations. In this way, nuclear command systems differed from prenuclear arrangements in which warning, threat assess-ment, and response often proceeded sequentially, in widely separated organizational fora, and with much time between the various steps. The loose coupling of warning, threat assessment, and response in prenuclear organizations was acceptable because entire nations could not be obliter-ated in half an hour with virtually no warning. Strategic military surprises prior to 1945 were often successful because the attacker benefited from the compartmentation of warning, assessment, and response.[96]

Tight coupling among warning, assessment, and response changes the character of military organizations in command of nuclear forces in kind, not just in degree, from their predecessors. Traditional organizations were arranged for information to flow vertically: orders from higher to lower levels, and information pertinent to warning and assessment from lower to higher. Nuclear command organizations demanded information from a variety of electronic and other sources almost instantaneously if retaliation was to be guaranteed. Therefore, they developed protocols to assure that missions can be performed even under the worst stresses of nuclear crisis management or actual war. One example is the status of the U.S. president relative to that of the nuclear force commanders. According to Bracken, the president functions primarily as a safety catch to hold back retaliation, instead of acting as the commander who triggers retaliation.[97] His role is exactly the opposite of the heroic military leader, as John Keegan has noted: The role calls for "post-heroic" leadership.[98] The role of the president and the principal national security advisors, including the topmost committee of military advisors embodied in the joint chiefs of staff, is to slow down the pace of events instead of speeding them up.

Regretably, there are no free lunches. The probability of avoiding a Type I error, such as mistaken retaliation, may be reduced at the cost of increasing the probability of Type II errors, such as refusal to authorize retaliation in a timely manner although an attack is actually in progress. Ashton B. Carter suggests that this trade-off between Type I and Type II errors is not always necessary, that there are some things that the United States or the Soviet Union can do that will simultaneously reduce the probability of both errors.[99] The protection of command centers on both sides from prompt destruction might be one of these. Those who are more pessimistic about the decision environments of nuclear crisis would argue that a trade-off at the margin between the two kinds of risk is inevitable. In addition, heightened levels of alert and special collection tasking for intelligence gathering platforms cost money, time, and trouble for officials. These organizational costs will involve marginal trade-offs in bureaucratic power, issue salience, and resources for the next time around. For these reasons alone, of the potential for disrupting precedent agreements on resources and prerogatives, most nations and military command organizations cannot go on alerts frequently, nor can they maintain them indefinitely. Thus, U.S. and Soviet nuclear command organizations will enter any serious crisis with little in the way of realistic experience in bringing strategic nuclear forces into higher states of readiness and maintaining them there.

These aspects of organizational structure and decision making also impact upon the prospects for U.S.-Soviet nuclear war termination, as did the doctrines discussed in the previous section. Clausewitz's friction is now a compound disability in which the statesmen are intellectually and psychologically detached from the machine. The warning, assessment, and decision making apparatus is self-feeding and self-sustaining. Officials assume that it is also self-correcting; in the case of simple component errors, so far they have been correct (that is, in the U.S. case, for we know precious little about the Soviet). This self-correcting system is built on cybernetic/organizational assumptions that the international environment will not generate stimuli beyond the ken of its preprogrammed routines. Supposing this equilibrium can be maintained in a crisis, after deterrence fails it is supposed to continue so that the United States can implement a flexible nuclear response. However, wartime conditions will drive actual control of information (and, thus, policy) downward in the organization and into previously off-channel directions, as the imperative of survival prevails over that of peacetime management.

CONCLUSION

During the past several decades of U.S. deterrence doctrine and operational nuclear strategy, reliance upon a greater margin of usefulness, not mere usability, has been judged necessary. This judgment has been made by public officials responsible for making the decision to use nuclear weapons if necessary, and it has been adopted as part of the planning process for the design and employment of U.S. strategic forces. From the early 1960s to the present, with varying degrees of intensity, the assumption has been that usable nuclear force converts by some metric into useful nuclear force. The conversion metric is thought to be theories and plans for the partial use of the U.S. and/or other NATO arsenal. This is to be accompanied by the appropriately designed communications, explicit and tacit, between adversaries during war. Theories, plans, and communications will allow for the control of escalation and the termination of nuclear war under the most favorable conditions.

This optimism about nuclear use is, as the introductory section of this chapter suggested, the result of conventionalization of nuclear strategy. It also invites the nuclearization of conventional strategy. Reacting to the arguments for nuclear usability, instead of mere usefulness, some advocates of conventional "deterrence" have conflated the meanings of deterrence and defense—to the detriment of both. Neither usable nuclear weapons nor stand-alone conventional forces will provide deterrence of war in Europe, since deterrence is based fundamentally on the fear of unacceptable societal punishment. However, a more conventional balance can make possible the control of escalation growing out of limited wars, should deterrence fail. A more basic question is whether strictly or mostly conventional balances can preclude war. This directs us to consider the issue of military stability in Europe in a postnuclear, if not postdeterrent, condition, a task that is undertaken in the next chapter.

NOTES

1. John J. Mearsheimer, *Conventional Deterrence* (Ithaca, N.Y.: Cornell University Press, 1983).

2. Ibid.

3. Robert Jervis, *The Illogic of American Nuclear Strategy* (Ithaca, N.Y.: Cornell University Press, 1984), 56–58.

4. For an expansion, see Stephen J. Cimbala, *Strategic Impasse: Offense, Defense and Deterrence Theory and Practice* (Westport, Conn.: Greenwood Press, 1989).

5. On dissuasion, see Edward N. Luttwak, *Strategy: The Logic of War and Peace* (Cambridge, Mass.: Belknap Press, 1987), 190–207.

6. See Leon V. Sigal, *Fighting to a Finish: The Politics of War Termination in the United States and Japan, 1945* (Ithaca, N.Y.: Cornell University Press, 1988).

7. I am grateful to David Tarr for this insight.

8. Glenn H. Synder, *Deterrence and Defense: Toward a Theory of National Security* (Princeton, N.J.: Princeton University Press, 1961). Excerpts of this appear in Robert J. Art and Kenneth N. Waltz, eds., *The Use of Force: International Politics and Foreign Policy* (Boston: Little, Brown, 1971), 56–75.

9. Thomas C. Schelling, *Arms and Influence* (New Haven, Conn.: Yale University Press, 1966).

10. See Richard K. Betts, "Surprise Attack and Preemption," in Graham T. Allison, Albert Carnesale and Joseph S. Nye, Jr., eds., *Hawks, Doves and Owls: An Agenda for Avoiding Nuclear War* (New York: W. W. Norton, 1985), 54–79.

11. Richard Ned Lebow, *Nuclear Crisis Management* (Ithaca, N.Y.: Cornell University Press, 1987).

12. Raymond L. Garthoff, *Detente and Confrontation: American-Soviet Relations from Nixon to Reagan* (Washington, D.C.: Brookings Institution, 1985), 771.

13. This is documented in Geoffrey Blainey, *The Causes of War* (New York: Macmillan, 1973), 35–56.

14. See Robert Jervis, Richard Ned Lebow, and Janice Gross Stein, *Psychology and Deterrence* (Baltimore: Johns Hopkins University Press, 1987); Robert Jervis, *Perception and Misperception in International Politics* (Princeton, N.J.: Princeton University Press, 1976); Alexander L. George and Richard Smoke, *Deterrence in American Foreign Policy: Theory and Practice* (New York: Columbia University Press, 1974); and Patrick M. Morgan, *Deterrence: A Conceptual Analysis*, 2nd ed. (Beverly Hills, Calif.: Sage Publications, 1983).

15. Richard Pipes, "Why the Soviet Union Thinks It Could Fight and Win a Nuclear War," *Commentary* 1 (July 1977): 21–34. For a Soviet perspective on past and present U.S. strategy, see Alexei G. Arbatov, *Lethal Frontiers: A Soviet View of Nuclear Strategy, Weapons and Negotiations*, trans. Kent D. Lee (New York: Praeger Publishers, 1988).

16. Jervis, *Illogic of American Nuclear Strategy* 29–33.

17. See David N. Schwartz, *NATO's Nuclear Dilemmas* (Washington, D.C.: Brookings Institution, 1987), passim, and Leon V. Sigal, *Nuclear Forces in Europe: Enduring Dilemmas, Present Prospects* (Washington, D.C.: Brookings Institution, 1984).

18. Background on this appears in Catherine McArdle Kelleher, "NATO Nuclear Operations," in Ashton B. Carter, John D. Steinbruner, and Charles Zraket, eds., *Managing Nuclear Operations* (Washington, D.C.: Brookings Institution 1987), 445–69.

19. Paul Bracken, *The Command and Control of Nuclear Forces* (New Haven, Conn.: Yale University Press, 1983), Ch. 5. Bracken's view is pessimistic on the controllability of nuclear war in Europe. Equally pessimistic is the judgment of Desmond Ball, *Controlling Theater Nuclear War* (Canberra, Australia: Strategic and Defence Studies Centre, Research School of Pacific Studies, Australian National University, October 1987).

20. On nuclear safeguards, see Donald R. Cotter, "Peacetime Operations: Safety and Security," in Carter, Steinbruner, and Zraket, eds., *Managing Nuclear Operations*, 17–74.

21. Gregory F. Treverton, "Theatre Nuclear Forces: Military Logic and Political Purpose," in Jeffrey D. Boutwell, Paul Doty, and Gregory F. Treverton, eds., *The Nuclear Confrontation in Europe* (London: Croom, Helm, 1985), 87–112.

22. Ball, *Controlling Theater Nuclear War*, passim.

23. Stephen M. Meyer, "Soviet Perspectives on the Paths to Nuclear War," Graham T. Allison, Albert Carnesale, and Joseph S. Nye, Jr., eds., *Hawks, Doves and Owls: An Agenda for Avoiding Nuclear War*, (New York: W. W. Norton, 1985), 167–205.

24. Marshal N. V. Ogarkov, *Vsegda v gotovnosti k zashchite Otechestva* (Always in readiness to defend the homeland) (Moskow: Voyenizdat, 1982) 60.

25. B. V. Panov, V. N. Kiselev, I. I. Kartavtsev, et al., *Istoriya voyennogo iskusstva* (History of military art) (Moskva: Voyenizdat, 1984).

26. Marshal N. V. Ogarkov, *Istoriya uchit bditel' nosti* (History teaches vigilance) (Moskow: Voyenizdat, 1985), 69. See also Mary C. FitzGerald, "Marshal Ogarkov on Modern War: 1977–1985," Center for Naval Analyses, Professional Paper 443, March 1986.

27. Ogarkov, *Istoriya uchit bditel' nosti*. In the same work, Ogarkov characterizes the U.S. military strategy of the Reagan years as one of direct confrontation (*pryamogo protivoborstva*), within which framework the Pentagon had adopted the concept of "air-ground operation" (*vozdushno-nazemnoy operatsii*) for the use of combined arms forces in European theaters of military operations during the conduct of wars with conventional weapons (69). Meanwhile, the Pentagon expected that U.S. strategic forces and NATO "Eurostrategic" nuclear forces "increases the possibility of achieving U.S. political and military aims in a 'limited' nuclear war in the European theater of war without its growing to a worldwide war" (68). With regard to these NATO hopes for escalation dominance by strategic and theater-nuclear counterdeterrence, Ogarkov suggests that "of course these hopes are pure utopia" (68).

28. See Christopher N. Donnelly, "Soviet Operational Concepts in the 1980s," in *Strengthening Conventional Deterrence in Europe: Proposals for the 1980s*, Report of the European Security Study (New York: St Martin's Press, 1983), 105–36. Lectures from

the Voroshilov Military Academy of the Soviet general staff given during the 1970s are now being declassified, with interesting insight into Soviet thinking about operational art and strategy. See Army Gen. I. V. Shavrov, "Osnovy i soderzhaniye voennoy strategii," (Principles and content of military strategy), *Journal of Soviet Military Studies* 1, no. 1 (April 1988): 30–53.

29. On the Soviet experience with encirclement operations, see V. A. Matsulenko, *Operatsii i boi na okruzheniye* (Encirclement operations and combat) (Moskow: Voyenizdat, 1983). I am grateful to John G. Hines and Col. Robert L. Stockwell for calling this to my attention. See also V. G. Reznichenko, I. N. Vorob'yev, N. F. Miroshnichenko, and Yu. S. Nadirov, *Taktika* (Tactics) (Moskow: Voyenizdat, 1984), Ch. 2.

30. Soviet Army Studies Office, *The Soviet Conduct of War* (Fort Leavenworth, Kans.: Soviet Army Studies Office, Combined Arms Center, 1987). See also John G. Hines, Phillip A. Petersen, and Notra Trulock III, "Soviet Military Theory from 1945–2000: Implications for NATO," *The Washington Quarterly* 9, no. 4 (Fall 1986): 117–37.

31. Col. Stanislaw Koziej, "Anticipated Directions for Change in Tactics of Ground Forces," *Przeglad Wojsk Ladowych* (Ground forces review) September 1986: 5–9. I am grateful to Dr. Harold Orenstein for translating this article.

32. Ibid.

33. Ibid.

34. Ogarkov, *Vsegda v gotovnosti*, 36.

35. Ibid.

36. A useful collection of pertinent writings is Derek Leebaert, ed., *Soviet Military Thinking* (London: Allen and Unwin, 1981). The chapter in this volume by Nathan Leites is of special interest for students of Soviet operational art and tactics.

37. Ogarkov, *Vsegda v gotovnosti*, 58.

38. V. D. Sokolovskiy, *Voyennaya strategiya* (Military strategy), 2nd ed. (Moskva: Voyenizdat, 1963), 22. This includes the argument that a majority of readiness and mobilization measures can be carried out ahead of time. For Gareyev's critique, see M. A. Gareyev, *M. V. Frunze: Voyennyy teoretik* (M. V. Frunze: Military theorist) (Moskow: Voyenizdat, 1984), 239–41.

39. Hines, Peterson, and Trulock, "Soviet Military Theory."

40. Gareyev, *M. V. Frunze*, Ch. 3, Part 3.

41. Richard Smoke, *War: Controlling Escalation* (Cambridge: Harvard University Press, 1977) 270–72.

42. Schelling, *Arms and Influence* passim.

43. Smoke, *War: Controlling Escalation*.

44. On this, see Bruce G. Blair, "Alerting in Crisis and Conventional War," in Carter, Steinbruner, and Zraket, eds., *Managing Nuclear Operations*, 75–120.

45. Ibid., 77–78.

46. See Graham T. Allison, *Essence of Decision: Explaining the Cuban Missile Crisis* (Boston: Little, Brown, 1971).

47. Elie Abel, *The Missile Crisis* (New York: Bantam Books, 1966) 167.

48. Khrushchev, quoted in Abel, *Missile Crisis*, 173.

49. Peter Pringle and William Arkin, *SIOP: The Secret U.S. Plan for Nuclear War* (New York: W. W. Norton, 1983) 126–36.

50. Charles Perow, *Normal Accidents: Living with High-Risk Technologies* (New York: Basic Books, 1984).

51. Luigi Albertini, *The Origins of the War of 1914*, Vol. II, trans. and ed. Isabella M. Massey (London: Oxford University Press, 1953). See also Richard Ned Lebow, *Between Peace and War: The Nature of International Crisis* (Baltimore: Johns Hopkins University Press, 1981).

52. See Alexander L. George, "The Development of Doctrine and Strategy," in Alexander L. George, David K. Hall, and William E. Simons, eds., *The Limits of Coercive Diplomacy* (Boston: Little, Brown, 1971), 1–35.

53. Schelling, *Arms and Influence*, Ch. 3.

54. Phil Williams, *Crisis Management: Confrontation and Diplomacy in the Nuclear Age* (New York: John Wiley and Sons, 1976).

55. Allison, *Essence of Decision*, 130.

56. Ibid.

57. Ibid., 124.

58. Ibid., 125–126.

59. Ibid., 138.

60. Schelling, *Arms and Influence*, 69–78, develops the concept of compellence.

61. Robert Kennedy, cited in Allison, *Essence of Decision*, 65.

62. Alexander L. George, "The Cuban Missile Crisis, 1962," Ch. 3 in George, Hall, and Simons, eds., *Limits of Coercive Diplomacy*, 86–143.

63. See Richard K. Betts, *Nuclear Blackmail and Nuclear Balance* (Washington, D.C.: Brookings Institution, 1987), 110–11.

64. Bruce G. Blair, *Strategic Command and Control: Redefining the Nuclear Threat* (Washington, D.C.: Brookings Institution, 1985), Ch. 3. And see John D. Steinbruner, *The Cybernetic Theory of Decision: New Dimensions of Political Analysis* (Princeton: Princeton University Press, 1974).

65. Martin Van Creveld, *Command in War* (Cambridge, Mass.: Harvard University Press, 1985), Ch. 7.

66. Edward N. Luttwak, *The Pentagon and the Art of War* (New York: Simon and Schuster, 1984), 50–52.

67. Samuel P. Huntington, "Organization and Strategy," in Robert J. Art, Vincent Davis and Samuel P. Huntington, eds., *Reorganizing America's Defense: Leadership in War and Peace* (New York: Pergamon Brassey's, 1985), 230–54.

68. There is now a large volume of material on maritime strategy. Capt. Peter M. Swartz, USN, has published several editions of his "Contemporary U.S. Naval Strategy: A Bibliography," and the 1986 edition appeared in the January 1986 issue of the *Proceedings* of the U.S. Naval Institute. This issue also contains the authoritative public exposition of the strategy by Adm. James D. Watkins, USN, then chief of naval operations. See also *Hearings*, Department of Defense Authorization for Appropriations for Fiscal Year, 1985, U.S. Senate, Committee on Armed Services, Subcommittee on Sea Power and Force Projection, March 14, 1984. See especially the statement by Admiral Watkins on p. 3869. I am grateful to Michael N. Pocalyko, Lt. Cmdr., USN for calling this testimony to my attention.

69. See Colin S. Gray, *Maritime Strategy* (Fairfax, Va.: National Institute for Public Policy, 1985).

70. See Barry R. Posen, "Inadvertent Nuclear War? Escalation and NATO's Northern Flank," *International Security* 7, no. 2 (Fall 1982), reprinted in Steven E. Miller, ed., *Strategy and Nuclear Deterrence* (Princeton: Princeton University Press, 1984) 85–111.

71. John J. Mearsheimer, "A Strategic Misstep: The Maritime Strategy and Deterrence in Europe," *International Security* 11, no. 2 (Fall 1986): 3–57.

72. Capt. Linton F. Brooks, "Naval Power and National Security: The Case for a Maritime Strategy," *International Security* 11, no. 2 (Fall 1986): 58–88.

73. Desmond Ball, "The Development of the SIOP, 1960–1983," in Ball and Jeffrey Richelson, eds., *Strategic Nuclear Targeting* (Ithaca, N.Y.: Cornell University Press, 1986), 57–83.

74. Desmond Ball, "Counterforce Targeting: How New? How Viable?" *Arms Control Today* 11, no. 2 (February 1981), reprinted with revisions in John F. Reichart and Steven R. Sturm, eds., *American Defense Policy* (Baltimore, Md.: Johns Hopkins University Press, 1982), 227–34.

75. McNamara, quoted in Lawrence Freedman, *The Evolution of Nuclear Strategy* (New York: St Martin's Press, 1981) 235.

76. Schelling, *Arms and Influence* 192–98.

77. See Freedman, *Evolution of Nuclear Strategy*, 303–12, 313–30.

78. Remarks prepared for delivery by the Hon. Harold Brown, Secretary of Defense, at convocation ceremonies for the 97th Naval War College Class, Newport, Rhode Island, October 20, 1980.

79. Jeffrey Richelson, "The Dilemmas of Counterpower Targeting," in Desmond Ball and Jeffrey Richelson, eds., *Strategic Nuclear Targeting*, (Ithaca, N.Y.: Cornell University Press, 1986), 159–70.

80. Requirements for a U.S. C^3I network suitable for war termination are outlined in Leon Sloss and Paolo Stoppa-Liebl, "War Termination: Targeting Objectives and Problems," in Stephen J. Cimbala, ed., *Strategic War Termination* (New York: Praeger Publishers, 1986), 99–119.

81. See Jervis, *Illogic of American Nuclear Strategy*, for analysis.

82. McNamara, quoted in David N. Schwartz, *NATO's Nuclear Dilemmas* (Washington, D.C.: Brookings Institution, 1983), 157.

83. Alain C. Enthoven and K. Wayne Smith, *How Much Is Enough? Shaping the Defense Program, 1961–69* (New York: Harper and Row, 1971).

84. Freedman, *Evolution of Nuclear Strategy*, 233.

85. Carl Von Clausewitz, *On War*, ed. and trans. Michael Howard and Peter Paret (Princeton, N.J.: Princeton University Press, 1976), 605.

86. Ibid.

87. See Jehuda L. Wallach, *The Dogma of the Battle of Annihilation* (Westport, Conn.: Greenwood Press, 1986).

88. Several of the chapters in Michael I. Handel, ed., *Clausewitz and Modern Strategy* (London: Frank Cass, 1986) explain this very well.

89. See Peter Paret, "Clausewitz," in Paret, ed., *Makers of Modern Strategy* (Princeton, N.J.: Princeton University Press, 1986), 186–216.

90. Clausewitz, *On War*, Book 1, Chapter 7, passim.

91. Ibid, 119.

92. Ibid.

93. Ibid., 120.

94. Richard Ned Lebow, "Clausewitz and Crisis Stability," *Political Science Quarterly* 1 (Spring, 1988): 81–110.

95. Van Creveld, *Command in War*, Ch. 7, covers information pathologies and command deficiencies evident during the U.S. intervention in Vietnam.

96. On the relationship among warning, intelligence, and surprise, see Richard K. Betts, *Surprise Attack: Lessons for Defense Planning* (Washington, D.C.: Brookings Institution, 1982), Ch. 4 and Ariel Levite, *Intelligence and Surprise* (New York: Columbia University Press, 1987).

97. Bracken, *Command and Control of Nuclear Forces*, 202.

98. John Keegan, *The Mask of Command* (New York: Elizabeth Sifton Books/Viking, 1987), 311–51.

99. See Ashton B. Carter, "Sources of Error and Uncertainty," in Carter, Steinbruner, and Zraket, eds., *Managing Nuclear Operations*, 611–40.

4

ATYPICAL WARS: BEYOND DETERRENCE?

Atypical wars are politico-military conflicts that will occur outside of the core security zones of the superpowers, and especially outside of Europe, and for which the Soviet and U.S. professional military establishments and policy elites have been least well prepared. War in Europe is now judged by many national security experts to be an off-line case for which stable deterrence at lower force levels is sufficient to guarantee against deliberate attack or inadvertent war.[1] Therefore, conflicts that were thought to be atypical in the past (hence, the chapter title) will now be typical, in terms of frequency of occurrence. However, atypical wars originating outside of Europe have the potential to involve the superpowers and their allies: The "escalation connection" between first and third world conflict can be made through deliberate involvement of allies or through catalytic expansion of a war.[2] Thus, the isolation of wars with the potential to inflict serious harm on NATO and Soviet interests from the European continent requires a "containment" strategy that disconnects East-West issues from the mélange of nationalism, religion, and other primordial value struggles occurring outside Europe.

Three defining characteristics of atypical wars can be identified. First, since the conflicts are located geographically outside of the superpowers' core security zones, they have ambiguous implications for their vital interests. Second, since U.S. and Soviet professional armed forces are structured and trained for high-technology combat in the main security zones of European, North American, and Soviet territory, atypical wars place new demands on the training and professional self-concepts of superpower military forces. The Americans in Vietnam and the Soviets in Afghanistan have learned this. A third characteristic of atypical wars is that they are more political than military in most instances; therefore, the ways and means of terminating them are more complicated. Atypical wars are often, although not always, revolutionary civil wars, and the struggle is over political legitimacy and primordial cultural values. Combat forces, even in advisory roles, have restricted applicability in many revolutionary situations.

Earlier chapters have examined high-intensity and high-technology warfare; if it occurs, this type of conflict has the largest consequences for policy and society. In this chapter I will explore some of the issues attendant to atypical wars. First, I will outline conceptual problems related to the development of a responsive U.S. capability for these situations. Second I will consider the issue of military professionalism as it relates to U.S. capabilities for the conduct of atypical wars. The discussion will then turn to the more philosophical issues attendant to political modernization and their implications for U.S. policy making. This third section has two parts: the first explores the problem of sociopolitical modernization and stability in general, and the second considers the social contract as a potential counter-paradigm to the Marxian one. A final section considers the problem of conflict termination as it relates to atypical wars in the category of low-intensity conflicts, while revisiting some of the earlier issues.

CONCEPTUAL ISSUES

Three generic kinds of failures mark U.S. efforts to understand atypical wars, including terrorist versions of those wars. The first is cultural or ethnocentric bias. The second is pinpoint policy planning and intelligence gathering. The third is unwillingness to acknowledge the distinction between temporary or issue adversaries and categorical adversaries.

Cultural or ethnocentric bias confounded U.S. political and military estimates in Vietnam, Iran, and Lebanon. The United States remains deficient in area specialists whose expertise can be mobilized on short notice in "crisis management" situations. It also must repair the damage done by the drawdown in university area studies programs that occurred during the 1970s. Most important, the United States must avoid cultural photo-interpretation or "Instamatic" anthropology in dealing with potential opponents of a statist or nonstatist variety. In the case of the latter, nonstatist actors may be especially difficult for intelligence agencies to understand or penetrate. Penetration takes time and requires patience, which are not always the preferred gifts of policymakers whose attentions are attuned to the next election.

This first issue is directly connected to the second, pinpoint policy planning and intelligence gathering. The "crisis management" mentality among defense and foreign policy officials derives from fixation upon management to the exclusion of strategy. Without a strategic map of where we are going in politico-military terms, policy analysts and bureau chiefs are apt to improvise their own strategic goals. The policy-making system becomes "sub-system dominant," and decentralized determination of goals and objectives displaces consensual goal seeking. Under these very frequently encountered conditions, successive approximation of desired goal states by top management is frustrated by the sub-optimization of their subordinates.[3] This sub-optimization has two consequences, one obvious and one not. The obvious one is that top policymakers may find their policies subverted or distorted. The not-obvious one is that, if these sub-optimizing organizations are intelligence or military organizations, they are more subject to penetration by hostile intelligence agencies or to confusion by smokescreens created by those opponents. Also, sub-optimizing agencies are prone to self-destructive delusions, as in the case of the CIA imbroglio over whether the defectors Yuri Nosenko and Anatoly Golitsin were genuine.[4] It is also the case that organizations do what they are organized to do, even if the environment calls for a very different response. The programmed response may be maladaptive to environmental conditions, but no other response can be improvised within available time constraints. The apparent paradox of Soviet missile construction in Cuba in 1962 according to trapezoidal patterns that were obvious giveaways to U.S. intelligence might be best explained by this tendency of organizations to repeat programmed behavior even when it is self-defeating.[5] Terrorists count on authorities who do the same thing.

Pinpoint intelligence gathering can be misleading because the larger context within which events are interpreted is confused with a very selective representation of that context. The North Korean invasion of South Korea in 1950 was at first thought by some U.S. analysts to be a possible feint that would be followed by a Soviet attack on Western Europe. Hitler's preparations for attack against the Soviet Union in 1941, although numerous in detail, were misinterpreted by the highest authorities, including Stalin, because of his preconceptions that Hitler's attack would come later, if at all, and with preceding political warning.[6] Warning indicators of Japan's intent to attack Pearl Harbor were masked by irrelevant information and by preconceived expectations that the attack would be initiated elsewhere in the theater of operations, if it took place at all.[7] In the case of U.S. and Western efforts to deter terrorism, intelligence about specific actions planned by terrorists may not be available until the last minute, if at all. Frequently, the terrorist groups are so loosely structured that they do not know or decide upon the exact targets until very late in the planning process. Resources expended in futile attempts at pinpoint prediction might be better used in attempts to understand the backgrounds, ideologies, and general operational methods of terrorists and their supporters.

The third and most general failure of "C^{3}I" (command, control, communications, and intelligence) in the Western sense is the failure to distinguish temporary or issue adversaries from categorical ones. Issue adversaries oppose U.S. interests selectively, on issues where there are genuine conflicts of interest. The IRA and the Armenian separatists have irreconcilable grievances against the governments of Northern Ireland and Turkey, respectively, but they do not necessarily oppose the broader geopolitical definitions of U.S. national interest. Terrorists supported by Iran and Syria in the Middle East, on the other hand, have clearly identified U.S. and West European officials and other citizens not only as targets of opportunity but also as fundamental political objectives. U.S. support for Israel stands in the way of Iranian and Syrian attainment of their foreign policy objectives, if those objectives are defined to include the subversion of Lebanese autonomy and the expansion of politically based Islamic fundamentalism. In similar fashion, the Soviet security services place emphasis upon the fundamental character of the United States as the principal enemy of the Soviet state, and Soviet intelligence gathering is appropriately tasked.[8] There is no automatic community of interest between Soviet intelligence and terrorist organizations outside the USSR, however, and in some instances the actions of these organizations may go farther than the Soviets might expect or hope.

The U.S. "command structure" for amorphous wars including counterinsurgency and counterterrorist operations is exceptionally porous. The director of the CIA is paradoxically charged with management of the entire intelligence community, a charge that is widely recognized as impossible to implement. The U.S. Congress has imposed itself upon the intelligence community (euphemistically named as it is) not only as a board of directors, but also as an auditor of operational decisions and their implementation. Although the disclosure requirements attendant to covert operations have been relaxed since the passage of legislation of Hughes-

Ryan, two oversight committees are still briefed in full and the inevitable leaks are made available through the U.S. news media to potential opponents (witness the September 1986 disclosures in the U.S. press about the National Security Council "disinformation" campaign against Khaddafy). Outside the CIA, its estimates are challenged by other agencies within the Department of Defense and by rival intelligence services. U.S. counterintelligence operates inside and outside of CIA control, with the FBI having jurisdiction over most operations inside U.S. territory. Department of Defense and CIA competition over ELINT (electronic intelligence) and HUMINT (human intelligence) resources and assets is expected politics. Finally, the multinational cooperation among UKUSA (United States, United Kingdom, Australia, New Zealand, Canada) intelligence organizations also involves significant elements of competition and distrust.[9] In short, the evidence is that the commanders are poorly controlled, and the controllers poorly commanded. Amorphous wars compound the difficulties attendant to intelligence gathering and policy planning. They are aimed at weaknesses in the decision making process for which appropriate remedies will not be easily devised, nor assuredly implemented.

MILITARY PROFESSIONALISM

Atypical wars are not only difficult to conceptualize. They also have two important implications for the U.S. military profession. First, they impact upon the relationship between the armed forces and the larger society. This involves important issues of values and legitimacy. Second, ambiguous wars also affect the military profession internally. Its norms, standards of ethical conduct, and sense of professional honor and mystique are all influenced by the kinds of training it receives and its suitability for the wars it is called upon to fight.

According to Sam C. Sarkesian, there exists in industrial democracies (including the United States) a potential tension between "military legitimacy" and "military posture."[10] Military legitimacy is subjective and is the cornerstone of congruity between the armed forces and society. Military posture is the organization, training, and coherence of the armed forces for the missions they have been assigned. These distinctions parallel to some extent those made by Samuel P. Huntington between subjective and objective control by a society of its armed forces. Subjective civilian control infuses the military with a social ethos that reflects the predominant values of the larger society. Objective civilian control relies upon a strictly defined sense of military professionalism in which values very discrepant from mainstream society are tolerated, or even encouraged.[11] Every society maintains a balance between objective and subjective control over its armed forces.

At this level alone, the issue of articulation between the armed forces and the society is complicated enough. In the United States, for example, subjective control is attained by primary educational and family inculcation of basic values about free speech, liberty, and human rights. Objective control is embodied in the constitutional requirement that the president shall be the commander in chief of the armed forces, and that Congress shall appropriate all monies for national defense or any other national function. The U.S. military officer corps stands between these two polar models, of ideal objective or subjective control, in its actual ethos and behavior. So do U.S. enlisted personnel, although they may feel the strains of professionalism less acutely.

However, in the case of amorphous wars, running from high level, programmatic terrorism at least indirectly targeted against the United States or its major allies (at one end of the spectrum) to the involvement of U.S. armed forces in wars in the Third World (at the other end), the problem of military professionalism becomes more complicated. The "high" end of the spectrum of amorphous wars occurs when U.S. armed forces take on combatant roles instead of advisory roles in areas outside the major U.S. security perimeter of North America, Japan, and Europe. As Sarkesian notes, low intensity conflicts, so-called, can include both combatant and noncombatant force employment.[12] When the United States moves from noncombatant (although still coercive) uses of military force to the actual involvement of U.S. forces in shooting wars, organized as U.S. units and operating under U.S. armed forces commands, then the threshold of low intensity war has probably been crossed. As the experience in Vietnam showed, any involvement of U.S. forces in actual combat under acknowledged U.S. political direction and command makes it an "American" war and increases the visibility of the conflict in domestic public opinion. Among other effects, this also increases the controversiality of U.S. involvement as well, unless it is a "splendid little war" that is over before public ambivalence and congressional antipathy have a chance to develop.

The step beyond low intensity conflict may take place once the U.S. armed forces, fighting as such, have begun to take casualties in significant numbers. But the threshold of amorphous wars is still preserved. Amorphous wars do not exclude the possibility of large numbers of U.S. casualties, even when Americans are used in noncombatant roles. A good example is provided by the bombing of the Marine barracks in Lebanon by terrorists in 1983. This took a large number of lives and increased the visibility and controversiality of President Reagan's policy. The lack of consensus among U.S. public officials and other elites about U.S. policy helped to make the strategy of "strategic terrorism" in Lebanon successful. There were several targets for this terrorist act, including the U.S. body politic in general, media and other opinion leaders, and the U.S. military profession itself.

Professional Bias

As has been noted by many writers, the bias of U.S. professional military training is against involvement in ambiguous conflicts. U.S. military officers and enlisted soldiers prefer to go into combat against a clearly defined enemy, with attainable objectives, and with strong public support. Given an ambiguous mission, they will rebel against it, inwardly at first, and then outwardly. This rebellion expresses itself within the ranks of the armed forces as well as outside it. In Vietnam, it was manifest in the "fragging" of officers by their own troops, or in unauthorized bombing raids that were concealed from higher authorities. One might add, parenthetically, that higher authorities did all they could to invite such disrespect and evasion. They depended upon an overburdened and highly bureaucratized chain of command that was more useful for making careers than it was for commanding forces to accomplish their wartime missions.[13] This was true on the military as well as the political side of the house. But, tragically and more innocently, they also failed to understand the kind of war they were fighting, and they imposed on that conflict a set of professional expectations that were at variance with the environment.[14]

The bias of military professionals extends into the larger U.S. body politic. Americans and their legislative representatives prefer wars that are scripted in Hollywood, with archtypical villains like Hitler and Tojo. They must be ended rapidly and decisively. And preferably at a small loss of life by substituting firepower for manpower. And the good guys should win in the end. Faced with this climate, public officials have expressed strong rhetoric about the need for U.S. responses to amorphous wars but have backed away from guarantees that military responses will produce political successes. The Reagan administration, for example, vacillated between supportive and antagonistic stances toward reformist elements in Central America. And in Nicaragua, the administration failed to persuade a majority of the U.S. Congress for several years (during the Boland amendment) that the Contras deserved financial support because the ambivalent character of that anti-Sandinista movement made its objectives suspect, and its competency questionable.

But compare the ambivalence of military professionals and public alike toward the possibility of low intensity war in Central America with U.S. combat forces with the same groups' reactions to U.S. "coercive diplomacy" in the Persian Gulf in 1987.[15] Professionals and public in general favored the commitment of U.S. naval forces to escort "reflagged" Kuwaiti tankers through the Persian Gulf. This was an example of noncombatant use of combat forces in an amorphous war. The Iran-Iraq war was not itself amorphous—anything but—but what was ambiguous and complex, in the ways that amorphous wars characteristically are, was President Reagan's understanding of the U.S. role there. Was the United States in the Persian Gulf as a neutral presence, guaranteeing against further escalation of the Iran-Iraq war? Or was it taking sides? Despite U.S. disclaimers, the United States soon found itself being shot at by Iranian forces and having to respond to maintain its credibility. The Iranians had got the United States committed to attempt "coercive diplomacy" in the Iranians' backyard and on terms that were guaranteed to make it appear that the United States was a combatant, on the side of Iraq. This, furthermore, had the side effect of strengthening the Ayatollah Khomeini's regime against its critics from within, who had become more dissatisfied as the war continued without any apparent resolution. So the Iranians managed to tie down significant maritime forces of a superpower in a bathtub of potential vulnerability without nearly so much controversy as had occasioned, for example, the elections held in El Salvador during Reagan's first term (which required that a U.S. congressional delegation journey to that country in order to observe the integrity of the electoral process on the spot).

Not only was the United States vulnerable to Iranian mines, speedboats carrying troops with various hand-held weapons, and Iranian-sponsored worldwide terrorism against U.S. targets. Also vulnerable was the U.S. military professional and public expectation about the noncombatant utility of combat forces in a war zone. These expectations need to be shaped and explained by the White House and the Department of Defense before armed forces are actually placed into the double jeopardy of interposition between combatants while declaring a policy of impartiality. The Reagan administration was either not fully aware, or chose not to tell, that the conditions under which "coercive diplomacy" (in the form of noncombatant missions for coercive political purposes assigned to combat forces) can work are very restrictive. First, the threatener must be able to communicate clearly what behavior is desired, or not desired, of the party being threatened. Second, the threatener must have the resources or capabilities to carry out the threat if compliance is not obtained. Third, the threatener must be willing to carry out the threat. Fourth, the costs to the threatener of carrying out the threat must not be greater than the costs of not carrying it out. And fifth, the costs anticipated by the threatener must not be greater than the perceived costs to the party being threatened, as the latter *perceives* them.[16]

In the case of the U.S. flotilla in the Persian Gulf protecting reflagged tankers, the last condition could not be satisfied even if the others could. The Iranians welcomed a more visible U.S. presence as a sign that they had provoked "the great Satan" into striking a comparatively weak opponent for reasons of meanness and spite. So did the Argentinians, when they took on the British in the war over the Falkland Islands, on the assumption that Britain probably would not fight, but if Britain did, then "nonaligned" sympathies would be with the Argentinians against a formerly global colonial power. This expectation was disappointed no doubt on account of longstanding memories, in the Third World and elsewhere, of the Argentine government's "dirty war" against its citizens during the 1970s. The Argentinians could not credibly play the role of Third World victim, nor could the Iranians with their international network of state-supported terrorism in Lebanon and elsewhere. However, the United States was unknowingly giving the Iranians all the ammunition they needed for marketing such an image.

Strategic Interests

The Iranian example can be stretched too far. One must also acknowledge that the United States and its allies have a strategic interest in maintaining the flow of oil through the Persian Gulf. The United States was also not unmindful of the deterrent effect upon the Soviets that the U.S. naval presence was certain to suggest. But this acknowledgment only qualifies the preceding point slightly. U.S. allies in Europe and Japan are much more dependent on Persian Gulf oil exports than is the United States itself. The outlet through the Strait of Hormuz has been the only option for many years, but future pipeline construction will allow for transshipment of oil across miles of desert country to other outlets. Iraq already has a head start on this option as a result of necessity, following Iranian attacks against tankers in the gulf that were carrying supplies from Iraq and

Kuwait. The oil issue also does not call for unilateral U.S. action as much as it does a multilateral NATO commitment to "out of the area" operations in the common interest. So one can still say that the Iranians "tar babied" the United States into a situation of disproportion between the ends obtainable and the means committed to obtaining them.

There is some irony, then, in the fact that the Reagan administration, which was committed to keeping Iran on the defensive in the gulf, also promoted the sales of U.S. weapons to Tehran in order to bargain for hostages. President Reagan denied this as a possible motive, but the evidence does not bear him out, and Senator Muskie's comment about "keeping hostage families away from the President" at the Iran-Contra report briefing is apropos.[17] The supposition that Mr. McFarlane's missions were designed to reach out to Iranian "moderates" suffered from the failure of any person in authority to identify who those moderates were, or what would be accomplished by them if they were to propose an accommodation with the United States to Khomeini. This episode, too, strained military professionalism, although in a different way compared to the gaffe in the gulf. In the case of the reflagged Kuwaiti tankers and their U.S. escorts, the United States was riding shotgun for Arab regimes that would just as soon keep their distance from U.S. foreign policy objectives, in general, and from U.S. military presences, in particular. Neither the Kuwaitis nor any of the other "moderate" Arab states on the gulf littoral would be interested in having a permanent U.S. base there. They are willing to have the United States step in to do what the Gulf Cooperation Council is unwilling or unable to do, but in their interests. Those interests are above all else the stability and survival of the regimes in power, which are for the most part traditional and authoritarian. So the United States finds itself standing against the tide of social change in the Persian Gulf in order to support its presumed national security interests, although our "allies" there do not perceive any consensual long-term interests of that sort.

In the Iran-Contra fiasco, the United States for reasons of hostage rescue or national security decided to influence the Iranians through "middle-men" including the government of Israel, which had its own interests in mind. Israel had been supplying arms to Iran in order to keep the Iran-Iraq war going (exactly the opposite of U.S. policy), on the assumption that this would limit Iraq's aspirations elsewhere. There is some indication that the initiative was taken on the Iran arms deal by Israel, and that Washington was persuaded to go along with a plan that the Israelis intended to carry out in any event. However, there remains the option to say "no," and the

Reagan administration did not say "no," thereby opening itself to the supposition that policy was based on the sentiment of the moment, or logical contradiction, or both.

In addition, the connection between arms sales to Iran and support for the Contras during a period of U.S. congressional prohibition for such aid was itself a controversial issue. The administration was perceived to be selling arms to the forces of darkness in order to support the forces of light, as it defined them. One year after the "connection" came to light in the U.S. news media, U.S. forces were sailing the Persian Gulf at war in fact, if not in declaration, with the Iranians. When the U.S. ship *Stark* was hit by an Iraqi missile (by mistake, presumably), the public and Congress discovered the risks of coercive diplomacy quite readily, but only after terrible cost. And, as in Lebanon, the forces had been placed into a war zone under rules of engagement appropriate in peacetime (this was soon changed after the attack on the *Stark*, following congressional, media, and public outcry). The frustration of military professionals who were tasked to survive in this nonwar but lethal environment must have been considerable. And students of military professionalism can have only sympathy for the commanding officer of the *Stark*, who was held responsible for the mishap and paid with his career.

Accountable Expertise

The last point bears further discussion in the context of military professionalism. The concept of professionalism includes the notion of an accountable expertise. Accountable expertise is a body of knowledge that can be held accountable for exercising discretion *within the limits of its assigned competency and jurisdiction.* Thus, Lieutenant Calley was properly put on trial for the charges attendant to the My Lai (Son My) massacre, on the grounds that an officer in his position had the discretion not to tolerate the kind of massacre that was committed there, and thus it could have been avoided. The situation with the attack on the *Stark*, and for that matter the bombing of the U.S. Marine barracks in Lebanon, was different. In the *Stark* case, the incompetency was at the top of both the military and civilian chains of command. The latter, including the president and the secretary of defense, had knowingly or unknowingly sent military forces into a war zone without rules of engagement that allowed for prompt retaliatory response to a perceived attack. In Lebanon, Marines guarding the barracks were not permitted to prechamber their ammunition and were thus unable to stop a truck bomber from driving within lethal distance. Military professionals put into this kind of situation are being used as substitutes for diplomats or as cyborg diplomat-warriors. However, they are not trained for diplomat-warrior roles, Marines least of all. The cases of Lebanon and the Persian Gulf cry out for multilateral peacekeeping missions, in the former case U.N.-sponsored, and in the latter, multilateral NATO engagement (given the futility of the U.N. cease-fire attempt in 1987).

Professional armed forces that are sent into combat with restrictions appropriate for embassy guards or homeguard police forces are asked to set aside their professional training for new norms. If they are expected to learn these new norms "on the job" so to speak, they and their superiors will be disappointed. Caspar Weinberger, to his credit, recognized the absurdity of the U.S. "peacekeeping" mission in Lebanon, although he failed to recognize as clearly the implications of conducting it and then leaving under pressure. Forces that are assigned policing duties against internal violence, as in Lebanon, must be drawn from the indigenous population wherever possible. In any case, they must mix with that population and acquire its affinities and trust. In the worst case, they are identified with the interests of one national or religious group against another, as the U.S. became identified with partisan Lebanese Christian causes. If amorphous wars of this type call for unilateral U.S. intervention, that intervention will in most instances consist of providing training and assistance to indigenous nationals. "Americanizing" a war rooted in domestic political causes, especially nationalistic and religious hatreds, makes the United States appear to be taking a "neo-colonialist" stance against somebody, even if the actual U.S. objectives are neutral with regard to intranational struggles. Even the United Nations has difficulty maintaining the image of neutrality in these kinds of situations, as its Congo operation in the early 1960s demonstrated.

Professional combat forces are unlikely to be able to maintain, simultaneously, an ethos appropriate for conventional war, paramilitary police operations and counterinsurgency, and coercive diplomacy. This is counter to U.S. notions that with technology we can have diversified forces to do all things for all clients. Certainly, the United States can diversify its forces and it is doing so, with more rapidly deployable, light divisions being created for that very purpose. But these forces, although more mobile, are not being educated and trained any differently than other U.S. forces, nor are they the products of a different culture and societal ethos. After the Vietnam War, the U.S. Army sought to distance itself from low intensity conflict and to concentrate on preparedness for large conventional wars (such as wars that might arise in Europe). The civil affairs and special forces branches retained an institutional interest in, and memory of, the kinds of training and education that would equip soldiers to understand foreign cultures and to be accepted by villagers as community builders and not destroyers.[18]

REVOLUTIONARY MOVEMENTS AND DEVELOPING SOCIETIES

Perhaps the most challenging problem for U.S. policymakers and planners has been to understand the dynamics of revolution in developing societies. For a government born of revolution, the United States has been remarkably insensitive to the aspirations of peoples worldwide for control of their own destinies. While U.S. political leaders and intellectuals have often insisted upon a Lockean political standard at home, they have tolerated a Hobbesian one abroad. Not understanding revolution, U.S. leaders have repeatedly embraced self-appointed tyrants and despots who proclaim that they are "against communism." It must be said, however painful the acknowledgment, that in Vietnam this problem defeated the U.S. military intervention before it began. The South Vietnamese government was unable to unify its people and to develop a sense of political effectiveness, which was prerequisite to prosecution of the war, with or without the United States. Analysts of the Vietnam War have looked at almost every other cause for the unfortunate outcome of that conflict. But the fact is that not even an additional 500,000 U.S. troops could have saved the South Vietnamese government from its own dry rot.

A revolution involves at least three issues. The first is who will rule over whom. The second is how the pie will be divided economically and socially. This means who gets what shares of status, income, and prestige. The third issue is legitimacy and valuation. What are the shared expectations that rulers and ruled will have with regard to questions of authority, right, and morality? Answers to these three sets of questions are never fully explicated in any sociopolitical order. Nor must the answers always be logically consistent. But they are useful diagnostic devices. If there is a great deal of contention among the public in general about these issues, however worded, then this is a barometer of trouble for the government. It is already marking time. If the first question is up for grabs (who rules over whom), then rebellion and dissent have become revolution in the truest sense.

Revolution in the truest or strictest sense implies that the form and meaning of government is in dispute. "Meaning of government" implies the set of expectations about its performance and accountability that a government communicates to its citizens. These meanings are embodied in three levels of organization or analysis: the persons who occupy positions of responsibility and accountability, public officials; the regime or constitutional structure; and the political community, that overarching set of publicly shared historical memories and cultural meanings.[19]

Necessary Evil

Let us pursue the point further. Americans are inclined to think of government as a necessary evil that should be limited to as restricted a scope as possible. In the U.S. creed, the individual should find fulfillment in the private sector. This is at least the U.S. ethos held even by persons who are public employees or public officials; note the ambivalent and apologetic explanation by business executives who agree to temporarily serve in government assignments. In many developing societies, however, "government" in the form of a tribal administration, religious hierarchy, military junta, or party politburo is not just a presence to be endured. It provides some authoritative political and social meanings for the general populace. In Iran, for example, the regime of Ayatollah Khomeini has returned to traditional Islamic precepts about the relationship between the individual and the state, in an attempt to provide additional meaning for both. This is an essential difference between governments or political systems that provide paychecks only and those that provide centralized symbolic meanings. In the first case, there may be controversy over who rules and over the distribution of spoils. But this controversy is unlikely to extend to the life-and-death persecution of opponents. In the second case, where essential meanings and definitions of selfhood are bound up in the struggle over who rules, the matter is different. Losing in the second situation is not only losing a share of the political and social pie. It is also a loss of face personally, a degradation of the spirit. One can see this in Lebanon, for example, where the civil war is rooted not only in competition for the spoils of political office, but also in religious and nationalistic fervor that allows for no middle ground.

The case of Iran in 1978 and 1979 is an especially interesting one, for it was a true revolution against the existing order by a disparate coalition of traditional and modern groups. Once the Shah had been deposed, these groups began to fall out, and dissidence against the Islamic republic is now expressed by the modernist elements of the anti-Shah coalition. This pattern, of a revolution in which traditional and modern opposition combine to overthrow ruling oligarchs, is not as uncommon as one might suppose. The Shah was an extreme example of ill health combined with last-minute loss of nerve. But the fate of his regime was sealed by his failure to deal with either traditional or modernist opposition in the most fundamental terms. His regime provided no supportive cultural and social meanings for the public at large to offset the claims of counter-regimes that they could provide alternative and better concepts. This is one of the strengths of Marxism, under the proper conditions: that it can provide a counterculture of shared meanings and aspirations for those who no longer derive their symbolic gratification from the society as it is. This might be thought a curious comment on Marxist influence. Most Americans, with their share-of-the-pie philosophy, see Marx as an economic reductionist, but he was hardly that. He was in fact a secular prophet, calling to account the societies of his day in what are properly described as religious terms. Capitalism, according to Marx, was the most productive force ever unleashed to his day. What was wrong with it was its method for achieving this production, which dehumanized the worker (however, it also conveniently created the working class with its revolutionary potential).

With regard to Western Europe and North America, Marx has been disappointed, and capitalism has not yet collapsed of its own internal contradictions. But the dialectical Marxist logic is better suited to providing a meaningful historicism for persons in developing societies who see regimes that have long since been delegitimized still clinging to power and status. In Argentina, the military junta had to lose a war in the Falklands before public opposition finally required their removal. U.S. scholars are inclined to look at aggregate data distributions in developing societies and to score those societies' revolutionary potential on indices of income maldistribution. But the matter of revolutionary potential, and the related problem of actualizing that potential, are not so simple. People have to know that they are not getting their fair share; they have to perceive that they can do something about it; and they have to be persuaded that the sacrifices made in doing something about it will be meaningful, in the sense in which that term is used above.

Myth and Revolution

This means that revolutions are very much about myth, in the objective rather than the subjective sense of that term. A myth is a motivational construct that is partly based on fact and partly not. Its purpose is to inspire people to action, not to define an analytical solution. Revolutions that change the form of government and transform the society (and some do one without really doing the other) are usually the results of clashes between some dominant myth and countermyth. The last statement does not imply, however, a Hegelian interpretation of history or revolution. It is not a matter of thesis and antithesis bound to result in a synthesis, as the clash of historically dominant great ideas was supposed to unfold. Revolutions are sometimes smashed into pieces by the authorities, and on other occasions the revolutionaries triumph. Indeed, it is a singular characteristic of some revolutionary leaders that their world views are absolutist and uncompromising. This is what makes them so appealing to fanatical followers, so threatening to their opponents, and so disturbing even to their potential allies. Hitler's single-minded obsessions helped to attract some very extremist and very loyal followers in the 1920s. A decade later, when Hitler sought to consolidate his power and obtain the backing of German business and military elites, these extremists were an embarrassment. So the result of collision between dominant and opposed myths is not necessarily a compromise. What does happen frequently is that the dominant myth absorbs some of the rhetoric of the insurgent one, and state policy reflects this in some concessions to the aggrieved parties.

Consider an example from an earlier century, the American Civil War, in order to perceive the importance of myth in motivating revolution or resistance. The Union was fighting to preserve itself, but a supportive mythology stressed the liberation of slaves and the South's alleged subservience to foreign influence. The American South, in terms of its own mythology, was fighting in order to preserve a special way of life against the encroachment of leading industrialists, bankers, and politicians of the "developed" North. The South was an American oligarchy defining itself as a state-in-waiting, waiting for the moment when the North would tire of the struggle and agree to secession. A similar decision was made by Moise Tshombe in the Congo in 1960, when he decided that mineral rich Katanga province was better off outside the newly independent Congolese state than in it. Both Tshombe and the American South were forced into political union by the sword, although neither could conceivably have defeated its opponent militarily. They represented threats that were not primarily military, but symbolic and mythological. If secession were permitted in either case, then the myth of a diversity of states in one American union, or the myth of a newly created and unified Congolese republic, would be disestablished.

Consider as well the retreat from colonialism that occurred after World War I and World War II. This required the replacement of one myth by another, and the process was harder to come by in some countries than in others. The British, for example, were able to retreat from the remains of empire with far less intranational upheaval than were the French or Portuguese. The Algerian war and the bitterness with which it was fought showed that the myths of colonialism and anti-colonialism were both held with religious intensity by their adherents. The Portuguese gave way only in the middle 1970s, after events in Angola had outrun their ability to control and had created within the Portuguese armed forces themselves professional and political turbulence. Now we can tie in the point about myth as it applies to the evocative symbols for societal evaluation with the notion of myth as it applies to professional symbolism. In the Portuguese case, professional symbolism called for army officers who emphasized their mission to defend that country against foreign invasion, and not policy-keeping duties in colonial Africa. The discontent of those officers who could not reconcile the myth of a Portuguese empire with the mythology and ethos of military professionalism almost brought down the Portuguese regime and threatened to disrupt the entire political community.

The reconciliation of professional military and social myths is also a challenge for the modern Soviet leadership, as it was for their predecessors. Two strains develop in this attempted reconciliation. The first is the tension between military-technical professionalism in the art of war and the sociopolitical priorities dictated by Marxist-Leninist theory. So, for example, Soviet military writers have asserted that nuclear war would have no winners and must be avoided. However, if the "imperialists" start such a war, the Soviet armed forces must fight until victory is secured.[20] This is not the contradiction it seems, because the sociopolitical logic tasks the political leadership to avoid war and the nuclear devastation of the Soviet Union. The Soviet armed forces are charged with defeating any opponent in war, of whatever scale. Once in war, military-technical logic predominates. Upon hearing this last observation, some Western observers fear the loss of policy or political control by Soviet rulers over their armed forces, with dramatic and negative consequences for escalation control. But the dominance of professional military and technical perspectives in carrying out war aims does not mean that officers preempt party elites in setting those aims. Quite the opposite is the case, and the Soviet leadership has established elaborate controls over military professional promotion and recognition to make certain that the situation remains the same. But the myth of military professionalism apart from political control dies hard, and it is in fact necessary in order to develop some cadre of well-trained officers who will do their job even when the state or party leadership is thought to be not entirely competent. The Soviet military leaders who marched into Berlin in 1945 were no more professional, by this standard, than those who died at the front in June 1941 in a resistance made hopeless on account of Stalin's willful disregard of his own and other intelligence sources about Barbarossa.[21] And the debacle of June 22 was in no small measure due to Stalin's purge of the Soviet high command during the 1930s.[22]

SOVEREIGNTY AND REVOLUTION

From the classical works of Bodin and Hobbes until the twentieth century, the term "sovereignty" seemed to describe correctly the lawful status and effective capabilities of the modern state. However, the growth of newly independent countries since World War II, and especially since 1960, has now created a situation in which the concept of sovereignty is under siege. This is not merely a semantic problem for political theorists. If the concept of sovereignty is not clearly understood, then the evaluation of revolution as a necessary or expedient tool for political actors cannot take place. Revolutionaries revolt against something. That something is not just an administrative apparatus. It is the idea that a certain way of making decisions about "the political" is rightful. The term "rightful" is itself an important and loaded one. Rightful rule making is rule making that is accepted as proper according to some societally approved standard. That standard may be derived from tradition, religion, law, or some other source. Any system of rightful rule making specifies a relationship between rulers or government and subjects or citizens. The connection between the expectations of followers and the behaviors of leaders in reaction to those expectations is what political scientists now call a "political system" and theorists formerly called a "polity."[23] A polity is a set of expectations about the rightful and effective political behavior of individuals and groups in a society.

All political systems, as Marx correctly saw, contain the seeds of their own destruction: They contain tendencies counter to the status quo that will bring the system down if they are not checked. The effectiveness of a political system is in how it deals with these countertrends. In the United States, for example, radical movements have been gradually absorbed into the mainstream Republican or Democratic political parties. But immediately prior to the American Civil War, there were too many radical and absolutist positions for the system to incorporate without breaking apart, at least temporarily. Whether a political system will withstand the pressures placed upon it by special interest and counter-elite groups depends upon its will to survive and its capacity to mobilize support. The Czar in 1917 had neither, nor did the Shah in 1979.

Revolutionaries can use power to oust the ruling elite and then to redefine the criteria for what is rightful rule. This seems to have happened in Ethiopia in the 1970s, when the regime now led by Mengistu overthrew Haile Selassie. The issue of rightful rule may be the stumbling block that causes the demise of the regime, as it was for Ferdinand Marcos in the Philippines. Sometimes ruling elites are ineffective at using power, and this in turn corrupts public perception of their legal and authoritative status. The Shah's inability to mobilize his own armed forces to suppress outbreaks of violence against the regime in 1978 was a signal to his opponents that he was vulnerable, and to fence-straddlers that he was perhaps not worthy of respect at all.

Revolutions are made by dedicated partisans, but they are won or lost among the greater mass of fence-straddlers and apathetics. It takes a small dedicated cadre to get a revolution started. In a developing society of the present day, this cadre must undermine the public perception that the government is effective and rightful with regard to its rule over its citizens. To do this, the cadre or nucleus first expands into villages and rural areas by what might be called "exemplary demonstration." Public works projects and citizen information programs (say, about health and sanitation) are used to gain a positive image in the villages. The next step is political propagandizing in order to establish villages as experimental laboratories in counterinsurgency. In this phase, villages are turned "inside out" by gradually weaning them away from allegiance to government officials and the state itself. Often this is a two-step process: The local officials are themselves vilified as corrupt and incompetent, and then the political system as a whole is delegitimized in the eyes of villagers.

The next step is to turn individual villages into lattice works or networks of anti-government political agitation and clandestine armament. Frequently, activists begin raiding patrols on government installations, in order to show that the ruling elite cannot protect its own officials. At this stage, the insurgents avoid large and organized military engagements with government forces.[24]

Consolidation of Power

From then on, in stages that are familiar, the revolutionaries gradually consolidate their political and military power until the ruling elite is deposed. In drastic instances the very nature of the polity is redefined, as in Czarist Russia in 1917, or in China in 1949. The so-called "Great Revolutions" usually have this character, of profound social transformation in addition to reconstruction of the polity or redefinition of the relationship between the general populace and ruling elites.[25] One might in this regard distinguish revolutions from revolts, and the American Revolution could be placed in the latter category. In its initial stages, it was a revolt against arbitrary policies of Parliament and the Crown, which the Americans felt were unjustly imposed against them. In other words, they (the Americans) were being denied their due as *English* subjects. However, at some stage during the rebellion, the process of goal transformation changed all this, so that the most influential leaders of the American Revolution no longer would settle for accommodation by Parliament of their (rightful) objections to its excesses. Now, the goal of the revolutionaries became the redefinition of rightful rule itself.

There is some skepticism among historians about whether the American Revolution was really a revolution in the most profound sense. I am not entering into this controversy. My definition has posited that revolution has taken place if the fundamental distribution of power *and* widely shared definition of rightful rule have been changed in significant ways. "Significant" is admittedly not a term that has been quantified, nor shall it be. The problem for most Western students of revolution has been that they define it only on one of the two characteristics noted above, that of power sharing (or, more frequently, wealth sharing). This reflects the bias of Western pluralist thought that revolutions—indeed, all politics—are about who gets what share of the pie. In the end this reduces politics to a political lottery in which the means justify the means. The issue of rightful rule is left out.

Marxists, who supposedly are obsessed with the issue of dividing the pie, are actually more acutely aware of the moral questions at stake in revolutions than are non-Marxist or anti-Marxist analysts. All politics is about the class struggle, and the class struggle is based not only upon relative deprivation of some classes compared to others, but also upon the illegitimacy of this deprivation (as seen by Marxists). The deprivation is illegitimate because it is dehumanizing, reducing people to commodities. And government is dehumanized to the extent that it participates in this deprivation. In addition, the Marxist argument draws powerful support from the determinism of Marxist historicism. The capitalists as individuals are not to be despised; some may be very personable, as during summit diplomacy. Capitalists as a class are to be deposed in order that history might be fulfilled, or at least the Marxist-historicist version of it. Thus, it is perfectly consistent for Soviet Marxists, for example, to consort diplomatically with President Reagan at summit conferences and to sign arms-control treaties, if these are temporary expedients on the way toward fulfillment of long-term Soviet political and military objectives. And Lenin in his applications of Marx and Engels was quite specific on the need for tacking day-to-day decisions with the wind of fortune; his apothegm to the effect that bayonets penetrate against mush, but withdraw after meeting steel, is well known.

What the Marxist paradigm provides for its adherents is a logically consistent model for explaining and predicting (if not prophesying) the triumph of revolution against regimes depicted as anti-Marxist. In the present day, this has come to mean revolutions against governments perceived as anti-Soviet. Since the Sino-Soviet split in world politics, the communist ideological monolith has shattered, and with it a transnationally and transculturally consistent interpretation of revolution. Again, what is important for discussion here is not that the PRC is, at this writing, experimenting with limited private production. It is that the PRC offers a countermodel of revolution to the Soviet one, and the countermodel has at times included the USSR as among the developed, "northern" status quo powers, opposed by the "southern" coalition of Third World developed and developing states. This fiction of Lin Biao was not long-lived beyond his own demise, but two communist centers of world revolution survive ideologically in Beijing and Moscow.

U.S. policy is more concerned with revolutions and insurgencies that seem to adopt the Soviet Marxist model, or to have adopted its rhetoric as a technique of mass mobilization and cadre motivation. U.S. pragmatism precludes the development of a countermodel that might be opposed to the monolithic mobilizing regimes in developing societies. U.S. and West European pluralism is based in a cultural medium of postindustrial mass consumption and social welfare legislation. These cannot simply be transferred to developing societies whose cultures are apt to treat pluralism as a sign of weakness, and party competition as an opportunity for graft and favoritism.

THE SOCIAL CONTRACT

Where, then, shall the United States go in order to offer a paradigm for development of the polity that can be competitive with the Soviet-Marxist revolutionary one? We are not speaking of improving Western propaganda here, but of something more fundamental. A proper normative and empirical understanding of revolution must be preceded by some theory of the policy itself. Where does it come from, and what sustains it? What are its functions, and what individual rights lie within it and outside it? It goes a long way toward tagging the problem, although without resolving it, to notice that U.S. secondary and university education deals insufficiently with this problem. Americans pride themselves on being educated as non-theoretically as possible, as the curriculum in most schools indicates.

It is also the case that not all amorphous wars spring from revolutions, nor from revolutions that are based in Marxist social analysis. The previous discussion of Marxist analysis above was used only as an example, counterpoint to the pretheoretical approach used in U.S. political and military explanations of revolution. The Marxist model has a sense of historical movement, a cause and effect argument, and a termination, although this last state of perfected communism is ever in the distance. To understand how such constructs or other ideological prisms can motivate persons to take up arms against their state and to depose it, U.S. and other Western analysts need some theoretical basis of their own. From theory follows policy applications, which are more than simple reactions to the events of the day.

There is such a theory or set of theories, although it has mostly gone out of fashion. This was known in the past as "social contract." The social contract provided a normative argument for why political societies must be created out of prepolitical societies. It also provided some constructive thinking about how the political societies, having been created, would be organized.[26] However, there is great subtlety in the theories of the social contract and much contradiction among their precepts. Modern versions of contract theory have tended to be very abstract, and even their prospective adherents (such as John Rawls and Robert Nozick) have found much of their intended audience to be uncertain about embracing modern contractualism.[27]

Briefly, we can say that Western contract theory deals with political origins and political management, or rightful rule. No consensual theory of social contract evolved from this literature contributed by Hobbes, Locke, Rousseau, and other political thinkers. Yet, all contract theories shared a common vantage point. They began with the individual and asked what the state or political association could do for that person. And only if the answer included some improvement upon the "natural" or prepolitical condition could a political association and its derivative government be justified at all.

Contract theory was not an historical allegory, since all real societies have had some political process for determining the nature of collective good and for resolving issues about rightful rule and its acceptance. The social contract is a deductive statement about political origins. It is made in order to derive an applied theory of the relationship between individual and state. And it puts the individual and his or her priorities into the driver's seat. Even Rousseau's "general will" had to be good for the individuals over whom it was imposed, however beastly the mechanics of imposing it. And Hobbes' sovereign was all-powerful only so long as the sovereign performed the appropriate functions of preserving order and security for citizens of the polity. Moreover, the order sought by Western contract theorists was not the order of the commune but the order of individuals who shared principles of political right, as Rousseau called them.

We are not doing a commercial for contract theory, only marking it as one framework through which U.S. analysts might develop some notion of political stability and revolutionary change. This would, in turn, provide some benchmark for armed forces that are supporting or resisting insurgencies in the name of U.S. foreign policy. Contract theory is one marker among many in Western thought in which the principles of rightful rule allow for some balancing of collective good and inherent individual rights. Military professionals must perceive that societal good and individual values are in balance, or military institutions will find it difficult to accept tasking that violates either. For example, U.S. soldiers in Vietnam were surprised and angered to find that grandmothers and children in villages were used as combatants on behalf of the Viet Cong. The line between peace and war, combatant and noncombatant, was blurred by U.S. standards. But those standards are themselves the result of a particular history and political development. The U.S. social contract has worked itself out, more or less, whereas the same issues in Vietnam remained to be resolved.

So, too, is the military professional's contract with the state primarily a normative one, a commitment to provide the state with professional expertise and honorific obligation. In turn, the officer expects the state not to provide to him or her a mission that has little or no public support. Members of the U.S. officer corps during the Vietnam War undoubtedly disliked being ostracized socially. That, however, is not new in U.S. military history. There is less excuse for allowing the armed forces to be politically ostracized. This is one of the risks of involving military professionals in extramural paramilitary operations, as in the Iran-Contra connection. The willingness of officers to carry out orders in a military chain of command is exploited by civilian leaders who have not bought into the same understanding of the relationship between the professional officer and the state. For civilians, the sense of obligation is a matter of loyalty to a particular administration, party, or political program. For U.S. military officers, the commitment is to carry out those functions and missions on behalf of the state with which officers are properly charged. It does not seem to me that taking the rap for the incompetency of civilian superiors is a proper charge, but recent trends in U.S. governmental practice may falsify this understanding. The U.S. military officer's social contract, like that which preceded the U.S. polity itself, is more a matter of collective conscience than it is a question of legalistic enforcement. In Vietnam, we saw the consequences of violating that contract, by placing the armed forces in a war that civilian leadership wanted "not to lose" for domestic political reasons, but for which it had no acceptable model of how to "win."

ENDING ATYPICAL WARS

The most difficult aspect of atypical wars, including some kinds of low intensity conflicts, is bringing them to an end. The problem of ending atypical wars is exacerbated by several conditions frequently associated with these kinds of issues. First, there are asymmetries in motivation on the part of the participants. Second, and partly on account of the first, there are differences in the willingness of the various sides to commit their resources to support their political and military objectives. Third, the effort to arrange a cease-fire or armistice does not necessarily end the fighting, although it may end the conventional military aspect of the struggle.

The first issue was found to be critical in the Vietnam War. The asymmetry in motivation favored the North Vietnamese and their allied forces in South Vietnam, as against the U.S. willingness to continue to fight. This was not so at the beginning of the U.S. military involvement with U.S. combat forces. But after several years of mounting casualties and domestic political unrest, it was clear that the Americans were not going to hold out, at least at their level of involvement at the time. President Johnson finally confirmed that the United States had been outlasted by the Vietnamese when he declined to run for re-election in 1968. This was Johnson's acknowledgment that he had lost the political war in Vietnam, meaning that the U.S. escalation could not be sustained any longer. This in turn signaled the North Vietnamese and the Viet Cong that they had only to bide their time until U.S. commitments declined to an acceptable level, and then they could topple the feeble politico-military structure of the government of South Vietnam.

In the case of the U.S. bombing of Khaddafy's headquarters in 1986, the Libyan dictator had underestimated the determination of the Reagan administration to make him a visible symbol of its anti-terrorism policies. Whether this equated to a success in a sustained campaign of counterterrorism was another matter. Terrorist organizations, unlike national states, frequently lacked "addresses" at which they could be attacked.[28] One could argue in theory for U.S. retaliation against the states that sponsored terrorism if the sponsors could be identified unambiguously. But the "terror network" is not so nicely strung together as to have one or a few vulnerable centers. Striking at terrorist headquarters does not have the same consequences, for example, as strikes at U.S. or Soviet nuclear command headquarters would have in a nuclear war. Terrorist organizations are like loosely structured ganglia, oriented around cellular components that may themselves be relatively autonomous. Striking at one ganglion or cell may simply cause it to regenerate in another location, with additional followers if the strike is excessively punitive and visible. In addition, one of the reasons why terrorists have been able to persevere in the face of much hostility from territorial states and their governments is that the terrorists have been able to co-opt the mantle of cultural nationalism better than some governments. In Lebanon, for example, the religious and secular cleavages among Muslims of different political persuasions make the state and the city of Beirut almost ungovernable except by extreme force, as in the Syrian occupation.

If asymmetry of motivation is one issue, another is the difference in resources that either side is willing to commit to a conflict. The United States in 1987 provided U.S. Navy vessels to escort reflagged Kuwaiti tankers in the Persian Gulf. The United States was motivated to ensure that the Iranians or Iraquis, and primarily the former, could not shut off the flow of oil to U.S. allies in Europe and Northeast Asia. This demonstrative use of coercive diplomacy relied upon the flexibility inherent in the widely dispersed maritime power of the United States. Had a major crisis in Europe or the Far East erupted during the U.S. escort melodrama in the gulf, the United States would have found itself forced to divert resources from the Middle East/Southwest Asia theater of operations to elsewhere. Although the Reagan administration was reluctant to identify the number of conventional wars it could fight while using its military resources at maximum capacity, it seemed apparent that it could not fight simultaneously on three fronts (Japan/Korea, Europe, and the Middle East/Southwest Asia) with actively deployed forces.[29] This might seem like mixing apples and oranges, but it is not. An amorphous war in the Middle East, growing out of U.S. coercion of the Iranians or from some other local cause, could spread into global conventional war that finds the United States fighting on many fronts. Of course, not all wars in the Middle East would be amorphous wars. If an Arab multifront coalition was threatening imminent destruction of the state of Israel or its armed forces in their entirety, U.S. objectives would not be ambiguous, although the timely availability of conventional forces adequate to the task could not be guaranteed.

The Vietnam War also provides evidence of the willingness of the United States and North Vietnam to commit their resources to the political and military conflict. Although it is a superpower with global commitments, the United States found its usable political and military power to be insufficient to dissuade North Vietnam from continuing the war. In part, this was because the United States was unwilling to commit more than a certain proportion of its resources to the conflict in Southeast Asia. Nuclear escalation was inappropriate to the circumstances, and the commitment of additional U.S. conventional forces was, by 1968, obviously not going to be sustainable in Congress. In addition, the Nixon administration rapidly signalled, after it took office in 1969, that it was committed to phased withdrawal of U.S. combat forces and to limitation of the U.S. military commitment in time and resources. Nixon obviously wanted to run for re-election in 1972 and needed to have created by that date at least the appearance, if not the fact, of U.S. combat disengagement. At the same time, he also had to guard his flank against a too-precipitate defeat of the South Vietnamese government by insurgents and/or North Vietnamese regulars, at least until after November 1972.

It might seem arbitrary to refer to the Vietnam War as atypical, for it was not a covert war, and it is arguable whether Vietnam fits the definition of "low intensity conflict."[30] Atypical wars are characterized by amorphous political and military purposes, regardless of their degree of public visibility, resource costs, or mixture of conventional and unconventional forces actually in combat. They are also characterized by professional uncertainties on the part of military officers and enlisted personnel as to the appropriateness of their missions and rules of engagement. The U.S. war in Vietnam fits both conditions. And, as we have been saying, it also proved to be problematical to terminate, on account of several factors typical of atypical wars. The second of these factors characteristic of atypical wars, and noncontributory to war termination, is the unequal willingness of the contestants to pay costs and suffer losses. The U.S. experience in Vietnam might suggest that high-technology, consumption-oriented societies could be less willing to suffer relative deprivation, as a result of combat losses and economic costs attendant to war, than developing societies. However, the Soviet experience in Afghanistan leaves the preceding verdict uncertain, since the USSR, while certainly deserving the "high-technology" label, affords a lesser priority to consumer preference, including consumer preference for the avoidance of war and its disruption of individual lives.

Cease-Fire versus Termination

The third dimension of atypical wars that makes them so difficult to terminate is that a military cease-fire is unlikely to be the end of the entire war, although it may mark the end of one phase. This also happens in conventional wars, as it did in Korea, but it is even more characteristic of unconventional wars or low intensity conflicts. The U.S. forces interposed in Lebanon during the first term of the Reagan administration were there as part of a multinational peacekeeping mission. This commitment followed on the heels of the near annihilation of Arafat's forces by the Israelis and the desire on the part of the Americans and their allies to limit the scope and duration of Israeli military activity in Lebanon. However, the U.S. and other forces sent to Lebanon in this role soon found the tasking of "peacekeeping" difficult to keep separated from the taking of sides in a brutal civil war, and one with strong roots in religion and nationalism. Effective peacekeeping operations could only be perceived as siding with the ineffective Lebanese government against its (mainly) Muslim opponents of various stripes. Separating the combatants in this divided country could not be distinguished from showing favoritism to one or another, and, thus, ideological fraternization of Americans with the goals of one or more Lebanese factions. Americans then became the targets of terrorists who saw the United States as no longer nonaligned in Lebanese cultural and religious strife.[31] The U.S. predicament in Lebanon in 1982–1983 shared some similarities with that of the United Nations in the Congo in 1960. The United Nations force sent to the Congo was supposed to restore order but maintain political impartiality among the various factions. In fact, order was restored eventually at the cost of suppressing the Katangese led by Moise Tshombe, by denying them the option of rebellion and secession.

Whether the war stops when the shooting does is also determined by the views of the relationship between war and peace that are held by the disputants. The Soviet view of this relationship differs in significant ways from the Western one. Entire volumes have been devoted to this topic, but it can be addressed here only in a very general way.[32] The Soviets have an essentialist, as opposed to an instrumental, view of the relationship between war and peace. Peace is not the antithesis of war, but a continuation of conflict under other-than-military auspices. This "Clausewitzian" heritage, of the causal connection between war and politics, is distilled through a prism of Marxist theory and Leninist practice supposedly in conformity with the theory. The theory is important, despite the emphasis in much Western scholarship on the Leninist character of the Soviet party and state. A Marxist perspective attempts to avoid wars that are not advantageous to fight; after all, wars are attributable to capitalism. Thus, the USSR will not be plunged into war through "adventurism," for which Khrushchev, having brought his colleagues near to the brink in Cuba in 1962, paid with his political demise.

Once engaged in war, the Soviets are going to expend as much blood and treasure as it appears necessary in order to accomplish their stated war aims. But wars can be ended on terms less favorable than those expected when war began, provided the acceptable, but lesser, terms are preferable to alternatives. Lenin made such a decision when he insisted that acceptance of the terms of Brest-Litovsk was in Soviet long-run interest, although to its apparent short-run detriment (and so opposed by some of Lenin's own entourage).[33] Speaking comparatively, one might wonder how the United States would have fared had it decided not to up the ante after Johnson's election as president in his own right in 1964. President Johnson might have decided, on the basis of his very large victory in the election of that year, to run the risk of "losing" South Vietnam, making the rearguard argument that no increase in U.S. commitment could substitute for a government that had lost popular support. We will never know. But Johnson chose to escalate in stages until the cumulative costs were perceived by the U.S. public and Congress to be excessive.

Soviets in Afghanistan: Cutting Losses

The Soviet predicament in Afghanistan in 1988, although dissimilar in geopolitical attributes from the U.S. commitment in Vietnam, shared some common decision making dilemmas. And these common dilemmas had to do with the character of amorphous war as related to the problem of war termination seen from the Soviet perspective. By the start of 1988, Gorbachev had clearly decided that enough was enough, with regard to the continuing commitment of large numbers of Soviet ground and tactical air forces. This did not mean that the USSR would now settle for a government in Kabul that was hostile to Soviet interests; it surely would not, especially if that government seemed to be the seedbed for insurrection in any of the Asiatic republics of the USSR. However, avoiding a government of this type would still leave a lot of room for choice among acceptable alternatives, including those installed by the Soviets in December 1979. If the Soviet leadership were willing to settle for an other-than-hostile regime on its border, it might be able to disengage combat forces from Afghanistan and even to leave open the choice of successor regime. Najidullah, former head of security, who was elevated to head of state, and his minions might survive the politics of the postoccupational era or they might not, but their fates could be decoupled from the Soviet perception of vital interests in the region.[34]

Regardless of the outcome in Afghanistan, Soviet views of conflict pertinent to amorphous wars are less predictable than they might be for war that threatened the Soviet homeland or the dominion of the USSR over Eastern Europe. In its relations with Ethiopia and Somalia a decade ago, the Soviet Union showed that it was prepared to shift its allegiance from one side to another if the shift resulted in a geopolitically favorable outcome in the Horn of Africa. In that instance, the USSR substituted a larger prize of intimacy with Ethiopia for the formerly cordial relationship with Somalia. In Angola, the USSR has encouraged Cuba to provide a praetorian guard for the MPLA (Popular Movement for the Liberation of Angola) government against both internal opponents (primarily Savimbi) and external ones (South Africa), as the Cubans have also done at Soviet behest elsewhere. Cubans and East Germans have also been welcoming Soviet exports to Third World states that want to wire up their security services along the Soviet model or some approximation of it. However, whether the Cubans will be willing to play this role as Soviet surrogates for very much longer is in some doubt. There is some obvious discontent among policymakers in Havana and among the Cuban armed forces over playing the role of "Soviet foreign legion." And the Soviets have some reason to doubt that the Cubans can be trusted to carry out their wishes without ever backing Soviet leaders into an unwanted confrontation with the United States.

One might argue, as Robert Bathurst has suggested, that the Soviet view of war termination comes into play when the last partisan is stood up against a wall.[35] Undoubtedly, the Soviets would fight with this kind of tenacity in any war that involved an invasion of their homeland, as the Great Patriotic War surely did. However, limited wars of lesser consequence are not going to go automatically to this extreme. Nor is the Soviet view of the potential of guerrilla warfare—to use one example of techniques common in amorphous wars—necessarily a favorable one. Lenin, in fact, was extremely skeptical of the accomplishments of irregular forces, and for very good reason. The Soviet Union under his leadership faced the immediate and vital need to reconstruct a loyal and effective professional armed force not dependent on the enthusiastic incompetence of amateur soldiers. Lenin wrote that "One should shun *partisanshchina* [guerrillaism] like fire" on account of "the arbitrary operations of individual detachments, the disobedience vis-à-vis the central power. It leads to ruin."[36]

And it is now apparent that as the counterinsurgent power, the USSR is willing to cut its losses, as it was in Afghanistan in 1988. The irony of "people's war" turned against the people's state by religious and nationalist revolutionaries is considerable. Soviet short-term political priorities and conditions indigenous to Afghanistan played important parts in turning this protracted conflict toward stalemate, and then into Soviet plans for withdrawal of combat forces. The USSR is concerned about its nationalities, even apart from those Islamic nationalities in its south central Asian republics. In 1988, the Soviet Estonian and Armenian nationalities were also restive. In February 1988, Western press reports based on information from Soviet dissidents suggested that as many as 100,000 persons took part in demonstrations in Soviet Armenia, on behalf of political reorganization that would reflect more faithfully nationalistic boundaries.[37]

Conditions within Afghanistan also contributed to conflict termination. The Afghani rebels (a loose coalition of at least seven different groups) could not hope to inflict a decisive defeat on the government of Afghanistan as long as Soviet combat forces remained there in large numbers. Once Gorbachev indicated a willingness to set a timetable for withdrawal of those forces (he made this explicit in his meetings with U.S. officials in December 1987), the negotiations in Pakistan between government and rebel forces took on a more serious cast. In the same fashion, the Nixon administration let the government of South Vietnam know that it no longer had a blank check on U.S. support. The U.S. "Vietnamization" policy would gradually phase out U.S. combat forces and eventually leave to South Vietnam the task of military self-defense and political reconstruction. Following this process, the government of South Vietnam did not survive, and the government of Afghanistan (from December 1979 until at least May 1988) may not survive either.

As these cases and others show, revolutionary "wars" in developing societies may be terminated in one sense although fighting continues in another. The Paris peace accords of 1973 supposedly terminated the war in Vietnam, insofar as the U.S. commitment to defense of South Vietnam was concerned. There were the usual statements by U.S. representatives about the right to return with combat forces if necessary, but everyone understood that public and congressional sentiment made this essentially impossible. The fighting between factions within Vietnam continued, however, until one side prevailed decisively. This more fundamental war, of the struggle for supreme power within Vietnamese nationalism, was thus not terminated until 1975, but the military outcome was for all practical purposes decided in 1973, or in U.S. domestic politics, in 1968.

As Fred Charles Ikle has noted in his seminal study of war termination, this raises the interesting question of whether the "treason of the hawks" or "treason of the doves" is more to be feared if an end to war, including revolutionary war, is desired.[38] The treason of the hawks is that they may insist upon continuing a war when it is politically pointless to do so. World War I provides an illustration in the behavior of members of both the Triple Alliance and the Triple Entente. The treason of the doves is that they may be willing to settle for less than optimal or attainable war aims if war termination becomes an end in itself. Ikle's verdict is that overall, governments have paid less attention to the treason of the hawks, which causes them to persevere in a pointless war.[39] Here, the relationship of military professionalism to public policy comes into play again. If armed forces are made to feel that it is "their" war that policymakers have abandoned, as U.S. forces did in Vietnam after 1969, institutionally dysfunctional behaviors are almost certain to result. The most surprising outcome of the U.S. military intervention in Vietnam was that the U.S. Army as an institution survived it. Elements of the French army reacted in a different way to the impending "surrender" of Algeria to nationalists, posing a constitutional challenge that required the personal charisma of Charles de Gaulle to defeat.

CONCLUSION

Most of the challenges to U.S. and Western national security in the next decades will not be invasions across the North German plain or the Korean demilitarized zone. They will be so-called "low intensity" conflicts with which the United States will find it very difficult to deal. It is frequently stated that the U.S. armed forces lack the training and equipment to perform well in such engagements. This may be so, but the argument here is that the United States is lacking in more fundamental political understandings prerequisite to successful involvement in atypical wars. These more fundamental understandings, absent as they are, then ripple into lack of political and military preparedness across the board.

Those understandings are, as we have seen, that the policy process for evaluating and applying intelligence is rarely adequate; that the military sense of professionalism is frequently compromised in atypical wars at the very time when a sense of unambiguous rightful duty is most important; and that there are alternative models to the Marxist one for social and political development, but these do not guarantee military success. Nor does military stalemate, desirable as that might be, guarantee a favorable political outcome. As one expert in national security studies has noted:

> Military intervention is usually a technique of last resort. Other instruments of policy are available and quite likely preferable in most circumstances. No matter how well informed, how wise and influential U.S. foreign policy is, this country cannot have absolute control over events. Many things will happen that are opposed to our interests and may have to be accepted for what they are. Not all radical movements or all revolutions constitute a threat to us. Not all gains by the Soviets are losses on our score sheet. Moreover, neither gains nor setbacks are likely to be permanent.[40]

What are the implications of arguments for U.S. and other major power options for the use of force outside of European and North Asian core security zones? Recent U.S. experience would suggest that there is some likelihood, under very favorable scenarios, for conducting hostage rescues; for interposing a trip-wire or plate-glass light infantry force into a hotspot as a deterrent; and for military aid and other kinds of security assistance to regimes that can use it effectively. What seems less likely to succeed are U.S. or Soviet efforts to fight extended Third World conflicts or to serve as the mediators or enforcers of peacekeeping operations.

NOTES

1. For a discussion of this in broader compass, see Offense-Defense Working Group, Commission on Long-Term Strategy, *The Future of Containment: America's Options for Defending Its Interests on the Soviet Periphery* (Washington, D.C.: U.S. Department of Defense, 1988). For perspective on unconventional wars and U.S. foreign policy, see Richard Shultz, "Strategy Lessons from an Unconventional War: The U.S. Experience in Vietnam," *Nonnuclear Conflicts in the Nuclear Age*, ed. Sam C. Sarkesian (New York: Praeger Publishers, 1980). For additional perspective on U.S. dilemmas in

low intensity conflict, see Sam C. Sarkesian, *Beyond the Battlefield: The New Military Profession* (New York: Pergamon Press, 1981), as well as the chapters by William P. Snyder and Roger Beaumont and by Alan Ned Sabrosky in *Nonnuclear Conflicts*.

2. See Francis Fukuyama, "Escalation in the Middle East and Persian Gulf," *Hawks, Doves and Owls: An Agenda for Avoiding Nuclear War*, eds. Graham T. Allison, Albert Carnesale, and Joseph S. Nye, Jr. (New York: W. W. Norton, 1985) 115–47.

3. Roger Hilsman, *The Politics of Policy Making in Defense and Foreign Affairs* (Englewood Cliffs, N.J.: Prentice-Hall, Inc., 1987): 179–203, and Graham T. Allison, *Essence of Decision; Explaining the Cuban Missile Crisis* (Boston: Little, Brown, 1971) 67–100.

4. David C. Martin, *Wilderness of Mirrors* (New York: Ballantine Books, 1980).

5. Allision, *Essence of Decision* 110.

6. Other factors were contributory in addition to Stalin's conviction that the USSR must avoid war if at all possible. Soviet appreciation of the implications of German operational-tactical doctrine was deficient. And repeated intelligence warnings were disregarded, including those from unimpeachable sources. See John Erickson, "Threat Identification and Strategic Appraisal by the Soviet Union, 1930–41," *Knowing One's Enemies: Intelligence Assessment Before the Two World Wars*, ed. Ernest R. May (Princeton: Princeton University Press, 1984) 375–423, esp. 418–20; and Barton Whaley, Codeword BARBAROSSA (Cambridge, Mass.: MIT Press, 1973).

7. Roberta Wohlstetter, *Pearl Harbor: Warning and Decision* (Stanford: Stanford University Press, 1962). Wohlstetter's assertion that the "noise" of irrelevant information drowned out the "signals" that would have revealed Japanese intentions is disputed in David Kahn, "The United States Views Germany and Japan in 1941," *Knowing One's Enemies*, ed. May, 500–01.

8. Jeffrey Richelson, *Sword and Shield: The Soviet Intelligence and Security Apparatus* (Cambridge, Mass.: Ballinger Publishing Co., 1986); John J. Dziak, "Soviet Deception: The Organizational and Operational Tradition," *Soviet Strategic Deception*, eds. Brian D. Dailey and Patrick J. Parker (Lexington, Mass.: D. C. Heath/Hoover Institution, 1987) 3–20.

9. Jeffrey Richelson and Desmond Ball, *Ties that Bind: Intelligence Cooperation Between the UKUSA Countries* (Winchester, Mass.: Allen and Unwin, 1986), 239–68.

10. The possibility of conflict between military legitimacy and military posture is explored in Sarkesian, *Beyond the Battlefield* Ch. 6,. esp. 91. See also Morris Janowitz, *The Professional Soldier: A Social and Political Portrait* (New York: Free Press, 1971), and Samuel P. Huntington, *The Soldier and the State: The Theory and Politics of Civil-Military Relations* (New York: Vintage Books, 1964; Cambridge: Belknap Press of Harvard University Press).

11. Huntington, *Soldier and the State* passim.

12. U.S. force employment in other than combat situations is discussed in Sarkesian, *Beyond the Battlefield* 63.

13. On the U.S. chain of command in Vietnam and its performance therein, see Edward N. Luttwak, *The Pentagon and the Art of War: The Question of Military Reform* (New York: Simon and Schuster, 1984), Ch. 1 and 2.

14. For an informative assessment, see Andrew F. Krepinevich, Jr., *The Army and Vietnam* (Baltimore, Md.: Johns Hopkins University Press, 1986).

15. Alexander L. George, "The Development of Doctrine and Strategy," *The Limits of Coercive Diplomacy: Laos, Cuba, Vietnam*, eds. Alexander L. George, David K. Hall, and William R. Simons (Boston: Little, Brown, 1971) Ch.1.

16. This is adapted by the author from George, Hall, and Simons, eds., *Limits of Coercive Diplomacy.*

17. President's Special Review Board (Tower Commission), *Report* (New York: New York Times/Bantam Books, 1987).

18. The role of civil affairs in army doctrine is discussed in Maj. David A. Decker, "Civil Affairs: A Rebirth or Stillborn?" *Military Review* 67, no. 11 (November 1987): 60–64.

19. David Easton, *The Political System* (New York: Alfred A. Knopf, 1953).

20. Michael MccGwire, *Military Objectives in Soviet Foreign Policy* (Washington, D.C.: Brookings Institution, 1987).

21. John Erickson, *The Road to Stalingrad*, vol. 1 (New York: Harper and Row, 1973).

22. On Stalin's purge of the military leadership of the USSR in 1937–1938, see John Erickson, *The Soviet High Command: A Military-Political History 1918–41* (New York: St Martin's Press, 1962), Ch. 14.

23. Ernest Barker's edition of Aristotle's *Politics* is very useful in explaining the difference between ideal and actual polities. See Ernest Barker, ed. and trans., *The Politics of Aristotle* (1958; New York: Oxford University Press, 1977), esp. 1ii–1iv.

24. The difference between insurgents and revolutionaries is one of nomenclature more than one of practice, in my judgment. Useful efforts to adjudicate the vocabulary of anti-statist political movements include Lawrence Stone, "Theories of Revolution," *World Politics* 18, no. 2 (January 1966): 159–76, reprinted in Sam C. Sarkesian, ed., *Revolutionary Guerrilla Warfare* (Chicago: Precedent Publishing Company, 1975) 27–46. The definitive study of Western revolutions remains Crane Brinton, *The Anatomy of Revolution*, (New York: Random House/Vintage Books, 1965). Important markers for the empirical study of political behavior in intra-national conflict settings include Harry Eckstein, ed., *Internal War* (Glencoe, Ill.: Free Press, 1964) and Ted Robert Gurr, *Why Men Rebel* (Princeton: Princeton University Press, 1970).

25. Brinton, *Anatomy of Revolution* passim.

26. *Social Contract: Essays by Locke, Hume and Rousseau.* Intro. by Sir Ernest Barker (1960; New York: Oxford University Press, 1977); Thomas Hobbes, *Leviathan*, ed. (New York: Washington Square Press, 1970).

27. A helpful discussion of contract theory in this context appears in W. J. Stankiewicz, *Aspects of Political Theory: Classical Concepts in an Age of Relativism* (London: Collier-Macmillan, 1976).

28. For discussions pertinent to this problem, see Neil C. Livingston and Terrell E. Arnold, eds., *Fighting Back: Winning the War against Terrorism* (Lexington, Mass.: D. C. Heath/Lexington Books, 1986).

29. On the strategy-force mismatch, see Richard Halloran, *To Arm a Nation: Rebuilding America's Endangered Defenses* (New York: Macmillan Publishing Company, 1986), Ch. 7.

30. The spectrum of U.S. deterrence-defense options is reviewed in Sam C. Sarkesian, "Nonnuclear Conflicts: Characteristics and Policy Issues," *Nonnuclear Conflicts in the Nuclear Age*, ed. Sarkesian, 5–35.

31. Luttwak, *Pentagon and the Art of War* 50–51.

32. A very useful collection is Derek Leebaert, ed., *Soviet Military Thinking* (London: Allen and Unwin, 1981).

33. Fred Charles Ikle, *Every War Must End* (New York: Columbia University Press, 1971) 82.

34. In the summer of 1981, two separate coalitions were announced, described by Western sources as "fundamentalists" and "moderates." Each had the same formal name: Islamic Unity of Afghan Mujahidin. The two coalitions came to be known as the Unity of Three (moderates) and the Unity of Six (later Seven, the fundamentalists). So-called moderates favored a democratic government for Afghanistan and Western assistance for their efforts to dislodge the Soviet-supported regime. Fundamentalists sought an Islamic government of the Khomeini type. See J. Bruce Amstutz, *Afghanistan: The First Five Years of Soviet Occupation* (Washington, D.C.: National Defense University Press, 1986), 96–101.

35. Robert Bathurst's "Two Languages of War," in *Soviet Military Thinking*, ed. Leebaert, Ch. 2. Bathurst also observes, "Whereas on every level, Soviet society is organized for struggle with a clearly defined victory, whether in the five year plan or on the battlefield, the USA seems to have given up the idea of victory in war as in diplomacy" (p. 32). See his comparison of Soviet and U.S. views of war termination in Robert Bathurst, "Some Problems in Soviet-American War Termination: Cross/Cultural Asymmetries" (Monterey, Calif.: Naval Postgraduate School, September 1988).

36. Quoted in Walter Laqueur, *Guerrilla: A Historical and Critical Study* (Boston: Little, Brown, 1976) 173.

37. *Philadelphia Inquirer*, 24 February 1988: 1.

38. Ikle, *Every War Must End* passim.

39. Ikle, *Every War Must End* 59–64.

40. David W. Tarr, "The Strategic Environment: U.S. National Security and the Nature of Low Intensity Conflict," *Nonnuclear Conflicts in the Nuclear Age*, ed. Sarkesian, 58.

5

MILITARY DECEPTION
AND DETERRENCE:
THE ART OF NOISE

Deception is one kind of stratagem. It is the nature of stratagems that they do not accomplish decisive aims in themselves. They accompany a well-considered operational plan for fighting war or for deterring it. Deception also involves a way of thinking about strategy and military operations. Deceiving a target state, its leaders, or its intelligence collectors and evaluators requires some knowledge of its decision-making process and national strategic style: How does it make decisions, and who makes which ones? This intelligence is not only the product of rigorous collection, but also of preconceptions that one side's political leaders and military planners have about another's. These preconceptions or belief systems determine the perspective from which intelligence on potential opponents is viewed.

This chapter considers the problem of military deception as a component of strategy and military operations. I first discuss the problem of threat assessment. This is first established as a species of uncertainty. I then consider the problem of threat assessment from two vantage points, although they overlap: the general estimation of capabilities and intentions of some states by others, and the problem of policymakers' expectations as related to vulnerability to deception and surprise. The relationship between deception and operational art is then considered. The "peculiar" problems of long wars, unexpected attacks, and other outcomes for which planners are infrequently prepared are treated separately. Finally, the use of electronic warfare in combination with deception is discussed, for the Soviet approach is unique.

This chapter draws from my article, "Mainstreaming Military Deception," *Journal of Intelligence and Counterintelligence* 3, no. 4 (1989), 509–535.

THREAT ASSESSMENT

Clausewitz reminds us repeatedly that the most certain thing about war is uncertainty.[1] This is so for at least two reasons. First, war is the realm of chance, and chance makes everything more uncertain. Second, there is the impact of friction on warfare. As Clausewitz notes, persons who have not actually experienced warfare will have difficulty appreciating the extent to which friction makes irrelevant even the most carefully thought out plans.[2] As he expresses it, "Everything in war is very simple, but the simplest thing is difficult."[3]

Friction, according to Clausewitz, is the only concept that corresponds to the factors that distinguish real war from war on paper.[4] The reason for this is not only that events are unpredictable. It is also the case that the parts of the military machine are not inanimate objects, but individuals, each having the potential to create friction.

By obtaining adequate intelligence about the opponent or by denying him intelligence, one might suppose that friction can be overcome and uncertainty eliminated. War is not as simple as that, nor are intelligence gathering and estimating. Clausewitz defines intelligence pragmatically: every sort of information about the enemy and his country.[5] Commanders and policymakers alike will identify with his next warning, with regard to the relationship between intelligence and war: Information in war is always transient and therefore unreliable.[6] Clausewitz's observations have more than historical interest. The acquisition and analysis of intelligence must have a purpose: that of anticipating, and negating, the plans of the opponent. War is, as Clausewitz has emphasized, a political act designed to obtain the objectives set by policymakers on behalf of the state. The process of acquiring and analyzing intelligence is sometimes apolitical, or subpolitical, in the sense that Clausewitz would not have preferred. Various parts of the intelligence and defense bureaucracy have their own vested interests and perspectives on what has been collected, and their own interpretations of what it means.

The enemy is not like us. This is the basic challenge for intelligence estimators and deception planners (and planners against deception). Eliot Cohen has suggested that failures in U.S. and other Western estimative intelligence are often caused by inability to appreciate the "otherness of the enemy."[7] One result of this insufficient appreciation of "otherness" is the temptation toward "mirror imaging." Thus, the U.S. decision to sell arms to Iran in 1985 was based on an assumption that the Iranian government was divided between "moderates" and "extremists" along the lines of pluralist systems.[8] As Gen. Maxwell Taylor noted in a message to National Security Advisor McGeorge Bundy, the U.S. military mission in Vietnam prior to 1965 had been charged with implementing a twenty-one point military program, a forty-one point nonmilitary program, a sixteen-point U.S. Information Service program, and a twelve-point CIA program "as if we can win here somehow on a point score."[9] Prior to the outbreak of World War II, both British "appeasers" and "anti-appeasers" assumed that the German leadership was similarly divided into factions for and against war in Europe. Both groups of British appraisers also assumed that Hitler could be deterred from aggression, if necessary, by the threat of war. Contrary to this widely shared supposition, Hitler wanted war—and by the summer of 1939, he was beyond deterrence.[10]

Historical Threat Assessment: Judging General Capabilities and Intentions

The major European powers before World War I, and the European and Asian powers between World War I and II, failed in significant ways to anticipate the wartime environment.[11] The kinds of misjudgments they made, about the most devastating and globally far-reaching wars of this century so far, are reminders of the humility with which intelligence analysts and academic students of intelligence need to approach their subject matter. In an overall sense, before World War I the major powers anticipated correctly the intentions or proclivities of their prospective opponents. But they were terribly wrong in their estimates of capabilities. How and why they were wrong is even more interesting. They got small things correct, but big things out of focus. Basic "order of battle" information was surprisingly accurate. Despite this surprising accuracy about details, the context for battle was misperceived. Thus, prewar military doctrine continued to emphasize the charging of prepared positions by forces that ran into the impassable hail of machine gun fire and barbed wire. Doctrinal fixities were followed even after the battles of 1914 and 1915 proved that a protracted war of attrition favoring the defensive was at least temporarily the dominant form of operational art.[12]

Before World War II, on the other hand, capabilities were more correctly understood, but intentions misjudged. The most obvious case in point was the surprise inflicted on the democracies of the West when Hitler and Stalin signed their nonaggression pact in 1939. The next most obvious case was the ability of Germany to surprise the Soviet Union on June 22, 1941 by launching Operation Barbarossa. Here we must pause to note that World

War II was full of surprises and stratagems of various sorts, but the two I have just mentioned are distinguished by their status as strategic surprises. That is, they were surprises that had important consequences for the overall geopolitical strategy of the relevant actors. By contrast, the German invasion and conquest of France in May 1940 can hardly be called a strategic surprise, since war had already broken out and the French anticipated a German attack sooner or later. However, the attack on France did achieve operational surprise, by arriving through the defiles of the Ardennes with fast-moving Panzer units, which then irrupted into the French rear, causing chaos and ultimate defeat.

The problem of surprise, especially in nuclear strategy, is closely related to the issue of preemption.[13] Preemption is an attack that is launched in the expectation that the opponent has already decided to attack, but before the opponent has in fact carried out the attack. The problem is closely related to the vulnerability of superpower nuclear forces, especially their strategic ones. If either side were to conclude, during a crisis, that its strategic retaliatory forces were vulnerable to nearly complete destruction by a surprise attack, then the expectation of the first side would be to launch its forces "on warning," despite the risk of inadvertent war. A modified version of this would be to launch "under attack" after sensors have confirmed enemy launch, but before targets have actually been struck. As a model for understanding planning guidance for U.S. strategic nuclear forces, this worst case assessment is not too misleading. But for other than conservative planning estimates, it is highly misleading. It drives analysis in the direction of "bolt from the blue" attacks and away from sources of conflict that are more probable.

This has been recognized by Graham T. Allison, Albert Carnesale, and Joseph S. Nye, Jr. of Harvard University in their study on the reduction of risks in the nuclear age.[14] They contrast the models used by "hawks," "doves," and "owls" to explain failures of deterrence (which apply to conventional as well as nuclear warfare). Hawks worry about appeasement as the proximate cause of war and counsel for defense preparedness as the key to successful deterrence. Doves worry about excessive provocation of potential opponents and recommend negotiation and diplomatic approaches to conflict resolution.

Owls are distinct from hawks and doves. Hawks and doves are, according to the Harvard investigators, both members of the same methodological family. They are perched on the branch of rationality, assuming that what causes war is a correct or incorrect assessment of the capabilities and intentions of potential opponents.[15] Owls emphasize factors that are less apt to be captured in assessments of the military balance or in intelligence forecasts. These include personality, decision-making biases, gaps in information, perceptual distortions, motivated biases, and other psychosocial dislocations of the process by which intelligence is gathered, focussed, evaluated, and directed into action channels. These other factors are related to the perceptions and expectations of policymakers and military planners during crisis and war. Of special interest to analysts of this persuasion is the transactional or relational character of the perceptions held by nations and national leaderships of one another.

From this metarational perspective, the balance of power or net assessment of combatant forces may be misleading. Particularly in nuclear crises, the personalities of decision makers and the perceptions that they hold may be more important. Thus, the Cuban missile crisis is an anomaly from the standpoint of new assessment. Khrushchev knew, and he knew that the Americans knew, that his military position relative to theirs was one of great inferiority in strategic nuclear forces.[16] U.S. explanations that he put missiles into Cuba in order to readjust the balance in his favor miss the point that, according to U.S. models of nuclear deterrence, he should never have dared to put them there. Having done so, the unpredictable Khrushchev placed President Kennedy in a dilemma: Kennedy had to threaten the possibility of (1) direct U.S.-Soviet conflict in order to induce the withdrawal of the missiles, and (2) general nuclear war if a Soviet missile launched from Cuba landed anywhere in the western hemisphere. Kennedy turned the tables on Khrushchev by adopting a "quarantine" that required the Soviets to desist from attempting to ship additional missiles to Cuba. But this did not prevent their efforts to complete construction of the missiles already there. Only U.S. threats conveyed through various channels to take forcible action against the missiles and Soviet personnel themselves, including possible air strikes or a Cuban invasion, obtained a reluctant Soviet withdrawal.

Two aspects of the crisis negotiations between U.S. and Soviet principals support the owlish perspective on crisis management. The first was the apparent difficulty the U.S. leadership had in understanding fully the implications of standard operating procedures activated by U.S. maritime forces. Thus, U.S. anti-submarine warfare was conducted against Soviet submarines in the Atlantic and elsewhere; some of these submarines were almost certainly nuclear armed.[17] A U-2 strayed off course and caused Soviet air defense fighters to scramble; Khrushchev later indicated that this might have been misconstrued as a U.S. bomber attack on Soviet territory.[18]

A second interesting aspect of the crisis was the conflicting messages received from Khrushchev with regard to the conditions for resolving the crisis. The first was rather conciliatory and focussed on the risk of war if disputed issues were not quickly resolved. The second, arriving one day later, was pessimistic and harsh in its demands for reciprocal U.S. concessions. The U.S. ExCom (the Executive Committee of the National Security Council, an improvised group of key Kennedy advisors) decided to deal with these conflicting responses by using the "Trollope ploy," in which the first—and preferable—letter was answered, and the second ignored.[19] This worked out successfully. One has the impression of a Soviet leadership that may have been divided about what to do, with an initial decision on the part of Khrushchev (to be conciliatory) having been overturned by Politburo colleagues. Nor can one be reassured by the need for U.S. and Soviet principals to communicate through the channels of Soviet embassy counselor (and suspected KGB head of U.S. operations) Alexander Fomin and ABC news reporter John Scali, under conditions that were unusual and auspices that were unattributable.[20] Backchannel negotiations are not uncommon in diplomacy, but the situation here was unique, and the Soviet approach to Scali suggested an urgency felt in Moscow that both sides might soon lose control of events.

Deception, Surprise, and Preconceptions

The Cuban case involved a situation in which time was short and the consequences of faulty decision making were potentially catastrophic. But additional time for policymakers and intelligence estimators does not always bring about improved decisions. On account of the biases and preconceptions of analysts, operators, and decision makers, surprises can be attained by attackers even against presumably well-informed defenders.

Two cases in point are the Nazi invasion of the Soviet Union in June 1941 and the Japanese attack on Pearl Harbor in December of the same year. Both Japanese and German military planners knew that their chances of fighting a long war to a successful conclusion were very small. Each planned a brilliant operational strike against an opponent who had received many intelligence indications of hostile intent and war preparedness. In the case of U.S. failure to anticipate the Japanese attack on Pearl Harbor, Roberta Wohlstetter's study found that the problem was not lack of sufficient information about Japanese intentions. The problem was a plethora of collected information that was not correctly analyzed. The reason for this, according to Wohlstetter, was that the correct "signals" with regard to Japanese intentions were blurred amid surrounding "noise" that suggested other, and equally likely, possibilities.[21] The noise factor has both quantitative and qualitative implications. The large number of misleading or irrelevant signals makes the correct ones harder to identify and isolate. The qualitative issue is that not all noise is equally irrelevant. Sometimes, estimates must be made before the prospective attacker has actually made an irrevocable move. One of the problems with anticipating surprise is that the attack planner can arrange feints in order to draw out the defender's probable responses. As the responses are catalogued, the attacker tries something else. If time permits, a successful option may be found.

The Soviet surprise by Operation Barbarossa seems even more difficult to explain than the U.S. surprise at Pearl Harbor. The Soviet leadership, including Stalin himself, received more than eighty warnings of German intentions to attack the Soviet Union in 1941, or of German preparations for an attack eastward, or both.[22] Yet these were disregarded, and the Soviet armed forces were caught largely by surprise and out of position when the invasion was launched.[23] Nor was this strictly tactical surprise, in terms of the exact timing and direction of the attack. It was also operational in the sense that the Soviets, despite their extensive espionage networks throughout Europe, failed to understand correctly the German method of warfare. The expectation of Soviet military planners was that the Germans, if they attacked at all, would fight a battle of several days with skirmishing and reconnaissance forces against Soviet covering forces along the border. Only after these skirmishes and probes had identified the most appropriate points for exploitation would the principal armor and infantry forces of the Wehrmacht be launched into the Soviet Union.[24] This expectation proved to be ill founded; the Germans hammered their way into Soviet territory from the very first hour with their crack ground and tactical air forces, in an effort to push the Soviets back along a broad operational front and to achieve a deep operational penetration that would disrupt the cohesion of the defense.

Part of the reason for the success of the German deception of the Soviets was Soviet self-deception. Stalin had decided that were Hitler to attack, the Nazi dictator would first issue an ultimatum. This would provide effective strategic warning of Hitler's intention.[25] The assumption was that, having issued this ultimatum, Hitler could be persuaded to delay any actual clash of arms by the pretense of Soviet concessions and political accommodation. This accommodation would last until mid-1942, when the USSR would be prepared for war. The Germans promoted another

Soviet self-deception: that Hitler would not attack the Soviet Union (thereby getting involved in a two-front war) without first subduing Great Britain or making peace. Thus, the Germans led Soviet analysts to believe that the military buildup in the east was a diversionary movement preparatory to the final phase of Operation Sea Lion, the German plan for the conquest of the British Isles.[26]

The most effective deceptions, and therefore military surprises, take the perceptual frameworks of the opponent and attempt to place misinformation—or encourage misestimation—within that context.[27] Consider, as an example, the U.S. decision-making problem with regard to the expectation of possible Japanese attack. It was not simply a matter of deciding whether Japan would attack, but where and when. Beliefs and expectations influenced estimates pertinent to those decisions. The U.S. expectation was that the Pacific fleet in Hawaii would act as a deterrent to Japanese attack on U.S. territory; for that reason among others, an attack in a southerly direction toward Indochina or Malaya was more likely. In fact, the Japanese, feeling that things would only get worse for them in the Pacific as time went on and seeing their options as "war now" or "war later," regarded the U.S. fleet in Hawaii as a target instead of a deterrent. The U.S. belief that the Japanese could not in fact conduct air-launched torpedo attacks in waters as shallow as those surrounding Pearl Harbor proved erroneous; the Japanese had modified their torpedoes to accomplish this mission, although the fact was unknown to U.S. intelligence.[28] U.S. values were also pertinent to assumptions about whether Japan would or could execute a surprise attack. According to David Kahn, some U.S. planners discredited the Japanese on ethnic or racial grounds as being capable of inflicting significant military damage to U.S. national interests.[29]

Whaley's analysis of Operation Barbarossa finds the "signal to noise ratio" not very helpful as an explanation for the German deception of Stalin, however compelling it might be for the surprise at Pearl Harbor. Instead, the Germans allowed the Soviet leadership to entertain alternative hypotheses about German intentions, and they supported those alternative hypotheses with active deception.[30] Several of these have been noted above. The Germans engaged in what military deception theorists now call "perceptions management."[31] They fed into the Soviet decision-making process a steady flow of official and unofficial reports that seemed to confirm Stalin's optimism about Hitler's unwillingness to attack the Soviet Union in 1941. They were also helped by the fact that these reports did not appear to be—and in fact were not—fully orchestrated from a central intelligence source. The fortuitous circumstance (for the Germans) was that there were a number of sources within Germany itself that were tapped by the USSR and unknowingly contributed to Stalin's misperception. This suggests that overly determined intelligence deceptions may backfire if they have a too-familiar odor. The best intended deception is one that feeds the opponent's preconceptions and, in addition, is helped along by seren- dipitous discoveries by his own intelligence sources.

INTELLIGENCE, DECEPTION, AND OPERATIONAL ART

Threat assessments may be accurate or not, and if accurate, they may still lead to less than adequate response. Accuracy is a matter of degree. The target of a deception plan need not be completely deceived for deception to contribute to a successful outcome. In fact, completely successful deceptions are rarer than partial ones—which, although partial, have devastating consequences. Once events move beyond peacetime or crisis-driven threat assessment into wartime operations, deception be- comes an integral part of operational art and strategy. So, too, does surprise.

The greatest surprise growing out of a modern war in Europe might be the refusal of both sides to use nuclear weapons. This would return the decision to the conventional battlefield, although not to a conventional battlefield like that of World War II or any time earlier. Robert Jervis has warned against the "conventionalization" of nuclear weapons—the prac- tice of discussing nuclear war fighting as if it were simply conventional war with more destructive weapons.[32] This error is certainly one to be avoided. An equally destructive error, and one to which Western military leaderships may well be more prone, is the assumption that modern war in Europe would rely upon the same "permanently operating forces" (to borrow Stalin's phrase) as the preceding one.

The Soviet view of a modern war in Europe apparently recognizes this. According to Christopher N. Donnelly, the Soviets conceive of the prepa- ration for, and conduct of, war in Europe (or elsewhere) as taking place during three major phases.[33] The first phase is the preparatory phase, one of setting the peacetime stage for war, should the Soviet leadership feel that a decision for war must be made later on. The connection between this stage and war if necessary is very difficult for Western observers to understand or accept. For the USSR, peaceful coexistence is not the same as conflict resolution; it is continuing conflict, along political, social, and economic lines, although the armed forces of the Soviet state are not involved in combat. Following the preparatory phase is the crisis phase, during which war is judged as possibly imminent, and the Soviet armed forces must expect to be involved in hostilities at any time. Finally, there is the decision for war itself, made only by the highest political leadership with the advice of military and other principals.[34]

Having made the decision in favor of war, the Soviet leaders would hope for a favorable outcome, relative to their intended objectives, in the shortest possible time, and without the use of nuclear weapons. Attainment of their objectives without nuclear escalation would require the most calculated and effective use of operational surprise, deception, and *maskirovka* (a Soviet form of military deception, implying camouflage, cover, or concealment and applicable at strategic, operational, and tactical levels).[35] In addition to military maskirovka, active measures and other forms of deception would be needed to divide the NATO alliance with regard to its political objectives. For example, one of the Soviet strategic and operational objectives during war in Europe must be to separate France from NATO. This is necessary to limit French military participation in the defense of West Germany. A longer-term strategic military objective would be to encourage U.S. military disengagement, partial or total, from the territory of Western Europe. The Soviet diplomatic and intelligence establishments would be tasked to accomplish these decisive aims during the preparatory phase, if at all possible.

Soviet operations for war in Europe would also, in all likelihood, involve the use of special operations forces (forces of special designation, or *spetsnaz*). These might be inserted behind NATO lines in order to create confusion in headquarters and disruption of key command and control nodes. The tasking and preparation of Soviet special operations forces could take place months, or even years, ahead of any actual outbreak of war. Western Europe is certainly blanketed by Soviet human and technical collection efforts. Spetsnaz teams have allegedly been organized for war or crisis time deployment against command centers, airfields, depots, nuclear weapons launchers and storage sites, and other time-urgent strategic and operational targets in Western Europe.[36] Western intelligence sources have reported that some 380 Soviet/Pact special designation forces have already been organized and tasked against appropriate targets in Western Europe, should the expectation develop that war is imminent.[37]

There is a danger in the exaggeration of Soviet special operations capabilities: They can easily get out of focus. Most of the time, spetsnaz forces will be engaged in *razvedka*, active reconnaissance and intelligence gathering in all its forms. Spetsnaz forces are not substitutes for conventional forces, nor are they "commandos" in the Western sense of the term. Nevertheless, they have significant, portable capabilities for behind-the-lines survival in wartime, and they will be tasked primarily to identify and designate high-priority targets for destruction by fire. Soviet military doctrine implies requirements for spetsnaz operations that are strategic, operational, and tactical in character. With regard to ground and tactical air forces, this might involve the following schematic. Strategic operations are conducted deep in enemy territory in order to disrupt national cohesion and to create demoralization of the opponent's body politic. Operational missions probably are assigned to front and subordinate commands to depths of 350 to 1,000 kilometers, involving GRU (the military intelligence directorate of the Soviet General Staff), airborne, and army level units tasked for military intelligence and sabotage. Tactical missions might take place at division level to a depth of 100 kilometers or less. Naval spetsnaz units support fleet and ground forces operations in strategic, operational, and tactical categories. In all cases, spetsnaz operations are to be coordinated with other force components in combined arms fashion throughout the theater of operations, and they "must be prepared to execute missions in both conventional and conventional-nuclear environments with all the critical timing, command and control, logistics, and other requirements which these entail."[38]

The Soviet political objective during the early stages of war in Europe will be to seek the sympathy or neutrality of as many members of the Western alliance as possible. They need not accomplish the permanent withdrawal of members from the alliance. Hesitation on the part of the Dutch, Belgians, Turks, Greeks, Danes, or others who might provide key components of defense along the Central Front or northern or southern flanks of NATO might suffice. Combined with operational/tactical penetrations that place NATO forces on the military defensive in West Germany and/or the low countries, the hesitation by several NATO European members to continue fighting could be decisive. Two or three NATO members fearful of nuclear escalation or of Soviet occupation of their own territory could leave the alliance little choice but to sue for peace under highly unfavorable conditions. The Soviet view is that such an outcome cannot be left to chance. The ground must be prepared beforehand.

This implies that strategic *military* defense, of the kind now discussed by Soviet military analysts, is not inconsistent with an offensive *political* strategy for dividing Western Europe and NATO. From the Soviet perspective, the propitious time for war is when the class struggle within the national political economies of the opposed coalition has rendered their collective counsel divided. Such a rendering can be aided by skillful Soviet diplomacy and disinformation, but the forces of history are in charge. Therefore, the opponent's disunity must be at the proper stage of development before any military attack has a chance to succeed. If the Soviets undertake a war of aggression at the wrong time, or are caught unprepared by NATO aggression (in their view, a strong possibility for this always exists, although NATO considers it impossible), then the USSR is going to lose. And for Soviet leaders, the loss of war in Europe would imply the loss of some control over Poland, East Germany, and Czechoslovakia, thus reversing history by overturning entrenched (at the time of this writing) communist regimes. In a very extended war, the East European members of the Warsaw Pact might not be very reliable allies, especially if the war was begun by the USSR according to plans and expectations that soon went awry.

The observation that the Soviets are on the political offensive even when they have assumed the military defensive is not a statement of cynicism. It is simple recognition that their military doctrine recognizes the importance of preparing the way beforehand for military success. For the Soviet leadership (as for Clausewitz), military success is political success—that is, the attainment of policy objectives for which the war is being fought. In the case of conventional war in Europe, let us suppose that the favorable political conditions have been created and that the polities of Western Europe are nearly comatose and ripe for the plucking. This still leaves Soviet planners with several dilemmas.

The first of these dilemmas is that NATO has a considerable force deployed in Western Europe, and particularly in Germany. The Soviets have either got to outflank it or overpower it. On a theaterwide scale, this will not be easy to do, even allowing for a maximum of tactical and operational surprise. A variety of studies by Western analysts have shown that projected outcomes from conventional war in Europe are very sensitive to assumptions about mobilization rates for NATO and the Pact, about the cohesiveness of the two alliances under wartime stress, and about a myriad of other factors both political and military.[39] When the usual disclaimers are edited out, not even pessimists in the West can deny that the Soviets are taking major risks under the best of circumstances.[40] Even the fulfillment of Soviet operational objectives on land in Europe leaves them with the problem of U.S. maritime power, which can be used to send U.S. reinforcements to Europe and to create other pressures on Kremlin decision makers. In the version of U.S. maritime strategy propounded during the term of office of John Lehman as secretary of the navy, this maritime tail-twisting included plans for direct attacks against the Kola peninsula from U.S. carrier-based airpower.[41]

The second dilemma for the USSR, in addition to the unpredictability of a conventional war in Europe, is the uncertainty attendant to the possible uses of nuclear weapons by either side. The Soviets will be prepared for the introduction of nuclear weapons, according to their doctrine, in the sense that their formations will be widely dispersed, their vehicles provided with NBC (Nuclear, Biological, and Chemical) protection, and so on. However, fighting under this "nuclear scared" posture is very different from actually experiencing nuclear blows, even if they are discrete packages aimed by NATO at "military" targets only. Apart from the psychological effects on leaders, commanders, and troops, the military effects from even small nuclear weapons will be highly destructive to enemy and friendly forces. West Germany is not a large country geographically, and much of the land battle would take place with NATO and Pact forces in "meeting engagements" involving rapid movement, alternating offensive and defensive tactical postures, and commingling of hostile and friendly forces. The Soviets have come to recognize that even the tactical uses of nuclear weapons might immobilize their own ground forces as much as they destroy enemy objectives.[42]

A third dilemma for Soviet planners would be the possibility of a protracted conflict, which would drain their national resources and expose their economic system as a hollow shell compared to the capitalist opponents. Here the analogies with World War II can be misleading. Neither the Soviets nor the Americans are in the same position as they were at the later stages of World War II. The United States has in many ways moved into the postindustrial era; its industrial mobilization potential for an extended, global war is at best uncertain. The Soviet Union would depend in an extended war on agriculture, transportation, and other sectors of their economy, which are barely performing at acceptable levels in peacetime. Neither could assume that an extended war would be to its obvious advantage, although there is some truth to Robert Komer's observation that the United States has many rich allies, while the Soviet Union has only poor ones.[43] This is so, provided that there is no adjustment of the prewar political lineup after war has begun, either by conquest or by intimidation. If Japan, for example, is removed from the "Western" or anti-Soviet camp, and Europe is the battleground, the West appears less overwhelming from an economic standpoint. According to Michael MccGwire of the Brookings Institution, Soviet military doctrine recognizes the possibility of a multifront, extended conventional war as a later phase of war in Europe, in which the USSR occupies much of NATO European territory but does not succeed in expelling the United States from the continent.[44]

GLOBAL OBJECTIVES AND INTELLIGENCE ESTIMATES

If the Soviets (and therefore, presumably, the NATO estimators as well) have accepted the possibility of extended, conventional war, there arises the difficulty of knowing what kind of intelligence is most important in a long war, as opposed to a short one. We might suggest that three of the more interesting intelligence targets, under such conditions, would be the possibility of leadership changes during war; the acquisition of new resources or the obtaining of greater leverage from old ones; and the character of unexpected attacks with "strategic" political effects.

As to the first, there is now suggestive evidence from the last major global, coalition war that the distribution of power within the Axis governments might have been more important for defeat of their military strategies (and for war termination with reduced losses), compared to the events as they actually unfolded. In the case of Nazi Germany, for example, there was substantial opposition to Hitler among the German general staff, and Admiral Canaris, the head of the Abwehr, sought throughout the period preceding war—and during it—to minimize Hitler's chances of success. On more than one occasion, signals were sent to the British indicating a willingness on the part of dissident members of the general staff and other collaborators to overthrow Hitler. The implication was that the British and allied powers should guarantee that Germany would be allowed to set up some post-Hitler government acceptable to the conspirators, and presumably without aggressive designs on Europe.[45] The British had good reason to be suspicious of many of these signals, since only with hindsight do we know the full extent of the various conspiracies against Hitler and his minions within the Third Reich. In addition, there was always the possibility that an attempted coup would fail, with an attributable powder trail leading back to London or to other Allied capitals. The point for present purposes is that, especially in the early stages of war and during some of the more important prewar crises (e.g., Czechoslovakia), there were apparent opportunities to exploit divisions within the German leadership to the advantage of the allied cause.

One problem was that the opportunities for exploitation of German leadership struggles during World War II were embedded in a tissue of misinformation, uncertainty, and intelligence confusion. This was also the case for allied understandings of the Japanese willingness to surrender in 1945, and on what conditions. Leon V. Sigal has studied the problem of war termination in the context of U.S. efforts to bring about the surrender and defeat of Japan.[46] He finds that U.S. policymakers were not always consistent about their own priorities and expectations, nor were they successful in communicating these to the Japanese. The Japanese political and military leadership was divided with regard to the acceptability of peace proposals. The key choices for the United States had to do with military estimates about whether conventional bombing and blockade of the Japanese home islands would suffice to bring Japan to the point of collapse, and thus induce surrender. Or would it be necessary to invade the Japanese islands with U.S. and Allied forces at a cost expected to be high in Allied and Japanese lives lost? Furthermore, the atomic bomb, once it had been tested successfully, offered an option that might induce more rapid surrender, although its use would involve tremendous civilian loss of life, collateral damage, and uncertain precedents with regard to the purpose of strategic bombing.[47]

The U.S. Strategic Bombing Survey after the fact determined that the Japanese could probably have been subdued without nuclear weapons or invasion of the homeland.[48] The blockade and conventional air bombardment could eventually have done the job. However, this estimate, as well as others that were more pessimistic about the effects of "more of the same," presupposed an allied intelligence reading of internal Japanese policy debates that was not available. Even after the Japanese "surrender" had been requested by the emperor of his military and political leaders, there were cliques within the Japanese armed forces who resisted. Fortunately, the resistance had been anticipated and was put down.[49] Present day arguments about whether it was necessary for President Truman to authorize dropping the bomb benefit from intelligence that was not available to U.S. policymakers at the time. Truman and Secretary of War Stimson believed erroneously that millions of casualties might result from invasion. There was undoubtedly some wishful thinking on their part, and on the part of the various bureaucracies that had developed the atomic bomb with the expectation that it would eventually be used.[50]

Hitler's reading of the British government during World War II was no better. He misjudged its intentions at critical junctures and continued to believe, in the face of all available evidence, that the British would sue for peace sooner or later if the United Kingdom was not invaded. In fact, official and unofficial German peace feelers only emboldened Churchill to try harder to bring about the total defeat of the Axis powers and their "unconditional surrender" according to the Casablanca formula. Hitler assumed that his correct reading of the British and French governments prior to his invasion of Poland in September 1939 would carry over into wartime assessments. He and his advisors misjudged the character of the British wartime coalition cabinet and the psychology of its leader.

In an extended war, it might be interesting to note whether there are divisions between hawks and doves in the enemy leadership, and whether the dovish faction can be used for leverage against the hawks in order to terminate the war.[51] For example, during their conflict with the Americans, the North Vietnamese obviously decided that the U.S. "center of gravity" was not in Saigon, but in Washington. Ho Chi Minh and General Giap could not manipulate U.S. officials or journalists as if they were members of their own intelligence apparatus. But the Vietnamese leadership could and did engage in one of the most successful cases of perceptions management since the end of World War II. The symbols of nationalism, revolution, and communism were fused with an image of a primordial society resisting a superpower to create division within the U.S. policy community, armed forces, and society at large. When the United States succeeded (as in certain tactical engagements with Vietnamese main force units), it still failed in the sense of being cast symbolically as an aggressive, anti-nationalist and neo-colonialist power. Part of the reason for the U.S. willingness to raise the ante in Vietnam was the U.S. expectation that the Vietnamese were vulnerable to coercive diplomacy—a gradual turning of the screw to influence the North to call off the insurgency that Giap was thought to control. But apparently the North Vietnamese Politburo was unable to compute the utility-maximizing curves that the Pentagon had expected. From their perspective the war was total, not limited. Thus, additional bombardment from U.S. air strikes only encouraged improvisations in providing war material land supplies. The same can be said for the Germans in World War II, who proved to be far more adaptable to U.S. strategic bombardment of their homes and factories than suspected by allied planners.

In this regard, intelligence estimates can go wrong at two levels. The leadership may be misexplained, and the vulnerability of organizations to the disruption of their cohesion, misunderstood. Destroying POL (petroleum, oil, lubricants) supplies is not equivalent to disrupting the capacity of an organization to reconstitute those supplies, or to find substitutes. And an opponent's leadership may be influenced in unexpected ways by attacks that are designed to discourage continued fighting. By all decision calculi known to scholars and analysts, Mao should have given up instead of going on the Long March and establishing a new basis for revolution in Yenan. Lenin should not have signed the agreement at Brest-Litovsk. And, contrary to suppositions based on the wisdom of hindsight, a group of systems analysts sent to assist Neville Chamberlain at Munich in 1938 might well have advised him to acquiesce to Hitler's demands, on the quite reasonable (although erroneous) assumption that Hitler could be placated.

If the present enemy leadership is difficult to understand, successors may not be any easier to fathom. The assumption that the German generals in World War II would have been more willing to settle for a *mutually agreeable* peace with Britain after 1939 requires some faith in their political perspicacity, which may not be justified. In World War I, the German generals were the hawks, not the doves, until the 1918 offensive in the West had obviously failed. Then they demanded that political leaders sue for peace, in order to save the remnants of the army and the German state. When this postwar German state turned out not to be authoritarian but democratic, elements of the armed forces blamed politicians for economic difficulties and military weaknesses. The Russian Revolution dispatched the czar with all of his ineptitude and brought to power a regime whose stability was uncertain. Allied efforts to see into the new Soviet regime were blighted by ideological assessments and Lenin's own uncertainties in developing his domestic and foreign policies. The regime that ruled in postrevolutionary France during the Terror seemed menacing to dynastic legitimacy throughout Europe. In fact, it was much less menacing to the existing order than the Napoleonic consolidation of autocratic power in the name of revolution.

Resources and Staying Power

A second kind of intelligence estimate that might be crucial in an extended war is whether one side can acquire additional resources—either economic, political, or military—during the course of war. Related to this, one wants to have estimated correctly the staying power of the opponent and his allies. Misestimates of this kind took place during both World War I and World War II, in addition to other occasions.

In World War I, Alliance and Entente planners expected a short war in which rates of mobilization and placing the first blows would be decisive. The problem of national and societal mobilization for a war of many years' duration was not addressed adequately by any of the various military intelligence or economic planning bureaus in democratic or authoritarian

Europe.[52] Nor were the costs of an extended war figured other than haphazardly. The possible loss of regimes suffered by Austro-Hungarian, German, and Russian elites was far from the minds of prewar military planners and intelligence estimators.

Before World War II, even fewer excuses were available to justify the erroneous assumptions about the duration of war or about its costs. Everyone had been through a rehearsal from 1914 to 1918. Yet, allied and Axis planners still focussed on operational instead of strategic issues. In fact, operational successes paved the way for strategic defeats and for intelligence estimates that led to those defeats. Hitler's invasion of the Soviet Union in 1941 was based on operational plans that would have entrapped the bulk of Soviet forces west of the Dvina and Dnepr, forcing the Soviets into a cauldron from which they could not extricate themselves. But no strategic plan had been developed for conquering the Soviet Union itself, as opposed to defeating its field armies. Such planning as did take place was counterproductive. The Nazis treated Soviet civilians in the Ukraine and elsewhere horribly, thus negating whatever potential anti-Stalinist sentiment they might have exploited.

As did Nazi Germany with regard to Soviet Russia, so did Imperial Japan with regard to the United States. The Japanese could not hope to win a long war with the United States; so they assumed a short war, followed by U.S. willingness to accept a peace settlement leaving Japanese naval power supreme in the Pacific basin. Prior to December 1941, some Japanese military leaders and intelligence estimates pointed specifically to the problem of an extended conflict against the United States, indicating that Japan had no hope of winning.[53] Ultimately, a negative argument against waiting to strike at U.S. possessions in the Pacific prevailed; hostilities were inevitable given U.S. policy, therefore the most opportune time for attack was now. Pessimism about the outcome of any long war against the United States was dispelled by the assumption of inevitable conflict in any case, added to the hope that somehow the United States could be induced to accept an indefensible position in the Pacific.

In the case of U.S.-Soviet global war under contemporary conditions, Soviet planners would have to confront economic weaknesses and the possibility that any protracted war would go against them. Therefore, they would have to change the balance of economic power quickly in order to forestall this outcome. The most obvious, but also dangerous, ways for them to accomplish this would be to occupy Western Europe and Japan. In a global war in which the status of Europe and Japan were still being contested, the U.S.-Soviet competition for resources in Southwest Asia might become important. If the war continued long enough, new weapons or new methods of employing old weapons might also create opportunities for either side to improve its position. During World War II, the Germans developed forerunners of modern cruise and ballistic missiles, although they lacked the sophisticated guidance, range, and nuclear delivery vehicles of the present. The consequences of Hitler's having developed and tested the atomic bomb before the United States was able to do so are too obvious to emphasize. As of 1930, the issue of who would be first in line was not yet decided; scientists in Britain, Germany, Denmark, and elsewhere were closing in on the secret of nuclear fission. Timely warnings from U.S. and other scientists to highly placed politicians, including President Franklin Roosevelt, contributed to the onset of the Manhattan Project and its ultimate success.

New methods of chemical and biological warfare might be attempted in an extended war between NATO and Pact coalitions that stalemated in Europe and remained below the nuclear threshold. The United States has expressed the concern that the Soviets have a sophisticated arsenal of chemical weapons and the best training of all military forces in using them. Chemical weapons were used in the Iran-Iraq war in the 1980s, including nerve gases and other agents. The Reagan administration sought permission from the U.S. Congress to develop binary chemical munitions for replacement of older munitions in the U.S. arsenal. These would be stored in separate compartments and mixed only in flight once their release had been authorized. Chemical weapons were not used in World War II on account of the fear by all sides of retaliation in kind. The same may hold for a future war, including an extended one, unless situations develop in which an opportunity for effective chemical use on the battlefield coincides with the possibility of disguising the identity of the user. Nations that might have misgivings about using nuclear weapons could be persuaded that chemicals are less escalatory as force multipliers in a given theater of operations. Biological weapons are potentially as dangerous to the user as to the victim. No one has demonstrated that they can be used in a controlled and selective way to disable enemy troops or civilians while protecting one's own. The use of biological agents in Europe would almost certainly be self-defeating for Soviet or NATO forces. Outside of Europe where Pact and NATO ground forces might not be in direct contact, the possibility could be higher that chemical or biological weapons would be exploited for tactical success. In addition to the problem of retaliation in kind, there is also the inhibition deriving from precedents in international law against gratuitous injury to noncombatants, and from international agreements to which the superpowers are signatories or sympathetic observers. At this writing, U.S. and Soviet negotiators, among others, are still attempting to work out an acceptable regime for the disarming of chemical weapons and the inspection of chemical manufacture facilities in both the East and the West. Should this bear fruit, the progress should be extended into biological arsenals, in conformity with the declared policies of both superpowers that they have no interest in using such weapons offensively.

UNEXPECTED ATTACKS

Decapitation

A third category of intelligence estimates is suggested by the preceding examples of off-line weapons that might be used in an extended war: the possible use of unexpected kinds of attacks with strategic—that is, militarily or politically decisive—effects.

The most generic form of these might be attacks designed to "decapitate" the political or military command system of the opponent. In a global or coalition war, this is easier said than done. One is dealing with a hydra-headed opponent who can regenerate leadership cadre to replace those that are defeated. Some leaders might think that in the case of war between NATO and the Warsaw Pact, even after it has spread outside of Europe, destruction of Soviet or U.S. leadership cadres would bring hostilities to an end. Even if this could be accomplished, that either coalition would lose its ability to continue fighting in some fashion is extremely doubtful. Much, of course, would depend upon where, when, and for what the fighting continued.

Changing the context from global conventional warfare to include the possible use of nuclear weapons in regional or transoceanic theaters of operations introduces other issues. U.S. declaratory doctrine for the use of strategic nuclear forces, and presumably some components of U.S. nuclear war plans, have included capabilities for attacking political and military command centers in the Soviet Union. The idea is that prompt attacks might be made against the military command centers that support the use of Soviet conventional and nuclear forces against time-urgent U.S. and NATO targets. Other U.S. nuclear weapons would be withheld from, but targeted against, the highest political and military command levels of the Soviet system: the party, state, and security services leadership without which the Soviet state is judged by some observers to be highly vulnerable to political disintegration. The Carter administration PD-59 (Presidential

Directive) issued in 1980 made clear U.S. capabilities to engage in this kind of targeting if the president so chose.[54]

This expectation that the Soviet high command can be credibly threatened with its own demise, or would be subject to destruction in the event deterrence fails, presents many problems. First, it may not be possible to execute the threat in a way that suggests countercommand targeting, as opposed to indiscriminate and widespread societal devastation. Much of the Soviet command system is located in the major cities of the USSR, especially in Moscow. Second, the Soviet command system is not so easily destroyed. As Martin Van Creveld has noted, command "systems" include organizations, technologies, and procedures.[55] The destruction of a leadership cadre, even if the membership could be isolated from the general population and identified, is something different from the destruction of an organization as pervasive as the Soviet high command.[56] Nor would the reciprocal version of the same problem, a Soviet countercommand attack against the U.S. command and control system, be easy to accomplish. An attack on the U.S. nuclear command system designed to preclude unacceptable retaliation against Soviet forces and society would have to expend thousands of warheads on U.S. targets spread throughout the United States.[57] The most successful Soviet preemption of this type would still leave thousands of U.S. strategic nuclear warheads at sea, perhaps disconnected temporarily from emergency action messages that would authorize their launch against Soviet targets. Eventually, these weapons would be expended; only the physical destruction of the U.S. ballistic missile submarines (SSBNs) would prevent retaliation. The clue to this is the absence of Permissive Action Links (PALs), electronic locks that require special codes to deactivate, on nuclear charges deployed at sea, including those carried on U.S. SSBNs.

Assassination

The second kind of countercommand attack that has been noted in the academic and policy literature, especially in the intelligence literature, is political assassination. This is thought to substitute surgical removal of an obnoxious ruler for unnecessary destruction of the property and values of his or her state and people. The idea of regicide is one that even medieval theologians would approve under certain circumstances; the king was, after all, responsible to God for the conduct of affairs of state and church, and having failed in that domain, subject to removal, including occasional removal by extreme means. Machiavelli's international milieu of Italian city-states was a hotbed of intrigues that included the use of assassination as a political tool. In more recent times, the U.S. CIA has been charged with complicity in attempts on the lives of Fidel Castro, Patrice Lumumba, and Salvador Allende; the first charge has been well substantiated by evidence appearing in congressional reports and academic studies.[58]

U.S. and other Western intelligence agencies think that the Soviets have probably assembled special designation forces with missions that include assassination of political and military principals in NATO Europe. Whether this is supposition on the basis of Soviet doctrine, or proved by hard evidence available from defectors and others with access to Soviet war plans, cannot be resolved here. But it is certainly plausible that political decapitation of unfriendly leaders, if not murder, has occurred to the USSR as a prewar stratagem. One could cause the downfall of certain regimes on the eve of war by discrediting them politically, through active measures that included forgeries, disinformation, and other efforts to shock their political colleagues and publics. The entrapment of NATO political leaders in compromising professional or personal circumstances, with the pertinent dossiers held in reserve for the future, cannot be excluded. How this can be done was illustrated by Admiral Canaris of Nazi Germany, when he sought to keep at arms length his rival Reinhard Heydrich. Canaris had compiled a dossier on Heydrich documenting personal indiscretions that, if revealed, would have damaged Heydrich irreparably in Hitler's estimation. He then informed Heydrich that the dossier had been safely deposited in Switzerland, ready for forwarding to the *New York Times* should anything happen to Canaris. This insurance obtained Heydrich's "cooperation" until Heydrich's death (by assassination, at the hands of allied special operations forces).[59]

Few nations have defended the systematic use of assassination, and most professional intelligence services consider the subject inappropriate for discussion in public fora. The feeling on the part of many scholars and intelligence practitioners is that elected politicians share a collective vulnerability, especially in democratic societies. Attacks by one side invite retribution. The feeling by national leaders that they are vulnerable to assassination somehow insults them personally. Nevertheless, Anwar Sadat was assassinated by dissident Egyptians possibly in collusion with other nationals. The United States bombed Khaddafy's desert headquarters with strategic FB-111s based in Britain and defended the attack as a response to Khaddafy-authorized murder of U.S. servicemen during a bomb explosion in a West Berlin discotheque. Domestic critics of the U.S. attack charged that the Reagan administration lacked sufficient evidence to point the finger at Khaddafy. The possibility cannot be dismissed that the attack on Khaddafy was exemplary, in the sense that it was designed for demonstrative intimidation of terrorists or of states other than Libya that might consider sponsorship of anti-U.S. terrorism.[60]

The CIA has found the topic of political assassination inexpedient to pursue with the U.S. Congress, and President Reagan's executive order precluding assassination as a legitimate policy tool followed in the wake of similar convictions expressed by Presidents Ford and Carter. Except in wartime, it is difficult to imagine any U.S. authorization being given, but that exception is precisely the issue here. World War II experience would suggest that a global East-West conflict would create an environment more permissive than the present one for U.S. and other allied special operations, including political kidnappings and assassinations.

Changing the Leadership

Coups fall somewhere in between political assassinations and conventional military attacks on government headquarters. A coup may be internally or externally instigated; those instigated internally can draw upon outside assistance, and vice versa. The anti-Hitler German plotters repeatedly sought assurances that the demise of the Nazi dictator would lead to supportive noises and actions abroad. Coups can sometimes involve inadvertent assassinations, in which the coup is set in motion with the aim of replacing the government but with indistinct plans for the old leadership. The killings of Allende in Chile and Diem in South Vietnam were inadvertent in this sense: Although not strictly ordered as a necessary condition for the success of the coups, they were by all indications not precluded by U.S. or allied policy. The major difficulty with externally instigated coups is that the successor regime may not be dependable or competent. The successors to Diem in South Vietnam proved to be even less competent than he, as political mobilizers of popular support, counterinsurgent administrators, and military leaders. Replacement of Marcos in the Philippines took place with the blessing of the Reagan administration only after it became clear that Marcos had lost all credibility at home and abroad, thus endangering U.S. interests. A repetition of the situation that occurred in Iran when the Shah's grasp fell apart was clearly possible if the United States did not divest itself of perceived connections with Marcos and his entourage. On the other hand, the U.S. government had evident uncertainties about the character of the regime that would succeed Marcos. Undoubtedly, the Aquino government would be more popular, but the question was its durability. To assure the latter, the United States was willing to place Marcos under virtual house arrest in Hawaii.

In Afghanistan, the Soviets intervened with military forces in 1979 to depose one Marxist regime and to install another that would govern more effectively according to Soviet priorities. This invasion with Soviet forces proved to be a political and military disaster. It set back relations with the third world, especially the Muslim part of it. It provided a rejuvenation of NATO and an excuse for U.S. rearmament, together with suspension by the United States of its participation in SALT negotiations. It consumed Soviet personnel and resources in a futile effort to subdue an indigenous population fighting for primordial religious and nationalist values. It cast the USSR as an arch-villain in a U.S.-scripted plot, as the Soviets had done when the Americans were rooted in Vietnam. Finally, it provided to the U.S. intelligence community a bonanza of information about Soviet military and paramilitary operations. Nor was it insignificant that the U.S. aid to Afghan rebels was the only uncontroversial covert action undertaken by the Reagan administration with the full concurrence and support of Capitol Hill.

The Soviet difficulties in Afghanistan and the U.S. difficulties in Libya suggest that arranging changes in political leadership, through coups or other means, is not as easy to bring about as it might have been in the days of Western colonial empires stretching from the Middle East to South Asia. As Metternich discovered to his dismay following the Congress of Vienna, and as the United States and other developed Western societies are finding out now, the virus of nationalism is something of which peoples are rarely cured once they have caught it. And this implies that leaders who have been displaced must be replaced by other leaders whose nationalist bona fides are also firmly legitimated.

With regard to the enemy leadership, a country's political leadership in time of war has at least three major tasks. First, it must maintain the most comprehensive view of political objectives despite changes in the opponent's objectives. Second, it must see through strategic deceptions perpetrated by the opponent's leadership. Third, the political leadership must understand the adversary leadership it is dealing with, or may have to deal with in the future.

There are numerous examples of political leaders giving insufficient attention to all three issues; the emphasis here is on the third, correct assessment of the adversary leadership. During World War I, it was not clear until too late to the autocratic regimes of Russia, Austria-Hungary, and Germany that battlefield reversals could culminate in the demise of polity and society alike. With regard to faulty intelligence assessment of enemy leadership, the kaiser's and the chancellors' subservience (on matters of policy as well as strategy) to the leadership of the German general staff was not correctly appreciated by allied threat assessors. Prior to the outbreak of World War II, German Air Force leader Hermann Goering was depicted by some foreign observers as a moderate who would restrain Hitler's more adventurist impulses. The Shah of Iran in 1978 was judged by President Carter and by U.S. intelligence assessments to be secure on his throne, and the mullahs were not evaluated as potentially significant political forces. The Reagan administration attempted to circumvent congressional restrictions against support for the Contras in Nicaragua by selling arms to the Iranians through middlemen, then rechanneling the profits to the pro-U.S. revolutionaries in Central America. One rationale for the willingness to sell arms to Iran, at the time labelled a terrorist state by President Reagan, was that the arms sales would influence moderates within the Ayatollah's regime, develop more sympathy for U.S. objectives, and result in the freeing of some U.S. nationals who were hostages in Lebanon. In 1945, as U.S. leaders considered the possibility of negotiating an end to the war with Japan, it was unclear to them who were the diehards within the Japanese cabinet and armed forces, and how important it was for the Japanese to preserve the institution of the emperor. The decision to use atomic bombs on Hiroshima and Nagasaki was made with no clear perspective on who among the Japanese leadership would be influenced more by atomic bombing than by other means, including the threat of invasion, continued conventional bombing of Japanese cities, or economic blockade.[61]

INTELLIGENCE, DECEPTION, AND POLICY

The entire point of deception is to deceive an opponent, or a prospective one. Therefore, some facts must be concealed from one's own government and policy elite. This is true in authoritarian and democratic systems, although the latter protest loudly. The question is how much self-deception can be practiced before the efforts to deceive the opponent become self-defeating. The compartmentation of information that goes on in all intelligence systems compounds the problem. People may have valid recall of their own experiences but may not have understood what was going on around them.

U.S. and other Western intelligence specialists will argue that the Soviets are not embarrassed by failure in deception operations and will devote any amount of resources to the task.[62] But deception has something to do with policy, and embarrassing failures are setbacks. Nor is there a checklist of U.S. successes and failures to tote up against the Soviet effort during the same period. Unfortunately, comparative studies of deception are rare. We now do have extensive work on military deception, especially in World War II, including both theoretical-conceptual frameworks and historical case studies.[63] There is a related literature on surprise attack and strategic military surprise. Some of this reflects directly on the Soviet view of surprise and deception.[64] Studies of strategic military surprise have suggested that attacker incentives and defender vulnerabilities offer almost equivalent probabilities for successful surprise.[65] There is a significant debate among specialists with regard to the relationship among collection, analysis, and surprise. Roberta Wohlstetter's assessment of the Japanese surprise at Pearl Harbor was that it resulted from a lopsided ratio of noise to signals that could only be disentangled after the fact.[66] On the other hand, Hitler's surprise attack on the Soviet Union was facilitated by a deception plan that contributed to Stalin's erroneous expectation that further political demands would precede actual war. The failure on the part of the USSR was not one of collection, but of incorrect analysis of many evident signals of Hitler's intent. Nevertheless, other intelligence services, not just the Soviet, judged Operation Barbarossa improbable until the attack was virtually imminent.[67]

Three points about "successful" deceptions (with politically or militarily significant consequences) can be found in this literature. First, the victim is to some extent guilty of self-deception or faulty assessment, which should have been seen through without the benefit of hindsight available to historians. Second, democratic governments are as vulnerable to deception as authoritarian, and vice versa. Experts find no correlation between form of government and vulnerability to intelligence deception. However, a relationship between continuity of intelligence personnel and vulnerability does seem evident. Having experienced hands on the job, and especially in the key linkage positions crossing interagency networks, avoids the need to reconstruct memory banks in each case and maximizes the potential for reliance upon conditioned reflexes. This is especially important for resolving competing estimates. The difficulty is that there are only so many "geniuses" to go around, and it sometimes takes unique circumstances to push them forward.[68] During the 1930s, the performance of British intelligence with regard to military estimation was simply dreadful.

Therefore, a third point that emerges from these studies (and one that is very pertinent to British intelligence in the 1930s) is that the policymakers are very frequently at fault when intelligence cannot provide the answers they seek. And when policymakers are deceived, it is as often on account of their own preconceptions, misperceptions, and emotional biases as it is due to lack of intelligence collection, lack of proper analysis, or enemy deception. The best enemy deceptions play into the primordial instincts of political leaders. These instincts are potential vulnerabilities if properly exploited. The best of these exploitable instincts is an overconfidence built of elitism or previously won victories "on the cheap."

Intelligence cannot provide answers to unintelligent questions. Predicting which move the opponent will make tomorrow is not an end in itself; the more important questions are why, and with what to follow. The performance of British intelligence improved markedly when the person asking the questions was Winston Churchill. Second, policymakers can structure the intelligence community for multiple advocacy, but the line between multiple advocacy and bureaucratic chaos is very fine. The Reagan administration preserved the line during its first term, with regard to Central American policy, but the line dissolved during the second term. The British problem in the 1930s was in the interagency coordination of assessments more than it was in the acquisition of pertinent information.[69] This is still a basic U.S. intelligence deficiency.

The incentives for an opponent to use peacetime or wartime deception include both opportunities provided by the target state and the potential payoffs should deception succeed, weighed against the risks and costs of failure. The availability of opportunities for deception and the prospective attacker's perception of the risk/payoff spectrum are distinct, although related, issues. For example, assertive counterintelligence not only reduces vulnerability, it also turns the payoff table inside out. Counterintelligence must not only ferret out potential spies and saboteurs; it must also allow some to live as double agents in order to play back the wrong message to the right ears.[70] In democratic societies, it must be said, counterintelligence is a necessary evil, and it bears watching. Good counterintelligence is gold. But all bona fide counterintelligence specialists are trained to look first for deception; soon, deception is all pervasive, even when events are innocent. When an entire security service adopts an ethos of this sort, one kind of vulnerability is reduced, but another, of self-paralysis, emerges.[71]

The most artful form of political deception is penetration of the higher ranks of an opponent's intelligence services, or counterintelligence services, with an enemy operative in place. The most widely publicized success of this type against the West was the Kim Philby case. Philby's name is now widely known, but his methods of obtaining his credentials and of legitimating his status within the British intelligence services are not so familiar. There are really two parts to the puzzle: the intelligence policy-making and recruitment context, which provided the opportunity, and the skillful way in which Philby exploited it. As to the first, rivalry characterized relations between the British foreign intelligence and domestic counterintelligence services (MI 6 and MI 5, respectively). Professional and organizational competition was exacerbated by personal rivalries within and between organizations. The assumption that MI 5 would have sole proprietary rights over activities on British territory, and that MI 6 would have exclusive jurisdiction abroad, soon broke down over the complexity of modern intelligence and counterintelligence operations.[72] There were also pronounced differences before, during, and after World War II in departmental ethos: MI 6 was more permissive of extraordinary measures as all in a day's work and was more freewheeling about appointments and promotions. This, in turn, led to distrust of one another's operational approaches to security, although, paradoxically, their theories of security shared a common premise: "the idea that the interlocking connections of the British middle and upper classes provided checks on people through their public schools, clubs, regiments and—when relevant—universities."[73]

Philby exploited this context during and immediately after World War II by using his considerable talents for ingratiation, diplomacy, and double-talking to rise within the secret world. There is controversy as to whether he might some day have attained the coveted top position as C, at the head of the Secret Intelligence Service. It seems implausible that his successful deception could have gone far enough, or long enough, to avoid a downfall sooner or later. But "later," in this instance, meant that Philby had already compromised many important Western intelligence and counterintelligence operations, from his position at the nexus of British and U.S. intelligence and counterintelligence cooperation. And it was certainly a coup of considerable proportions for Philby to have been selected to head the newly created British intelligence effort directed against the USSR in 1944.

One might argue that an episode this extreme could not recur, but complacency is never warranted. Peter Wright, former British counterintelligence operative and author of a bestselling book banned in the United Kingdom, raises the possibility that a former head of British counterintelligence was actually a Soviet agent.[74] Had Philby never existed, the contention would seem less plausible. Wright stirred additional controversy with his suggestion that other "moles" have escaped the counterintelligence dragnet on account of sloppy procedure or lack of political interest at the uppermost levels of government. The problem for the reader who was not on the inside of these battles is the problem of judgment forever suspended in midair. Unless all the participants live long enough and squeal on one another at equal volume, history is the residue of tendentious pleading.

The effort to winkle out moles within one's own intelligence apparatus also has autolimitations, with regard to the stamina and morale of one's own security services. Security services, both those operating abroad and those tasked with internal security, depend upon a certain degree of mutual trust and respect among professionals who share a common background and commitment. This requirement holds true regardless of personal frictions, or of competitions for influence that occur among organizations in any bureaucratic setting. It is when the internecine struggle spills over from "he or she is my competitor" to "he or she is my enemy" that organizational paralysis awaits offstage. The United States has gone through several periods of intra-intelligence and interagency mistrust of this sort: the McCarthy era, the Watergate/CIA investigations by the U.S. Congress, and the Iran-Contra affair during the Reagan administration. Only the first *explicitly* involved efforts to identify and purge traitors within the government machine. But the others, Watergate/CIA and Iran-Contra, involved charges that intelligence professionals were misused in counterintelligence roles (spying on U.S. citizens) or in commingling private and public activities in ways that distorted U.S. intelligence and policy objectives (Iran-Contra).

On the other hand, counterintelligence failures promise large costs, and additional intelligence resources are no guarantee against them. The Pelton, Howard, and Pollard cases in the United States were all revealed during the 1980s, although they had roots further back chronologically. The common thread, connecting them by genotype to Philby, Burgess, and McLean, is that there were abundant clues in the personal behavior of the U.S. spies that were noted *en passant*, but not acted upon or appreciated in their fullest significance. Ronald Pelton was ideally placed within the Soviet group at the U.S. National Security Agency (NSA) to have access to a great deal of sensitive and compartmentalized information. His previous disciplinary problem in the air force and personal bankruptcy while at NSA failed to alert officials to his possible role in subversion, even after a 1982 report revealed the almost certain compromise of the highly sensitive U.S. submarine intelligence-gathering program, Ivy Bells. Jonathan Jay Pollard, analyst for the U.S. Naval Investigative Service, spied for Israel; he claimed for years that he worked for *Mossad*, the Israeli foreign intelligence service, but listeners refused to believe it (shades of Guy Burgess getting drunk and declaring that he was working for the Kremlin). The most notorious case of the 1980s, the Walker espionage ring, involved the penetration of U.S. naval cryptographic communications systems used for operating the U.S. fleet during peacetime and in wartime. In the late 1970s, Adm. Isaac Kidd had reported that the Soviets were reacting so successfully to U.S. Atlantic Fleet exercises that he became suspicious. He had prepared a staff report that concluded in favor of a security leak, in all likelihood a radioman with broad access to cryptographic material. The report was examined by NSA but not followed up until 1985, when John Walker was exposed by other means, and after great damage.[75]

Cases such as this suggest to many U.S. audiences that counterintelligence can never be overdone. The danger in this "remedy" is that the counterintelligence tapeworm can consume the host. This has happened in authoritarian and totalitarian systems, as Stalin's military purge and subsequent disaster in June 1941 attest. The Soviets, having experienced this firsthand, wanted no repetition. The relevant organs were used to support the efforts of the armed forces high command in World War II, not to subvert the leadership of STAVKA. As Beria reached for power after the war, his colleagues, seeing an incubation of permanent purge, dispatched him. The message was not lost on Khrushchev or on his successors. The great fear can carry the seeds of its own destruction. Vigilance is an exercise in observation and in proportion: Magnifying threats out of proportion in order to further partisan domestic agendas makes a country more, not less, vulnerable to external threats. Moreover, the Stalins, Robespierres, and Chairman Maos (in the 1960s) who depend upon a fear state for rule risk the coming apart of the post-fear state in the hands of successors who are less charismatic, less ruthless, or less competent (or less in all three respects).

ELECTRONIC WARFARE AND DECEPTION

Electronic warfare is well known in Western armed forces and is generally well thought out at a tactical level. The Soviet approach is more holistic. At an operational or operational-strategic scale, the Soviet concept of radio-electronic struggle (*radioelektronnaya bor' ba*) includes measures to deny the efficient use of the electronic spectrum to the opponent, to preserve the security and combat efficiency of Soviet uses, and to contribute to the commander's overall design of military operations. Toward these ends, the radio-electronic combat of the Soviet armed forces is designed to operate on the opponent's intentions and capabilities before battle begins and during it.

The *Dictionary of Basic Military Terms*, edited by Col.-Gen. A. I. Radziyevskiy, reflects the Soviet view that control of the electromagnetic spectrum begins with the acquisition of adequate intelligence. Included in this is the acquiring of electronic intelligence (*radiotekhicheskaya razvedka*), which is defined as "detection of enemy radio-technical facilities and determination of their characteristics by reception and analysis of their signals."[76] Electronic intelligence may be acquired by many means, including *radiopoisk* (radio search), *radioperekhvat* (radio intercept), and *radiopelengatsiya* (radio direction-finding). The security of one's own troop control is preserved from electronic sniffing or interference by several means, including radio silence (*radiomolchaniye*).[77] Also important for preserving communications security is radio camouflage, *radiomaskirovka*, which is "the complex of organizational and technical measures directed toward hindering enemy conduct of radio reconnaissance."[78] Radiomaskirovka measures include restricted uses of communications equipment, changes in operating frequencies and call signs, and special measures to misinform enemy radio reconnaissance.

Troop control under modern conditions means that commanders will have to deal with operations that are widely dispersed geographically and involve forces of massive size. Thus, the role of troop control has risen so much that "more and more it acquires the significance of a major sector of military affairs" based on scientific principles.[79] The ability to foresee the development of combat operations holds an important place in the theory of troop control. Foresight is inconceivable "without a profound knowledge of the organization, equipment, and tactics of the enemy, as well as without precise and detailed calculations."[80] Foresight is based on constant knowledge of the situation that is at least one step ahead of the rate at which the opponent acquires pertinent information. Razvedka is thus partly untranslatable, having the connotation of intelligence and reconnaissance combined, and it must provide information so that decisions can be made within the decision cycle of the opponent. The control time the Soviet commander requires to go through his decision cycle of obtaining, processing, and transmitting information, when added to the time required to carry out his decision, should be less than the critical time after which obtained information is obsolete.[81] However, under modern combat conditions obtained information is more perishable than formerly, on account of the greater amounts of destruction due to firepower, geographically dispersed and highly mobile operations, and improvements in the accuracy with which conventional weapons can be delivered over longer ranges.

Of special concern to Soviet planners are the impending developments in air-land battle and the use of electronics and communications technologies as force multipliers. An informative assessment of the prospects for ground forces in the remainder of this century and beyond appeared in September 1986, in the Polish *Ground Forces Review* (*Przeglad Wojsk Ladowych*). The author identifies the "basic directions" of change in the tactics of ground forces as follows: (1) transformation of traditional land operations into air-land operations, (2) increased importance of mobility in troop operations, (3) development and dissemination of the practice of combat operations within enemy formations, especially raiding operations, (4) initiation of battle at increasingly greater distances, and (5) growth in the significance of the "information struggle," having as its goal the steering of the enemy in the direction of one's own plans and intentions.[82] The information struggle has many implications:

> The struggle in the sphere of information ultimately boils down to the effect on the command and control system of the enemy (chiefly through his reconnaissance system). Winning this fight means *the ability to steer the enemy in the direction of one's own plans and intentions*. In the face of the growth in the effectiveness of strike means, the ability to steer the enemy, to impose one's will upon him, and to completely deceive him will have increasingly substantial significance for the course and results of combat operations.[83] [Italics mine]

Taken as a whole, the development, electronization, and automation of systems for reconnaissance, directing fire, command and control, communications, and radioelectronic warfare implies that managing information will assist strike means and, in some cases, will independently prejudge the results of the engagement, sometimes even during the preparation phase.[84] This is especially so with regard to the reconnaissance-strike (operational) and reconnaissance-fire (tactical) complexes on which AirLand Battle and FOFA are dependent, and which the Soviets are concerned to nullify.

Conventional deep strike can be nullified by attacking the launch platforms, by interfering with or destroying the communications between reconnaissance and strike platforms, or by deceiving the opponent with regard to the probable location of targets. According to V. G. Reznichenko and colleagues, the potential of enemy weapons for mass destruction of reconnaissance-strike complexes makes obsolete previously thought out tactics. Today, combat operations involve the entire depth of the orders of battle of the belligerents simultaneously. Therefore, combat missions must be determined, not according to lines as was previously done, but in relation to important areas or objectives, in order to undermine the stability of enemy defenses.[85] Defenses are no longer based on defensive positions and zones, but on groupings of enemy fire weapons coordinated with the first and second echelons. Troops no longer advance from one line to the next. Instead, they penetrate deep into enemy defenses and develop the offensive while coordinating their actions with airborne forces landed in the enemy rear.[86]

Not all the lessons of previous wars are irrelevant, however. The importance of concentration of maximum force on the main attack sector remains. However, the way in which this is to be done has changed. The speed and destructiveness of modern weapons mean that it would be neither possible nor advisable to create the kind of densities of personnel and equipment in breakthrough sectors that were encountered in the Great Patriotic War.[87] Moreover, deeply deployed defenses saturated with fire weapons cannot easily be penetrated. Therefore, according to Soviet experts on tactics, the main emphasis should be placed on creating not so much a quantitative as a qualitative superiority over the enemy.[88]

The organizing of decisively dominant forces on the main attack sectors that are qualitatively superior has other implications. Strong artillery groups must be created for use in the first echelon, capable of supporting advancing troops throughout the duration of the entire battle. These artillery groups would be tasked to destroy enemy offensive nuclear and chemical weapons, artillery, reconnaissance-strike complexes, multiple rocket launchers, tanks, antitank guided rockets, infantry-fighting vehicles, electronic installations, air defense equipment, and remote mine-laying sources.[89] Tactical airborne forces must now be used to capture and annihilate some of the most important enemy objectives, including offensive nuclear weapons, operating high-precision weapons systems, and command and control posts and communications centers.[90]

The competent Soviet commander must have the foresight to anticipate enemy plans not only for the initial phase of battle but subsequently. Plans must be meticulous and made well in advance. In preparing an offensive battle plan, commanders must recognize that the volume of tasks has grown more complex while the time for carrying them out has decreased. Commanders follow the usual process of preattack assessment of their own forces and those of the enemy. In addition, they need special insight in order to reveal the enemy's plan and the options available to him.[91]

This is not altogether new, just more difficult to do even with the modern adjuncts of aerial and space reconnaissance and sophisticated radio DF and ELINT (electronic intelligence) platforms. But the exactitude of the mission of establishing clearly the enemy's plan and deployments is old hat. It was emphasized by Wellington at Waterloo and throughout his career, and by Grant during several important campaigns in the American Civil War. There is no substitute for the commander who, as John Keegan has succinctly put it, knows and sees what is happening on the battlefield.[92] When it is not possible to do this in person, and under modern conditions it frequently is not, then the commander must rely on a personal staff (and today, on modern automated decision aids) as surrogates and supports. The danger is that the electronics and computers will be depended upon to the extent that the commander's own intelligence appreciation and reconnaissance appraisals are not finely honed. The commander is supposed to reflect experience, judgment, and other qualities that Clausewitz combined under the rubric of "military genius." But this leaves undecided the critical issue of how much leadership to exert from the front, so to speak, and how much from the rear.[93] Nowadays, "from the front" means being personally involved and skeptically appraising what comes out of the electronic ether. "From the rear" means maintaining a distance from the seemingly most threatening and immediate events in order to observe the overall development of trends and tendencies.

The instruments of electronic warfare or, as the Soviets say, radio-electronic struggle, are part and parcel of the commander's tool kit. There must still be developed the strategic instincts and command habits to go with the tools. This obviously involves schooling and training, but something more. There are cultural, social, and even personal dimensions to what people do when they are shot at. Clausewitz explained that the stress upon commanders comes not only from the fear of losing, but from the fact that they must participate in and observe the wastage while it is in progress. Maintaining a clear view of events in the unfolding nightmare of battle requires steel nerves, determination, and compassion at the same time: "an intellect that, even in the darkest hour, retains some glimmerings of the inner light which leads to truth."[94] The resistance that challenges the psychological strength of the commander is only in part due to the enemy's activity. The other part is the weight of anxiety and the commander's sense of responsibility on his or her capacity to make decisions. Clausewitz notes that the commander must endure the stress of seeing his comrades killed and wounded in battle, which cumulatively saps his moral and physical strength.[95]

Thus, Napoleon's incredible insight into tactics and operations does not fully explain his ability to hold together his decimated forces as they retreated from Russia in 1812. Nor, for that matter, does it fully explain the willingness of the *Grande Armée* to follow him into Russia in the first place. Skill in leadership requires tactical and technical proficiency, but much more. The troops will follow only those commanders who are steadfast despite the confusion of their surroundings. Thus, the age of automation promises to make available more information, and more rapidly, during peacetime rehearsals and simulations. But once war begins, automated confusion may reign, with commanders thrown back on their own abilities to sort the wheat from the chaff in information environments of uncertainty, deception, and chance.

CONCLUSION

Too often, deception is taken as something sui generis in military art, as a war-within-a-war important unto itself. I suggest instead that it is applicable to problems of deterrence and military strategy, but as a component of the larger puzzle of complex decision making under uncertainty, with all that this implies. On the matter of conflict between superpowers or their military coalitions, nuclear deterrence and conventional war fighting are intertwined in the fashion of a double helix. Thus, inadequate conventional denial capabilites invite nuclear escalation, but with perverse implications that neither the Americans nor the Soviets can fully control. For example, were the Soviets to create the "successful" deception that they possessed a conventional, theater strategic war-winning option for conflict in Europe, this might not redound to their advantage. Instead of increasing deterrence stability, it might motivate the West to seek its own versions of conventional surprise attack and, in the event either side were so emboldened as to try its luck, provoke nuclear escalation anyway.

If the problems of intelligence and deception with regard to superpower relations are sufficiently intimidating to their respective intelligence establishments, this chapter has demonstrated the sorry track record of major powers dealing with so-called low intensity conflicts. Outside of Europe, U.S. and NATO intelligence is mostly targeted against non-Western cultures, petty tyrannies of all descriptions, and terrorist desperados at war on behalf of statist and nonstatist agendas. Until now, Western intelligence failures in these milieus have not redounded in loss of control over a process of escalation that then spilled over into war in Europe. No one can guarantee that the past will be prologue for the future in this regard. The deception capabilities of non-European states may increase along with the lethality of their high-technology weapons, and so, therefore, may their capacity to create global wars out of regional conflicts.

NOTES

1. Carl Von Clausewitz, in *On War*, Michael Howard and Peter Paret, eds. and trans. (Princeton: Princeton University Press, 1976).

2. Ibid., 119.

3. Ibid.

4. Ibid.

5. Ibid., 117.

6. Ibid.

7. Eliot Cohen, "The No-Fault View of Intelligence," *Intelligence Requirements for the 1990s*, ed. Roy Godson (Lexington, Mass.: Lexington Books, 1989), 71–96, citation p. 72.

8. Ibid., 77.

9. Leslie H. Gelb with Richard K. Betts, *The Irony of Vietnam: The System Worked* (Washington, D.C.: Brookings Institution, 1979), 117.

10. Ernest R. May, "Capabilities and Proclivities," in *Knowing One's Enemies: Intelligence Assessment before the Two World Wars*, Ernest R. May, ed., (Princeton: Princeton University Press, 1984), 503–42, citation pp. 520–21.

11. Ibid., 504.

12. Ibid. One can do no better to appreciate the context of war on the western front during World War I than to read John Keegan's account of the Somme, in John Keegan, *The Face of Battle* (New York: Viking Press, 1976), Ch. 4.

13. Richard K. Betts, *Surprise Attack: Lessons for Defense Planning* (Washington, D.C.: Brookings Institution, 1982), Ch. 8.

14. Graham T. Allison, Albert Carnesale, and Joseph S. Nye, Jr., *Hawks, Doves and Owls: An Agenda for Avoiding Nuclear War* (New York: W. W. Norton, 1985).

15. Joseph S. Nye, Jr., Graham T. Allison, and Albert Carnesale, "Analytic Conclusions: Hawks, Doves, and Owls," *Hawks, Doves and Owls*, eds. Allison, Carnesale, and Nye, 206–22.

16. See Graham T. Allison, *Essence of Decision: Explaining the Cuban Missile Crisis* (Boston: Little, Brown, 1971).

17. Allison, *Essence of Decision*, 138.

18. The U-2 was reported to have been on a "routine air-sampling mission" when it went off course. See Allison, *Essence of Decision*, 141.

19. The second letter came Saturday, October 27, reversing the Soviet position taken the previous day, and now insisting that U.S. missiles in Turkey would have to be withdrawn in return for the removal of Soviet missiles from Cuba. See Elie Abel, *The Missile Crisis* (Philadelphia: J. B. Lippincott/Bantam Books, 1966) 167–71. Abel, reflecting the views of U.S. principals, says that the idea of trading Jupiter missiles in Turkey for Soviet missiles in Cuba "had a glittering symmetry," but that Kennedy and his advisors rejected it. If general war occurred, the president felt it would occur not on account of Jupiter missiles stationed in Turkey, but because "the Russians had tried by stealth to alter the balance of forces between East and West" (p. 171). A reasonable argument can be made that the offer was symmetrical, however, since the U.S. government had debated removal of the Jupiters from Italy and Turkey (along with Thor IRBMs) since early 1961, and Kennedy finally decided to do so in August 1962.

20. Abel, *Missile Crisis*, 156.

21. Roberta Wohlstetter, *Pearl Harbor: Warning and Decision* (Stanford, Calif.: Stanford University Press, 1962).

22. Barton Whaley, *Codeword BARBAROSSA* (Cambridge, Mass.: MIT Press, 1973).

23. See S. P. Ivanov, *Nachal' nyy period voiny* (The Initial Period of War) (Moskva: Voyenizdat, 1974). The introduction notes that on the eve of war with Germany, the Soviet economy was still operating according to peacetime standards; that the Soviet government limited the deployment of forces in the Western military districts of the USSR along the border near areas of likely attack; and that the directive ordering that forces of the border military districts be made combat ready was not issued until the early hours of June 22, 1941.

24. John Erickson, "Threat Identification and Strategic Appraisal by the Soviet Union, 1930–1941," *Knowing One's Enemies*, ed. May, 375–423.

25. The Reich foreign ministry invented or first utilized the cover story of impending ultimatum, suggesting that German behavior might be dependent on Soviet conduct, shortly before May 17, 1941. This became the most important set of rumors in the weeks preceding the German invasion of the USSR, but there were others: authentic information posing as rumor; misleading information spread by the Germans as part of their deception campaign; and plausible speculation. See Whaley, *Codeword BARBAROSSA* 175–77.

26. This was the so-called contingency hypothesis. See Whaley, *Codeword BARBAROSSA*, 223.

27. See Robert Jervis, "Perceiving and Coping with Threat," *Psychology and Deterrence*, eds. Robert Jervis, Richard Ned Lebow, and Janice Gross Stein (Baltimore: Johns Hopkins University Press, 1985) 13–33.

28. Irving Janis, *Groupthink: Psychological Studies of Policy Decisions and Fiascoes*, 2nd ed. (Boston: Houghton Mifflin, 1982) 85.

29. David Kahn, "United States Views of Germany and Japan in 1941," *Knowing One's Enemies*, ed. May, 476–502.

30. Whaley, *Codeword BARBAROSSA* 221–46.

31. See John J. Dziak, "Soviet Deception: The Organizational and Operational Tradition," *Soviet Strategic Deception*, eds. Brian D. Dailey and Patrick J. Parker (Lexington, Mass.: Lexington Books, 1987) 3–20, and Richard J. Heuer, Jr., "Soviet Organization and Doctrine for Strategic Deception," *Soviet Strategic Deception*, eds. Dailey and Parker, 21–54. See also John J. Dziak, *Chekisty: A History of the KGB* (Lexington, Mass.: Lexington Books, 1988), and Ladislav Bittman, *The Deception Game* (New York: Ballantine Books, 1972).

32. Robert Jervis, *The Illogic of American Nuclear Strategy* (Ithaca, N.Y.: Cornell University Press, 1984).

33. See Christopher N. Donnelly, "Soviet Operational Concepts in the 1980s," *Strengthening Conventional Deterrence in Europe: Proposals for the 1980s* (New York: St Martin's Press, 1983) 105–36.

34. Donnelly, "Soviet Operational Concepts," 112–18.

35. Heuer, "Soviet Organization and Doctrine," notes that maskirovka is conducted at three levels: strategic, operational, and tactical. There are four broad categories of maskirovka, including camouflage, simulation, feints and demonstrations, and disinformation. Maskirovka is a military operational term, not an intelligence concept. See also Roger Beaumont, "On the Analytical Challenge of Maskirovka," *Intelligence and Intelligence Policy in a Democratic Society*, ed. Stephen J. Cimbala (Dobbs Ferry, N.Y.: Transnational Publishers, Inc., 1987) 197–222.

36. Cap. Erin E. Campbell, "The Soviet Spetsnaz Threat to NATO," *Airpower Journal* 2, no. 2 (Summer 1988): 61–67.

37. Desmond Ball, *Controlling Theater Nuclear War*, Working Paper No. 138, Strategic and Defence Studies Centre, Research School of Pacific Studies, Australian National University, Canberra, October 1987.

38. John J. Dziak, "The Soviet Approach to Special Operations," *Special Operations in U.S. Strategy*, eds. Frank R. Barnett, B. Hugh Tovar, and Richard H. Shultz (New York: National Strategy Information Center, 1984) 95–120, citation 104–05.

39. For current information and estimates, see Congress of the United States, Congressional Budget Office, *U.S. Ground Forces and the Conventional Balance in Europe* (Washington, D.C.: U.S. Government Publishing Office, 1988). Generic approaches to estimation of the conventional balance in Europe include the statistical force comparison approach; the combat-modelling approach; and the decision-making simulation approach. In the end, these are all scenario dependent. For an interesting effort to combine aspects of these and other approaches in an innovative way, see Paul K. Davis, *The Role of Uncertainty in Assessing the NATO-Pact Central Region Balance* (Santa Monica, Calif.: RAND Corporation, 1988), and Paul K. Davis, *A New Analytic Technique for the Study of Deterrence, Escalation Control, and War Termination* (Santa Monica, Calif.: RAND Corporation, 1986).

40. See Benjamin S. Lambeth, "Uncertainties for the Soviet War Planner," *International Security* 7, no. 3 (Winter 1982/1983): 139–66.

41. Robert W. Komer, *Maritime Strategy or Coalition Defense?* (Cambridge, Mass.: Abt Books, 1984), and John J. Mearsheimer, "A Strategic Misstep: The Maritime Strategy and Deterrence in Europe," *International Security*, 11, no. 2 (Fall 1986): 3–57, and in the same issue a rejoinder by Capt. Linton F. Brooks, USN, "Naval Power and National Security: The Case for the Maritime Strategy," 58–88.

42. John G. Hines, Phillip A. Petersen, and Notra Trulock III, "Soviet Military Theory from 1945–2000: Implications for NATO," *The Washington Quarterly* 9, no. 4 (Fall 1986): 117–37. On the other hand, Soviet command arrangements facilitate rapid transition from nonnuclear to nuclear operations. See U.S. Army, *The Soviet Army: Operations and Tactics*, (Washington, D.C.: Headquarters Department of the Army, 1984), Ch. 3 and 4 (FM 100–2–1), and John Erickson, Lynn Hansen, and William Schneider, *Soviet Ground Forces: An Operational Assessment* (Boulder, Colo.: Westview Press, 1986) 26–27.

43. Robert W. Komer, "Strategymaking at the Pentagon," *Reorganizing America's Defense: Leadership in War and Peace*, eds. Robert J. Art, Vincent Davis and Samuel P. Huntington (New York: Pergamon Brassey's, 1985), 223.

44. Michael MccGwire, *Military Objectives in Soviet Foreign Policy* (Washington, D.C.: Brookings Institution, 1987) 67–89.

45. See Anthony Cave Brown, *Bodyguard of Lies* (New York: Harper and Row, 1975).

46. Leon V. Sigal, *Fighting to a Finish: The Politics of War Termination in the United States and Japan, 1945* (Ithaca, N.Y.: Cornell University Press, 1988).

47. See also Fred Charles Ikle, *Every War Must End* (New York: Columbia University Press, 1971), and Paul Kecskemeti, *Strategic Surrender: The Politics of Victory and Defeat* (Santa Monica, Calif.: RAND Corporation, 1958).

48. U.S. Strategic Bombing Survey (Pacific), *Japan's Struggle to End the War*, Report no. 2 (Washington, D.C.: 1946) 13, cited in Sigal, *Fighting to a Finish*, 9.

49. Ikle, *Every War Must End*.

50. Sigal, *Fighting to a Finish*, Ch. 4, esp. 175–223.

51. Ikle, *Every War Must End*, passim.

52. For evidence, see May, "Cabinet, Tsar, Kaiser: Three Approaches to Assessment," *Knowing One's Enemies*, ed. May, 11–36.

53. U.S. leaders apparently made little use of military intelligence in planning deployments and in procuring military forces. The focus was on U.S. capabilities. According to David Kahn, "Such matters as whether Germany had 100 divisions or 300 and whether Japan had 10 carriers or 20 were not even raised when policy-makers examined the basic issues of strategy." See David Kahn, "U.S. Views of Germany and Japan," *Knowing One's Enemies*, ed. May, 477–78.

54. Walter Slocombe, "The Countervailing Strategy," *Strategy and Nuclear Deterrence*, ed. Steven E. Miller (Princeton: Princeton University Press, 1984) 245–54; Desmond Ball, "The Development of the SIOP, 1960–83," *Strategic Nuclear Targeting*, eds. Desmond Ball and Jeffrey Richelson (Ithaca, N.Y.: Cornell University Press, 1986) Ch. 3.

55. Martin Van Creveld, *Command in War* (Cambridge, Mass.: Harvard University Press, 1985).

56. See Harriet Fast and William F. Scott, *The Soviet Control Structure: Capabilities for Wartime Survival* (New York: Crane, Russak/National Strategy Information Center, 1983).

57. Ashton B. Carter, "Assessing Command System Vulnerabilities," *Managing Nuclear Operations*, eds. Ashton B. Carter, John D. Steinbruner, and Charles A. Zraket (Washington, D.C.: Brookings Institution, 1987) 555–610.

58. The combined effects of the Hughes-Ryan Amendment, other legislation of the 1970s, and the establishment of Senate and House intelligence oversight committees in 1976 and 1977 on CIA capabilities and proclivities for covert action are aptly described by John Ranelagh, *The Agency: The Rise and Decline of the CIA* (New York: Simon and Schuster, 1986) 616.

59. Brown, *Bodyguard of Lies*, 158.

60. U.S. intelligence now apparently believes that the La Belle Discotheque bombing was the work of Syrians or Iranians instead of Libyans.

61. See Sigal, *Fighting to a Finish*, passim.

62. Raymond S. Sleeper, ed., *Mesmerized by the Bear: The Soviet Strategy of Deception* (New York: Dodd, Mead, 1987).

63. Donald C. Daniel and Katherine L. Herbig, eds., *Strategic Military Deception* (New York: Pergamon Press, 1981), and Dailey and Parker, eds., *Soviet Strategic Deception* are collections including many expert analyses.

64. P. H. Vigor, *Soviet Blitzkrieg Theory* (New York: St Martin's Press, 1983).

65. Klaus Knorr and Patrick Morgan, eds., *Strategic Military Surprise: Incentives and Opportunities* (New Brunswick, N.J.: Transaction Books, 1983). This contains very useful chapters by the editors and by Michael Doyle, Michael Handel, and Richard Betts.

66. Wohlstetter, *Pearl Harbor*. See also Ariel Levite, *Intelligence and Strategic Surprises* (New York: Columbia University Press, 1987), Ch. 2.

67. Whaley, *Codeword BARBAROSSA*.

68. On Donovan and the OSS, see Ranelagh, *The Agency*, Ch. 1–3, and Thomas Troy, *Donovan and the CIA* (Frederick, Md.: University Publications of America, 1981).

69. See Donald Cameron Watt, "British Intelligence and the Coming of the Second World War in Europe," *Knowing One's Enemies*, ed. May, 237–70 and Christopher Andrew, *Her Majesty's Secret Service* (New York: Viking, 1986).

70. Roy Godson, ed., *Intelligence Requirements for the 1980s: Counterintelligence* (New York: National Strategy Information Center, 1980); Roy Godson, ed., *Intelligence Requirements for the 1990s* (New York: National Strategy Information Center, 1989), Ch. 4.

71. See David C. Martin, *Wilderness of Mirrors* (New York: Ballantine, 1980).

72. Bruce Paige, David Leitch, and Phillip Knightley, *The Philby Conspiracy* (Garden City, N.Y.: Doubleday and Co., 1968) 115–16.

73. Paige, Leitch, and Knightley, *Philby Conspiracy*, 117.

74. Peter Wright, *Spycatcher* (New York: Dell Books, 1987).

75. See Bob Woodward, *Veil: The Secret Wars of the CIA, 1981–87* (New York: Simon and Schuster, 1987) 447–49, 478–79, and John Barron, *Breaking the Ring: The Rise and Fall of the Walker Family Spy Ring* (New York: Avon Books, 1987).

76. Col.-Gen. A. I. Radziyevskiy, ed., *Dictionary of Basic Military Terms* (Slovar' osnovnykh voennykh terminov) (Moskva: Voyenizdat, 1965). Published under the auspices of the U.S. Air Force, Soviet Military Thought Series, p. 185. For Soviet experience in World War II, see M. M. Kir'yan, *Vnezapnost' v nastupatelnykh operatsiyakh velikoy Otechestvennoy voyny* (Surprise in offensive operations of the Great Patriotic War) (Moskva: Nauka, 1986). Kir'yan classifies surprise as strategic, operational, and tactical, and he notes:

> In the contemporary situation, when reconnaissance possibilities have grown along with the increase in the scale of wars, it is extremely difficult to totally conceal preparations for large operations. It is a perfectly realistic mission to conceal their real scales, however, particularly the focus of measures being carried out, the concept and axis of the strike, and the time at which active combat operations are to be started.

(Excerpted from the foreword). See also Chapter 1, "Steps Taken to Achieve Surprise during Preparations for Offensive Operations."

77. Radziyevsky, *Dictionary of Military Terms*, 184.

78. Ibid., 183.

79. Col. Gen. N. A. Lomov, ed., *Nauchno-tekhnicheskiy progress i revolyutsiya v voennom dele* (Scientific-technical progress and the revolution in military affairs) (Moskva: Voyenizdat, 1973). U.S. Air Force Soviet Military Thought Series, p. 165.

80. Lomov, ed., *Nauchno-tekhnicheskiy* 170.

81. Lomov, ed., *Nauchno-tekhnicheskiy* 167.

82. Col. Stanislaw Koziej, "Anticipated Directions for Change in Tactics of Ground Troops," *Przeglad Wojsk Ladowych* (Ground forces review) September 1986: 5–9. I am grateful to Dr. Harold Orenstein for translating this article.

83. Koziej, "Anticipated Directions," 5–9.

84. Koziej, "Anticipated Directions," 5–9.

85. V. G. Reznichenko, I. N. Vorob'yev, and N. F. Miroshnichenko, "Combat Missions," in *Taktika* (Tactics) (Moscow: Voyenizdat, 1987), Ch. Four, Part 3.

86. Reznichenko, Vorob'yev, and Miroshnichenko, *Taktika.*

87. Reznichenko, Vorob'yev, and Miroshnichenko, *Taktika.*

88. Reznichenko, Vorob'yev, and Miroshnichenko, *Taktika.*

89. Reznichenko, Vorob'yev, and Miroshnichenko, *Taktika,* Ch. 4, part 4.

90. Reznichenko, Vorob'yev, and Miroshnichenko, *Taktika.*

91. Reznichenko, Vorob'yev, and Miroshnichenko, *Taktika,* Ch. 4, part 5.

92. John Keegan, *The Mask of Command* (New York: Penguin Books, 1988), 311–51.

93. Keegan, *Mask of Command,* 311–51.

94. Clausewitz, *On War,* 102.

95. Clausewitz, *On War,* 102.

6

ESCAPING THE NUCLEAR REVOLUTION: ANTI-NUCLEAR DEFENSES AND DETERRENCE

So far, we have seen that there are inescapable tensions built into the theory and practice of nuclear deterrence, and that conventional deterrence is not an escape from these. There is one other possible approach to a union between prenuclear strategic thinking and postnuclear technology, in order to escape the limits of nuclear deterrence. If conventional deterrence will not work, then nuclear transcendence will. Nuclear weapons can be made obsolete, or so incompetent relative to strategic non-nuclear weapons, that dissuasion against aggression will no longer depend mainly on atomic reprisal. As in the case of conventional deterrence as an attempted escape from the paradoxes of nuclear strategy, so, too, for anti-nuclear defenses: The appeal runs the ideological gamut from military mavens of new technology to the academic and policy priesthood that despises nuclear weapons for their own sake.

Therefore, the subject of anti-nuclear defenses, SDI, and so forth cannot be avoided. It will be approached here, however, in keeping with our overall objective of focussing on the relationship between coercion, or force, and policy. Unfortunately, much of the popularity of anti-nuclear defenses to both the political Right and Left in the United States springs from a desire to return to the golden age of imagined U.S. nuclear invulnerability. In this imaginary past, questions of actually using nuclear weapons during war, or employing them as coercive instruments during crisis, remained buried in the agendas of research specialists, far from public visibility. The invulnerable past is as imaginary as the invulnerable future, based now on weapons poised in the sky to shoot down weapons of mass destruction based on earth. This is not a prejudgment of the value of any particular U.S. or Soviet defense technology.

The more inclusive question is not whether impressive gadgets can be built, for surely they can. And some of them, by the next century, will undoubtedly work. But spaceborne sensors, weapons, and command and control systems will not be added to a tabula rasa, but to an existing framework of U.S.–Soviet adversary partnership. If the character of U.S. and Soviet policy changes, then this partnership will change as well, and with it the perceived reasons for maintaining military establishments. And a critical question for U.S. policy elites in the next decade or so is whether highly competent missile defenses will be congruent with an emerging Soviet military doctrine of defensive sufficiency, or on a direct collision course with it.

On the subject of the relationship between coercion or force and policy, the great Prussian military theorist Carl Von Clausewitz offers insightful observations especially pertinent to the comparison of offense and defense. I will use some of Clausewitz's frame of reference as a conceptual pivot to analyze the problem of anti-nuclear strategic defenses, asking whether defense is the superior form of war, and if so, what this might mean for nuclear or postnuclear deterrence. It turns out that one can argue for a supremacy of the defensive, but Clausewitz helps us to see that this implies (if correct at all) the supremacy of a defensive *mission or function*, not a technology or tactic.

OFFENSE AND DEFENSE: IS ONE FORM SUPERIOR?

Anti-nuclear strategic defense is an extremely visible issue, in the wake of President Reagan's Strategic Defense Initiative. SDI was given birth by the president's speech of March 23, 1983, in which Reagan called upon the U.S. scientific community to provide technologies that would eventually make nuclear weapons obsolete.[1] The president asked whether it would not be better to save lives than to avenge them, and so attempted to steal the high ground not only of technology, but also of political rhetoric, from his opponents.

Rhetoric aside, one could divide the proponents of SDI into essentially two groups: the anti-nuclear "transcenders" who sought newer generations of technologies in order to base the prevention of war on something other than deterrence, and the "reconstructionists" who sought to rebuild deterrence from what was felt to be a precarious base of almost total reliance upon offensive retaliation. Opposition to SDI grew quickly in the academic and scientific communities. In 1983, the Reagan administration empaneled two prestigious study groups, one on technology and one on future strategy, to study the technical and strategic feasibility of ballistic missile defense.[2] Their prognoses were generally favorable, although the group studying the strategic future came down more favorably for limited, as opposed to total, defenses.

Clausewitz was more aware of the importance of the mission or function of defense than any of his contemporaries. He was sufficiently emphatic to make the following controversial assertion:

> So in order to state the relationship precisely, we must say that *the defensive form of warfare is intrinsically stronger than the offensive.*[3]

There were numerous reasons why the defensive form of warfare was the stronger. The concept of defense, according to Clausewitz, was the parrying of a blow.[4] Its characteristic feature was awaiting the blow.[5] The defense was the stronger form of war because the defender was protecting his own territory against invasion. The attacker would have to make the first move, thus revealing the essence of his strategy. Assuming that both sides have equal means, Clausewitz notes that the objectives of defense are usually "preservation and protection," which are easier than attack.[6]

In Chapter 3, Book 6 of *On War*, Clausewitz discusses the relationship between attack and defense in strategy, having previously addressed tactics (although with implications for strategy). The main factors in strategic effectiveness, according to Clausewitz, are the advantage of terrain; surprise; concentric attack; fortresses to strengthen a theater of operations; popular support; and the exploitation of moral factors.[7] He notes that the first obviously favors the defender, and the second the attacker. In Chapter 5, "Character of Strategic Defense," he reiterates that defense is "simply the more effective form of war." However, he is now most emphatic about the relationship between offense and defense, and I shall come back to that in a moment. In one of the most interesting and important passages pertinent to his argument on behalf of defense as the stronger form of war, Clausewitz notes that war serves the purpose of the defense more than that of the aggressor. Only aggression calls forth defense, and war along with it. Aggressors are always peace-loving, like Napoleon Bonaparte: They prefer to take over countries unopposed.[8]

Strategy, according to Clausewitz (and as noted in an earlier chapter of this book), has to do with the coupling of political purpose with military force. He is now adding something very important to the observation that war is the continuation of politics by other means. The addition is the implication that military force can be used for dissuasion or coercion, as well as for actual combat. Force can serve to persuade potential attackers of the small probability of their success, in addition to inflicting costs upon attackers if they are not deterred.[9] It can be used as an instrument of anticipatory influence; if the defender is potentially able to resist the attacker, the chances are greater that the attacker will forego the attempt. Thus, the resistance provided by defenses exerts costs against attackers (denial of their gains and objectives) and creates for them the risk of further punishment (I will discuss this more below).[10]

Before examining the connection between defense and offense, it is worthwhile to pause at this point in order to make some further connections between Clausewitz and contemporary concerns. There are two other reasons why defense is the stronger form of war. The first is time, or the importance of time in strategy and tactics. The second is friction, already mentioned, or the sum total of forces that cause plans to go awry and the unexpected to complicate designed moves. Time favors the defender in that he can regroup and draw upon the additional resources of the nation, its economy, and its people. Friction complicates all warfare, but it complicates matters for the invader more than it does for the defender. The attacker must take the risk of committing himself to some plan of action that will constitute the first move. Once committed, the attacker can no longer disguise hostile intent, and he has given away the gist of the war plan. The defender, having awaited the first blow and now being apprised of the attacker's opening gambit, can react.

Benjamin S. Lambeth of the RAND Corporation once wrote an article entitled "Uncertainties for the Soviet War Planner."[11] In this article, he noted how Soviet planners would, in contemplating an attack against the United States with nuclear weapons, be restrained by their estimates of various uncertainties that looked very different before and after deterrence had actually failed. According to Lambeth, this is also true for Soviet assessments of their prospects in major conventional wars:

> At almost every level of conventional force employment, Soviet commentary emphasizes the importance of such critical intangibles as leadership, awareness, and flexibility, none of which can be counted on in adequate measure at the proper time.[12]

Thus, uncertainty avoidance would undoubtedly extend into Soviet estimates of the likely success of any nuclear first strike. During the presidential campaign of 1980, the issue of a potential "window of vulnerability" with regard to the possible destruction of U.S. land-based missiles in a surprise attack became national press copy. The concern was expressed by Reagan and by public advocacy groups (such as the Committee on the Present Danger) that the Soviet Union might, using only a portion of its ICBM force, destroy the bulk of the U.S. ICBM force in a surprise attack. The USSR would then be in a position to coerce the U.S. president, who would be told that if the United States retaliated against Soviet cities, the Soviet Union would do likewise to U.S. cities. Thus, the United States would be forced to capitulate.[13]

This scenario illustrates, with regard to the case of U.S.-Soviet nuclear deterrence, the assessment by Clausewitz that defense is the stronger form of war. The United States is in a position to await the Soviet first strike and then to retaliate with its remaining weapons. Unless the USSR has a defense of its own, to absorb the U.S. retaliation, its first strike will be followed by catastrophe. The attacker must run incalculable risks in order to accomplish his objective. This is true for either superpower as long as the cities of both are subject to retaliatory destruction.

Commonly, this scenario and others like it are misread to imply the predominance of offense over defense in the nuclear age. But this misreading confuses defensive *tactics* and *technologies* with defensive strategy. Waiting to absorb the first strike of your opponent and then retaliating is a defensive strategy; preemption is an offensive strategy. Given an approximately equal balance of superpower strategic nuclear forces ("equal means"), the defensive strategy is more contributory to the objectives of policy than an offensive one. The preeminence of defensive strategy is supported by the predominance of offensive technology.

Conversely, an offensive strategy with regard to superpower strategic nuclear deterrence would be dependent on an improvement in defensive technologies. If either the Americans or the Soviets were to acquire nearly perfect or perfect defenses, while the other lacked defenses, the first superpower would be able to coerce the second. The side without defenses would be vulnerable to the first strike of the opponent, since the opponent's defenses would limit the effectiveness of any retaliation.

Thus, a true window of vulnerability might open up if one side deployed defenses and the other did not, assuming that offenses stayed essentially equivalent. However, a static situation for offenses is improbable as long as new defenses are being deployed. Each side will be racing to make sure that its offenses retain their ability to penetrate the opponent's defenses unless and until offenses are totally disarmed. Maintaining the penetrability of each side's offensive forces will be necessary to support the continuation of a defensive strategy. If either side doubts that its offenses can still penetrate the opponent's defenses, after having absorbed a first strike, then it must make the necessary corrections or lose the benefit of deterrence.

Clausewitz's notion of defense was sensitive to this problem of the interaction between offensive and defensive forces, and between offensive and defensive tactics. This second aspect of defensive strategy called for the defender to take the offensive at the most favorable opportunity; that is, after the attacker's forces had passed their "culminating point."[14] During an attack, the force of that attack gradually diminishes. When the attack reaches a point at which the remaining strength is sufficient only to go on the defensive and wait for a peace settlement, the attack has passed its culminating point.[15] This allows the defender to gain superiority, which is the necessary prelude to the attainment of ultimate victory.

This passing of superiority in battle from attacker to defender, and the determination by the latter of the attacker's culminating point, is important for the attainment of the defender's military and political objectives. The defender must go on the offensive; a purely passive and reactive strategy will never lead to the accomplishment of war aims. The transition to a counterattack must be accepted as an inherent tendency in defense and is one of defense's essential features.[16] The sudden transition to the offensive is the "greatest moment" for the defense.[17] To Clausewitz, a victory achieved by the defensive is not turned to military advantage; it is allowed to whither away unused. This is a serious mistake.[18]

This applies to conventional war and deterrence, with which Clausewitz was well acquainted, and potentially to nuclear deterrence. The shield is meaningless without the sword, or without the threat of retaliation in response to aggression after the initial attack has been halted. In the case of conventional war in Europe, for example, NATO assumes that it will not suffice to stop a Soviet advance at the Rhine, but that it will have to force onto the USSR the decision to return to the status quo ante or to use nuclear weapons. Samuel P. Huntington has taken this application one step further in his proposal for NATO to consider a conventional retaliatory offensive simultaneous with any Pact invasion of Western Europe.[19]

Huntington's logic is deserving of further discussion in applying Clausewitz to contemporary problems. Huntington suggests that conventional retaliation should be given more emphasis, and nuclear retaliation less, in NATO strategy. Conventional retaliation into Eastern Europe would pose a symmetrical, controllable threat to Pact attackers without relying on early nuclear escalation, which might not be a credible threat or a controllable response. Conventional retaliation would then be the "flashing sword of vengeance," fulfilling Clausewitz's recommendation for a counterattack that accomplished NATO's political objectives. Nuclear retaliation might jeopardize those objectives if it led to uncontrolled escalation.

On the other hand, from Clausewitz's standpoint, of the proportionality between political ends and military means, NATO is an alliance made up mostly of European members. And the European members of NATO would prefer the deterrence of *any* war in Europe to the more credible retaliation against conventional aggression (while containing war below the nuclear threshold). To West Germans especially, any war on the Central Front is a decisive calamity, even if the Western alliance system ultimately "wins." The U.S. priorities might emphasize containing war below the nuclear threshold so that it remains conventional, and preferably in Europe. Europeans would prefer that it not take place at all, even if this means that the availability of a credible conventional retaliation is less certain.[20]

From the Soviet standpoint, allowing an attacker to reach the culminating point of success and then flashing the sword of vengeance in retaliation, is analogous to their experience in World War II. Of course, the USSR did not actually allow Hitler to get the jump on its forces, but once the war had begun, the Soviet strategy in general was to fight a strategically defensive war until the time was appropriate for counteroffensives on a large scale. It took some time for the Soviet ground and tactical air forces to be properly equipped and trained for the large operational maneuver that would characterize their combat with the Germans in the USSR from 1942 on.[21] Meanwhile, they were to conduct a strategic holding action, which included selective counterattacks when the Germans became threatening to strategic targets (e.g., Moscow). In the case of Napoleon's invasion of Russia, the French actually took Moscow and still fell short of fulfilling the requirements for causing the Russians a strategic defeat. The Russians abandoned the capital and left a ravaged city to Napoleon, regrouping and striking later against Napoleon's retreating armies.

In World War I, the Germans seemed to have reached their culminating point of success after the Russians ceded to their demands at Brest-Litovsk and plans for the offensive in the West in 1918 were made amid great optimism. As late as July 2, 1918, the kaiser and his warlords expected to deal a decisive blow against the Entente in the West, while holding onto an expanded greater Germany in the East, which included the Ukraine and other Soviet territory.[22] This expectation was very much against the realities of German economic and military resources, which were already stretched to the limit. The fifth and final German offensive in the West, which proved to be disastrous, opened on July 15. On July 18, U.S. and French attacks forced two German armies into retreat behind the Marne, and the strategic offensive had decisively passed to the Allies. The kaiser's confused anger at the sudden shift in momentum, on behalf of the Allies and against the Germans, is reflected in his comments of September 2:

> The campaign is lost. Now our troops have been running back without a stop since July 18. The fact is, we are exhausted. I cannot understand what they have been doing at Avesnes (the G.H.Q.). When the offensive was opened on the Marne on July 15, I was assured that the French had only 8 divisions left in reserve, and the British perhaps 13. Instead of this, the enemy assembles a crowd of divisions in the forest of Cotterets, unnoted by us, attacks our right flank and forces us to retreat. Since then we have received blow after blow. Our armies can simply do no more.[23]

Amazingly, political and military leaders of the Reich who met on August 14 at Spa, with the emperor presiding, continued to hold the hope that the military—and, therefore, political—situation could be rescued. Ludendorff stated that the German high command had set the aim of "gradually paralysing the enemy's will to fight by a strategic defensive."[24] This would have astounded Clausewitz, in view of the balance of forces and national capabilities that now remained. How the Allies, having been augmented by the Americans, were to be paralyzed by a defensive strategy in the West was not laid out. Of course, the earlier miscalculations of 1916 and 1917, which led the Germans to adopt unrestricted submarine warfare and thereby brought the United States into the war, were precursor disasters on a strategic scale. In retrospect, one can see that the culminating point of success for the Germans was passed once the United States was committed to war, although the culminating point on the battlefield was delayed until 1918.

Sometimes the culminating point comes and goes without being exploited. The case might be made with regard to the French and British failure to exploit German vulnerability in September 1939, immediately after Hitler's attack against Poland, and during the period of "phoney war" until May 1940, when Hitler launched his attack against France. In the first ten days of September, the Germans could spare only covering forces, and those very much under armed, to maintain the Siegfried Line on their western front. The French had great superiority in the numbers of men in combat divisions that could be brought to battle in the West, and an equally impressive superiority in numbers of tanks (several thousand on the French side, none on the German). Although the French air force was insubstantial relative to the German, the British could have augmented it with bombers capable of striking against key German force and infrastructure targets. The likelihood was that during the first two weeks or so of German fighting in Poland, a strong French and British attack against Germany's western front would have collapsed it, and thus permitted a strategic offensive into the Ruhr causing potentially catastrophic losses to Hitler's regime.[25] Instead, during early September 1939 and thereafter, the British and French were convinced by their intelligence estimates that they would have to assume the strategic defensive until Germany attacked in the West. Adopting the strategic defensive decreased their security instead of increasing it, because they allowed potential culminating points to pass without shifting from the defensive to the offensive at the proper moment. By May 1940, the Germans had finished off Poland and had built up considerably their forces capable of attacking westward, which they proceeded to do.

As John J. Mearsheimer has noted, the British and French were deterred from assuming the offensive by the prospect that, if it failed, they would be worse off than if they did not act.[26] There may have been some expectation that, while the fate of the Poles was being sealed, there was still opportunity to negotiate some kind of peace agreement between Germany and the western Allies. The Germans had forestalled the need to fight a war on two fronts by signing the nonaggression pact with the Soviet Union. The British and French had these and other reasons for justifying their postponement of any invasion until it was too late. The point is that the defensive strategy allows only certain windows of opportunity for the defender to turn the tables against the attacker. If these are not used, the defensive strategy is self-defeating. It is not, as Clausewitz noted, simply the absorption of punishment until the attacker gets tired or distracted onto another target.

Another implication of the counteroffensive component of any successful defensive strategy is that the counteroffensive should exploit the confusion that is bound to mark the conduct of an offensive (compared to a defensive) operation in a cumulative fashion. The culminating point of success for the offense, and the time at which the advantage may pass to the defense, may be marked by the paradox (for the offense) of ground forces moving forward while their cohesion has begun to come unstuck.

This is one of the major risks of blitzkrieg operations, with their emphasis on rapid and decisive thrusts into the opponent's rear by armored spearheads accompanied by tactical air power. As happened to the Germans in the Soviet Union in World War II, their fast-moving *panzer* divisions left behind the slower-moving infantry and horse drawn vehicles. Sometimes it seemed as if the Germans were fighting two different wars within the same operation.[27] As Edward Luttwak has noted, the modern battlefield will be scrutinized by electronic and other sensors, but:

> Today there are technical means of observation that can monitor the action as it unfolds, but it is still the defense that can best assess the ongoing results of aerial attack within its own area of control. . . . That information advantage, and the possession of all means in place, can enable the defenders to react with broad means against the deep-attack "system" of the attackers. . . .[28]

Another—and related—advantage for the defender, especially in the modern, high-technology information environment that would exist in Western Europe, is the consecutive nature of operations and the uncertainty that this introduces into the calculations of the attacker. For example, with regard to NATO or Pact efforts to exploit sensors and terminal munitions for deep attack, a number of systems and processes have to work in harmony. The breakdown of any link in the chain spells trouble:

> Similarly, in deep-attack systems the initial sensors *and* the relay transmissions *and* the control centers *and* the missiles or manned aircraft *and* the terminal munitions must all function correctly one after the other, whereas the defenders can defeat the entire system's ability to attack any given set of targets by successfully neutralizing just one of the links.[29]

It is no coincidence that Luttwak was drawn to this inference by his awareness of Clausewitz's discussion of raiding cavalry and the "countermeasures" cavalry would have to oppose in sequence (eluding pickets, maneuvering around larger forces, locating a convoy, scattering the convoy escort, and so forth).[30] There is also an analogy between the defensive anti-air warfare suites on modern U.S. cruisers (Aegis class) and the offensive weapons that would be opposing them. But to see this naval analogy with regard to strategy, we must invert the relationship of offensive and defensive technologies and tactics.

The carrier anti-air warfare suite is analogous to the SDI missile defense system. The defense poses layers of intruders between the offense and its targets. This does require that the offense show its hand, as in the case of a nuclear first strike or a conventional invasion crossing borders in Europe. But the problems of information management and consecutive operations do not favor the "defender" in this case, nor in the SDI case, as they did on land, because the objective of sequential operations on land is the acquisition and holding of territory. Relative to this objective, the information regime available to the defender—so long as his forces are not actually dislodged from that territory and his overhead "eyes and ears" electronically blinded—remains advantageous compared to that of the attacker. In the problem of air- and sea-launched attacks against carriers, the information management problem for the defender is greater. Ghosts must be distinguished from real threat objects, which must be classified and then acted upon in a very time-urgent manner. The disaster of the USS *Stark* in the Persian Gulf in 1987 and the accidental downing of an Iranian civilian airbus in 1988 by the USS *Vincennes* illustrate the problematical information regimes available to naval defenders who have the best-deployed technology relative to the mission at hand. As in the anti-air warfare case, the BMD information management problem is much more difficult than the offensive one, at the tactical and operational level. In fact, it may not be manageable at all if pessimists about the future capabilities of BM/C^3 software can be taken at their word. However, this pessimism is neither proved nor disproved at the moment. The point is that any missile defense system, and especially one deployed partly or totally in space, will have to perform with unprecedented fidelity under untried conditions, coordinating the massive data inputs that will be required to synthesize sensors, communications, weapons platforms, and other components of the system.[31] The information burden on the offensive battle management system will be of a lesser, although still drastic, kind. One might well ask whether either offensive or defensive BM/C^3 systems will perform as expected under the stress of nuclear combat, and the sensible answer would be no.

Notice, on the other hand, that in the case of anti-carrier missile attacks or attacks on strategic nuclear forces protected by anti-nuclear defenses, the defensive strategy is not to await preemption and count on attrition of the attacker's forces. These defensive operations and tactics might be forced on the side that has taken the strategic defensive. But the defensive side might, consistent with Clausewitz's teachings, use the operational and tactical offensive to its advantage. Consider the case in which NATO has been attacked in Europe and seeks to maintain the capability to reinforce Europe despite adversary efforts to prevent reinforcement. To maintain control of the sea lanes of communication that connect Western Europe to North America, the United States and Allied naval forces might have to conduct forward maritime operations well north of the Greenland–Iceland–United Kingdom gap (GIUK, or GIN for those who prefer to define the line as Greenland–Iceland–Norway). The contest for operational advantage in the North Atlantic might take U.S. and Allied surface and submarine forces into the Norwegian Sea and other territorial waters at the very time that those areas are being contested by Pact attackers. Former U.S. Secretary of the Navy John Lehman may have gone too far in envisioning early carrier battle group attacks against the Kola peninsula, which the U.S. admirals would be unlikely to conduct in any event. But the assumption by U.S. naval planners that the next war might not allow them the luxury of an operationally defensive strategy, as opposed to a strategically defensive one, is one that can and has been defended by experts.[32]

ANTI-NUCLEAR STRATEGIC DEFENSES: COMMAND AND CONTROL

The filtration model of ballistic missile defense has characterized many descriptions of it, including those offered by Reagan spokesmen. The first, or "boost" phase, layer intercepts attacking missiles during the first three to five minutes of powered flight, and before they have dispersed their warheads from the "buses" that they carry aloft for that purpose. Thus, boost phase defenses have great leverage against MIRVed ICBMs, thought to be the most destabilizing components of U.S. and Soviet arsenals. The second, or post-boost, phase occurs as the warheads are dispensed and allocated to their preprogrammed targets; this phase takes several minutes also. The longest, or midcourse, phase occurs as the re-entry vehicles arc through space on their designated trajectories for some fifteen to twenty minutes. Finally, re-entry vehicles descend into the atmosphere and close in on their targets during the suitably named re-entry phase.

Actually, each of these phases of attack presents a somewhat different problem to the defender. In the boost phase, the rising boosters must be distinguished from the hot infra-red plume that makes them visible and detectable to space-based sensors. There is very short time for the engagement. And since the premium for boost phase defense, relative to the attack price that it can impose on the offense, is very high, any prospective attacker will be inclined to attack the defenses first. Thus, before any defenses can be activated against the terrestrially based ballistic missiles (land or sea launched) for which they have been tasked, those defenses must first defend themselves against anti-defense preemption (defense suppression). One interesting legal question, with regard to U.S. or Soviet space-based boost phase defenses, is whether attacks against them constitute acts of war or acts of war prevention. It could be maintained that one side's attempt to deploy an effective boost phase defense was an attempt to deny to the other side the capacity to retaliate against a first strike. Thus, attacking such a "destabilizing" BMD system would, according to this line of argument, uphold deterrence. Whose hardware was being destroyed might matter less than who was threatening deterrence stability.

In the midcourse phase, there is a comparatively long time for engagements of attacking re-entry vehicles, perhaps twenty minutes. But the problem of discrimination, of warheads from decoys, now intrudes. The problem is that discrimination results from the deception that the offense will attempt to use in order to confuse the defense. It may attempt to make warheads look like decoys, or vice versa. The defense must then have some way of deciding when it is being tricked, unless it has so many interceptors that it can waste them improvidently. One of the technical challenges for SDIO (Strategic Defense Initiating Organization) is to provide for midcourse discrimination, and it has investigated a variety of options, including the use of particle beams.[33] The reader will recognize the analogies with problems of strategic deception alluded to earlier. One possibility is that the attacking side will expend many dummy re-entry vehicles with a small proportion of good ones against the BMD system. The real thrust of the attack would be based on other, and probably atmospheric, weapons. If the BMD system performs well, it uses its effectiveness against a secondary front of the attack. If the BMD system performs poorly, the attacker gets a bonus of additional re-entry vehicles that escape attrition. Such a strategy and its accompanying deception might correlate with an anti-boost defense deception to deploy many unarmed ICBM launchers throughout the countryside.

In the terminal of re-entry phase, the RVs (Re-entry Vehicles) are descending through the atmosphere very rapidly, and the atmosphere sorts the RVs from the decoys because the latter are lighter. Now the problem is not discrimination, but to react rapidly against the remaining warheads and intercept them before they detonate within the destruction radius to which their targets are vulnerable. Some of the attacking warheads may be salvage fused so that they detonate when interceptors are attempting to collide with them. Thus, the incoming RVs should be intercepted as high in the atmosphere as possible. The United States and the Soviet Union have experience with terminal defenses, in the form of the once-deployed U.S. Safeguard system and the currently deployed Soviet modified Galosh system. The U.S. system grew out of earlier BMD efforts at terminal defense (e.g., Sentinel, Nike-X). Earlier versions of terminal defense systems suffered from the limitation that the use of nuclear-armed interceptors would be required. Thus, the collateral damage from a successful defense might be prohibitive. SDIO emphasized non-nuclear terminal defenses, building upon technology developed for the Low Altitude Defense System (LOaDS) by the U.S. Army.[34]

Although each of these phases of the defense presents unique problems of technical and tactical measures versus countermeasures, the entire synergy of the defense is even more complex. If the boost phase defense does not succeed, the rest of the system will be overwhelmed. Moreover, the other parts of the system must know with high confidence just how well the boost phase defense has done. Some method must be developed for "birth-to-death" tracking of threat vehicles from the time of launch to the time of interception. This means that attacking launchers or re-entry vehicles not destroyed in one phase must be handed over to the next. Accurate information must be passed among space-based sensors, weapons-carrying satellites or other platforms, space-based communications links, and ground stations from which national command authorities will conduct the battle. To accomplish all of this, a battle management system for command and control of the various phases, to assure that the conduct of operations in one phase does not interfere with the actions taken in others, will be necessary.

The requirements for writing software to accomplish integrating the various phases of any BMD system will be imposing. There are two generic approaches, although any actual system might borrow from both. The first is to design a centralized, top-down system that attempted to allocate all interceptors according to the most efficient (i.e., cost effective) scheme. The objective would be to destroy the greatest number of targets for the smallest expenditure of interceptors. Another approach would be modular, bottom-up, in which the various parts of the system might be deployed step by step. No single part would be expected to sustain itself against a dedicated attack. As the various pieces were fitted together, software would be designed to be fault tolerant of the sub-system limitations. Only at the end of the process would the entire system be coagulated, and even then, some higher (but presumably acceptable) degree of inefficiency would be tolerated, compared to the top-down system.[35]

The top-down system has the advantage of central coordination and efficiency in the allocation of interceptors against targets. It has the disadvantage that a centralized, tightly coupled system is subject to catastrophic failure if the "brain" of the system is destroyed. The bottom-up system has the advantage of flexibility and survivability even if one or more nodes are destroyed or disabled. The disadvantage of the bottom-up system is that parts of the system may do what is optimal for them, but not for the system as a whole.

Moreover, the success or failure of any missile defense system depends on survivability more than it does on its efficiency. Paul H. Nitze indicated that survivability and cost-effectiveness at the margin were the two criteria that any BMD system must meet before it could be considered for deployment.[36] Once an attack seems imminent, however, the criterion of survivability will mean much more. The two important issues will then be the impact of defenses on crisis stability, and their effectiveness at limiting damage if deterrence fails.

It might be thought that defenses are obviously good for crisis stability. Crisis stability is the condition such that neither superpower feels an incentive to strike first on account of being more vulnerable to first strikes as opposed to retaliatory strikes. The difference between the expected value of striking first compared to striking second is the best measure of crisis stability. However, crisis stability is not guaranteed by a small difference between expected values of preemption and retaliation. Desperate attackers motivated by domestic political impulses or irrational fears can (and historically have) launched attacks when the odds suggested that defenders could prevail. Overly optimistic crisis managers have pushed confrontations to the brink in the expectation that the adversary will back down, only to find that the opponent is resolved not to yield.[37]

Thus, the U.S. position at the Johnson-Kosygin talks in 1967, that defenses were destabilizing and should be limited or prohibited altogether, drew understandable criticism from the Soviet premier, who responded with the commonsense observation that offenses destroy, while defenses provide protection.[38] By the time SALT I was concluded in 1972, the Soviets had apparently joined the Americans in recognizing that, under some conditions, defenses could be destabilizing of a strategic equilibrium.[39] The Soviets had not, as some U.S. spokesmen had hoped, adopted the U.S. strategic doctrine of mutual assured destruction. But they had recognized that crude and vulnerable defenses were very much like ineffective and vulnerable offenses: They invite attack on themselves, and so contribute to crisis instability.

They do this because, as Clausewitz would have recognized, defenses and offenses do not exist in separate realms, but influence one another. The U.S. offenses and defenses have implications for each other, and for the Soviet offenses and defenses. From the standpoint of crisis stability, defenses that are more vulnerable to attack than the offenses they are protecting (if that is their mission) add nothing positive to the equation and may contribute something negative. It depends in part on the stability of the balance of offenses, without any defenses. If the U.S.-Soviet offensive force balance is highly stable, then the addition of vulnerable defenses may make little difference other than wasted money. But if the balance is thought to be unstable or undergoing a period of change, as it was during the mid- to latter 1960s, then the addition of vulnerable defenses may detract from crisis stability.

The vulnerability of defenses, in turn, rests on the offensive counter-measures used against them. If these countermeasures are cheaper to deploy or to prepare than the costs of deploying additional increments of defense, once the basic defense infrastructure has been deployed, then the defenses are not "cost effective at the margin," as defined by Nitze. The problem is that the marginal cost effectiveness of any BMD system cannot be determined until a basic system is first built and deployed, and then the action-reaction of countermeasures and counter-countermeasures (with associated costs) takes effect. This, in turn, has implications for the influence of defenses on crisis stability. If it turns out that, having built U.S. defenses, they are not marginally cost effective compared to Soviet offensive countermeasures, then the United States has invested a substantial sum in order to provide to the Soviet Union an inviting target.

Now, it might be objected here that limited U.S. defenses, even if they are vulnerable and not marginally cost-effective, will be valuable in complicating the Soviet calculus of attack. Therefore, they provide additional insurance against any crisis-borne first-strike temptation that the Kremlin leadership might harbor. This point must be considered within the context of overall Soviet and U.S. defense postures and the incentives or disincentives they would otherwise have for nuclear attack. The insurance provided by any U.S. BMD system must be weighed against the effects of that system on crisis stability, other things being equal. This means that defenses might be a net positive if they were survivable, cost-effective, and capable of defending only military or command targets of the kind that would be preferred objectives of a first strike, but not of a second.

Even after having met these criteria of survivability, marginal cost-effectiveness, and nonprovocativeness, defenses must be justified, according to the reasoning of Clausewitz, on grounds of preferred strategy. In Chapters 7 and 8 of Book 6, he suggests two grounds. First, the defender establishes the ground rules for his conduct although he is not yet certain of the plans of an attacker. Second, attackers can fall short of their objectives in two ways: They can perish by the sword, defeated by the defender's armies as close to his border as possible, or they can be defeated by their own exertions.[40] In the case of any U.S. SDI system, for example, the ability to establish ground rules might be demonstrated in the capability for preferential defense of some targets and a comparative willingness to sacrifice others to light attacks. The preferential defense scheme would not be known to the attacker. The exhaustion of the attacker by his own exertions would also seem applicable to a very comprehensive SDI system if the various layers of the defense worked in harmony and not against one another.

We must remember, as Clausewitz did, that offensive and defensive strategies should not be confused with offensive and defensive technologies or tactics. Whether U.S. or Soviet defenses are used offensively or defensively, in a strategic sense, depends upon the tasking prescribed for them in war plans. For example, although during the 1960s the U.S. declaratory policy was assured destruction, strategic target planning allocated many warheads to the task of damage limitation. Damage limitation was the use of U.S. strategic forces to destroy the opponent's forces in order to prevent those forces from being used against U.S. targets. From the U.S. standpoint, this was a preferable way of targeting weapons assumed to be used in the early stages of any war, as opposed to using them against Soviet cities. However, from the Soviet standpoint, the damage limitation mission described by the McNamara Pentagon appeared very similar to the objective of preemption. This is, in fact, a problem with counterforce targeting strategies as a whole: They appear to the prospective opponent to be a provocative, and perhaps trigger prone, approach to the use of force that could tip a crisis over from peace into war.

So, defenses for the purpose of damage limitation, it might be argued, are no worse than offenses for the same purpose. At least the defenses of one side cannot be pointed at the offensive retaliatory forces of the other, thereby raising fears of preemption. This is literally true, but strategically misleading. The defenses of one side *that also has deployed offenses capable of attacking major portions of the adversary's force target set* are, in fact, pointed at the retaliatory forces of the other side. The defenses and offenses used together by one side might threaten to deny the other side an acceptable (i.e., adequately deterring) retaliation. I mean "adequately deterring" in two senses here. First, the side with offenses and defenses combined may be able to coerce the side with offenses only in a crisis. Second, after deterrence fails but before war has escalated to all-out exchanges, the side without defenses will feel that it is already losing. It will have fewer incentives to limit its retaliation and to engage in controlled exchanges, for it has no hope of limiting damage to its population and society even from limited enemy attacks. Thus, the asymmetry between an attacker with both offenses and defenses and a defender with offenses only is more meaningful in limited, as opposed to total, nuclear war. The side with offenses and defenses can launch limited (although still very destructive) attacks against its opponent in the hope of exerting intrawar deterrence or compellence. The other side must respond with disproportionate retaliation, in order to overcome the opponent's defenses, or see its bargaining position gradually reduced to something negligible.

This is not to argue for defenses by the back door, as a mechanism for war termination if both sides have them, allowing for the safe conduct of limited nuclear wars. No such safety can be guaranteed. But defenses can add to crisis stability if they provide protection *not otherwise available* and at acceptable cost for offensive forces that would be destroyed in preemptive attack if undefended. Thus, the U.S. MX/MPS "racetrack"-basing scheme of the Carter administration, had it been deployed, would probably have required eventually some kind of active defenses to increase its leverage against the numbers of ICBM warheads that the USSR could, with unlimited fractionation, have thrown against it. The MX/MPS system was cancelled by Reagan in favor of silo-based MX/Peacekeeper deployments. Had the United States gone the MX/MPS route, it would have found an expensive technical solution that created several strategic problems. First, MX/MPS would act as a "warhead sponge" and invite even more Soviet warheads onto the continental United States in the event of war. Second, it depended upon arms-control agreements to limit Soviet warheads and yields—which, by a suitable combination of point and barrage attacks, could have defeated it. Third, it depended, as do most ICBM defense schemes, on launch under attack, a procedure that a well-designed surprise attack will make very difficult to execute.[41]

Following the recommendations of the Scowcroft Commission, the Reagan administration attempted to resolve the issue of ICBM modernization by deploying fifty MX/Peacekeepers in silos (with an additional fifty later allocated for deployment in rail-garrison basing), while proceeding with research and development on the Midgetman small, single warhead, land mobile ICBM.[42] The idea behind Midgetman was that its mobility would provide higher survivability than silo-based ICBMs, and its single warhead would make it a less attractive target than a MIRVed ICBM. Thus, the arms-control community favored Midgetman and the Pentagon planners favored MX/Peacekeeper for its damage limitation capabilities. From the standpoint of strategy, the irony was that the case for MX or for Midgetman was weak unless they were deployed together, and then costs became prohibitive. The case for Midgetman survivability depended upon limiting Soviet barrage attack capabilities; that for MX rail garrison on surviving, despite barrage attacks if sufficient warning were available. The targeting of mobile missiles was more than a problem of allocating individual weapons to discrete targets because the targets moved and were to some extent concealed.

The more pertinent strategic issue was whether the United States needed additional land-based "prompt counterforce" or whether it could depend upon sea-based systems (Trident II submarine-launched ballistic missiles and sea-launched cruise missiles) for strategic counterforce. The Scowcroft Commission pointed to the value of having multiple basing modes for U.S. strategic forces. The Soviet Union would be forced to attack U.S. bomber bases and missile silos with somewhat different flight profiles and weapons to target allocations. This resulted in a trade-off between additional U.S. ICBMs, or bombers, which would escape destruction depending on the preferred Soviet plan.[43] What was not addressed in this discussion was why the USSR would attack either the bomber or the ICBM force if it could not assuredly destroy the U.S. ballistic missile submarine (SSBN) force as well. Otherwise, the Soviet Union would be vulnerable to societal devastation even after destroying much of the U.S. ICBM, or bomber, forces—or both.

The U.S. response to this question, when it has been addressed, is that ICBMs provide unique offensive capabilities that other components of the strategic "triad" do not offer. They are the weapons most capable of attacking the hardest targets promptly, including the Soviet missile silos and command bunkers. According to the Scowcroft Commission, these targets are the most highly valued by the political and military leaders of the Soviet Union.[44] The Soviet leaders, according to this reckoning, value most highly the preservation of both their political control and their military power. Therefore, these are the points of greatest vulnerability, and threatening to attack them provides the most credible deterrent.

Even if this reasoning about what the Soviet leadership values most is not disputed, and there are reasons to do so, the requirement for U.S. weapons that can credibly threaten to destroy Soviet forces and leadership *promptly* is not so clear. From the perspective of strategy (which is, according to Clausewitz, guided by a political aim), U.S. planners would want to assure the eventual, instead of rapid, destruction of these targets. Their immediate destruction in wartime would leave the Soviet Union with no incentive to withhold any component of its retaliation, and thus destroy whatever possibilities remained for negotiated war termination. There is another problem in the assumption that these targets should be attacked promptly. The assumption is that attacking physical things like missile silos is a task comparable to attacking a leadership group and its cohesion and control. However, these are two very different tasks.[45] Destruction of members of the Soviet political and military elite does not guarantee against their replacement by others who are more belligerent and who might want to continue fighting until their arsenals had been exhausted.

There is also a difference between a national command authority and the totality of cohesive forces that hold together a responsive military capacity. Organizations can survive the death, destruction, or incapacitation of leaders. Hitler's high command was riddled with dissension and treason. Stalin was psychologically distraught to the point of decision-making incapacity in the days immediately following Operation Barbarossa. The performance of the German Wehrmacht on the Eastern Front is judged by historians to have achieved a standard of combat effectiveness in operations and tactics not matched by any other combatant in World War II. This remained true whether the Germans were fighting on the offensive or the defensive, when they were outnumbered, when they faced superior firepower, and so on. Under conditions of military retreat and guiding political incompetency, which would have shattered the cohesion of most other armies, the Wehrmacht held fast, costing the Russians many times the casualties per effective unit inflicted upon the Germans. One can go too far with this, as some historians have, and imagine that the Wehrmacht was some kind of military superforce, but it was not. It maintained its cohesion under duress as a result of superior training, experience, and a philosophy of mission-oriented tasking that allowed junior commanders to make decisions appropriate to their levels of responsibility and battlefield assignments.[46]

Another issue pertinent to strategy, in the sense that Clausewitz intended it, is whether the United States plans to destroy the Soviet leadership or to credibly threaten to do so, and thereby inhibit the successful management of nuclear crises. Presumably, what one wants out of crisis management is to escape from war while avoiding significant political and military losses. A Soviet leadership that felt vulnerable to prompt decapitation might reach the stage of desperation sooner than one that did not. On the other hand, there is every likelihood that, having decided that war is inevitable, the USSR may include attacks on U.S. national command authorities and other C^3 components among its earliest salvos. This is not necessarily the mirror image of U.S. target planning, which apparently envisions attacks on the highest Soviet leadership only in the latter stages of a war. One would hope that the Soviet high command would appreciate the difference, although it can be forgiven for cynicism.

The protection of national command authorities in Washington and Moscow, together with the protection of other important C^3 targets from prompt destruction, has been suggested as one method by which partial defenses might contribute to strategic stability. One might say that this is a conceivable cure for the disease of command vulnerability, but it is not necessarily the best one, given the side effects of defenses on stability. The case that defenses can protect command targets in a cost-effective manner, compared to hardening, dispersing, and concealing them, remains to be made. As I noted above, ICBMs that demand their own missile defense systems for survivability are in danger of removing themselves from candidacy for feasible deployment. The competition, in the form of submarine- and bomber-delivered "stealthy" weapons, is becoming more formidable, and the case for ICBMs with their allegedly unique properties, weaker. The need to make the ICBM mobile and the possible need to provide missile defense for it are two clues to its impending doom as a preferred system for strategic nuclear deterrence and for limiting damage if deterrence fails.

Perhaps the strongest argument for partial defenses is that they could contribute to stability by making extended deterrence more credible. They could do this in either of two ways. First, U.S. missile defenses protecting the U.S. retaliatory forces that would otherwise be vulnerable would raise U.S. confidence in its second-strike capability. This would contribute to deterrence and improved crisis management, compared to a situation of suspect force survivability. The key qualification here is "forces that would otherwise be vulnerable." Second, partial U.S. or NATO defenses could be deployed in Western Europe as an enhancement of its anti-air defenses. Theater ballistic missile defenses could help to deter the use of (and limit the destruction caused by) short-range ballistic missiles, including conventionally armed SRBMs employed as components of a Soviet theater-strategic air offensive.

Whether the arguments for partial defenses as supports for extended nuclear or conventional deterrence make sense depends on several factors. The first is whether the same increment in stability can be accomplished by arms control instead of investment in additional force structure. Second, any defenses deployed must appear to be incapable of subsequent expansion into larger, and perhaps destabilizing, deployments. Third, partial defenses deployed in Europe are as dependent for their credibility as are offenses on a plausible explanation of how NATO will manage the process of escalation. For if NATO cannot manage, the expansion of limited war into total war is assured, with or without defenses. The only case in which this roadblock need not be surmounted is the hypothetical one in which the technology of defenses is totally dominant over the technology of offenses. We will take up that hypothetical situation in the last section. First, we must address the issue of NATO command systems, doctrinal assumptions about escalation control, and the probability that those systems and doctrines could provide for escalation management after the nuclear threshold has been crossed. To do so, we need first to consider the difference between deterrence and compellence—or, rather, the distinction between deterrent missions and compellent missions for nuclear forces.

DETERRENCE, COMPELLENCE, AND U.S. NUCLEAR STRATEGY

Insights into Clausewitz's observation that defense is inherently the stronger form of war, and related observations about U.S. nuclear strategy, can be derived from contrasting the notion of compellence with that of deterrence. The concept of compellence is an active form of deterrence, according to Thomas C. Schelling.[47] Deterrence is intended to persuade the opponent not to start an action that we do not want him to start. The objective of compellence is to undo or stop an action that the other side has already undertaken. Alexander George has suggested that the "stop" and "undo" forms of compellence offer another gradation: "stop doing" is milder than "undo" what you have done.[48] In the Cuban missile crisis, to apply Schelling's distinction, the United States was exercising deterrence prior to the discovery of the missiles in Cuba. Once they were discovered, the U.S. government had to resort to compellence to get them out.

This was, in fact, one of the difficult decisions to be made by President Kennedy and his advisors. They had to use an active form of deterrence because the Soviet missiles were already being constructed and would be ready in a short time. The blockade of Cuba sufficed to prevent the USSR from delivering any additional missiles to Cuba. But it did not by itself remove them. Kennedy had to use a combination of threats and incentives to do that. The threats were not entirely controllable, holding out the possibility of a clash between the superpowers, which neither wanted. For example, the United States could easily have attacked Soviet SAM (surface-to-air missile) sites protecting the medium-range ballistic missile (MRBM) construction areas. For that matter, the United States could have successfully invaded Cuba, deposed Castro, and installed a regime of its liking, had the cost seemed proportionate to the risk. It clearly was not. Kennedy and his advisors feared that Khrushchev would attack in Berlin, where U.S. and Allied forces were vulnerable, in response to a Cuban invasion or air strikes that killed Soviet troops in Cuba. The invasion and air strike options were not suitable because they were not proportionate to the objective. The objective, as the president repeatedly reminded members of the ExCom, was not to get into a war with the Soviet Union, but to get the missiles out of Cuba.

U.S. grand strategy or high policy and the commitments following from that strategy will help to determine the balance between reliance upon nuclear deterrent, or compellent, threats. Since the formation of NATO in 1949, the United States has been committed to the forward defense of Western Europe along with fifteen of its allies. However, the original conventional force goals for NATO were never reached, or even approached. Since the 1950s, NATO has, to a greater or lesser extent, depended upon nuclear weapons to substitute for its lack of conventional forces (I am accepting NATO judgments of the conventional force requirements only for purposes of discussion). As a result, even after the adoption of flexible response in 1967, the United States and its West European allies remained locked into a declaratory policy that guaranteed the eventual use of nuclear weapons, if not the early use.

The result of this nuclear umbrella over NATO Europe, for U.S. strategy, is twofold. First, the United States by implication requires nuclear forces that can serve not only as deterrents, but also as compellents. In the event of an outbreak of conventional war in Europe, NATO would attempt to restore the status quo ante by compelling Warsaw Pact forces to abandon their objectives and return to their own territories. However, this might not be possible with conventional forces alone. Therefore, NATO has declared that it will use nuclear weapons based in Europe, and perhaps those in North America, if need be, rather than lose a conventional war in Europe.

There are strategists and politicians who doubt that the United States will actually use nuclear weapons in the event unless the Soviets do. Others doubt any NATO willingness to use nuclear weapons. Nevertheless, I take the alliance strategy as it has been approved by the member governments as authoritative.

The second implication of the requirement for U.S. nuclear weapons, including strategic nuclear ones, to act as compellents is that the requirement is more straining of credibility than the more passive form of simple deterrence is. For U.S. or other NATO nuclear weapons to be used as compellents during war in Europe, they must be perceived to be at least equivalent, and preferably more than that, to Soviet theater and strategic forces. Yet this requirement is hard to meet, and if met, it becomes disadvantageous to other policy objectives, including arms control and deterrence stability. Given the numbers of strategic and theater-nuclear weapons deployed by the Soviet Union and the United States, the meaning of superiority in this context is not clear, if indeed it has any meaning. One might argue that one side or the other should be able to fight a nuclear war in Europe, or across the U.S. and Soviet continents, and win it in a classical fashion. However, nuclear weapons are not classical weapons, and a more un-Clausewitzian idea is difficult to imagine. So, while falling short of the number of weapons that poses to the Soviet Union the possible loss of its deterrent, the United States and NATO must somehow obtain compellent pressure once a conventional war has been launched.

To see this dilemma more clearly, let us imagine two axes, as indicated below. One axis (horizontal) represents the dimension from the most passive forms of deterrence to the most active forms of compellence. The second axis (vertical) represents the degree of control or the confidence we have about control of nuclear weapons and nuclear escalation, once they are used. Each of these dimensions represents a continuum instead of a two-option set. The question of interest is the match between force and command system capabilities and the degree of activeness that policy requires from those forces and command systems. The problem with current NATO strategy is that it rests in cell 4, although the cell can be subdivided into greater and lesser degrees of compellent requirements and control stresses.

Degree of "Activeness"

Degree of Control	Passive Deterrence	Active Compellence
Most Control	1	2
Least Control	3	4

This assessment is borne out by expert analysts who have reviewed the NATO command and control system. Paul Bracken notes that the complexity of crisis and wartime decision making could pose problems for NATO, even if we grant that its doctrines for the use of nuclear weapons have all the necessary integrity. According to Bracken:

Complexity of decision making contributes to deterrence because it raises the risk that the military aspects of a crisis would get out of political control. Once nuclear weapons dispersal has occurred, the forces of decentralization and delegation and the ambiguity of command authority make nuclear usage so unpredictable as to create a threat that no attacker can discount.[49]

This is the familiar "incalculable risk" or the "threat that leaves something to chance" on which NATO has relied for so much of its deterrent. In conventional war, the destruction of the opponent's forces or the disruption of his cohesion was followed by a predictable outcome, his surrender. The issue with nuclear weapons is more complicated. A loss of control over their dispersal or authorization could spell disaster for both sides instead of one. One writer insists that, given the choice between "using them or losing them" with regard to nuclear weapons based in Western Europe, NATO will surely choose to lose them.[50] In this view, the risk of inadvertent nuclear escalation in Europe once nuclear weapons have been dispersed from storage is overstated here. However, the choice may not be an all-or-nothing one. The problem is more subtle than that, from a command and control standpoint.

The survivability of many of these weapons depends on mobility and concealment. Consequently, they are carried by mobile armies, ships at sea, and dispersed aircraft. The inventory control problems of such a force are immense, especially in an environment where communications are disrupted and coherent political authority may not exist. In the event of conflict, possession of nuclears might become one of the few symbols of authority, and military commanders might be reluctant indeed to return them to centralized, and vulnerable, storage.[51]

In other words, a plausible compellent tasking for NATO nuclear weapons must provide for putting the proverbial genie back into the bottle after it has been permitted to escape. This is provided that the NATO political authorities can be persuaded to grant nuclear release in the first place, and that decision is far from automatic. Thus, while SACEUR and perhaps other military commanders were requesting nuclear release, a process that might require between twenty-four and sixty hours, the situation on the ground or at sea could change enormously.[52]

Nor is this all. The willingness of NATO political leaders to stand fast in a crisis would depend upon their expectations of maintaining control over events if crisis deteriorated into war. Their expectation of maintaining control would be related to their optimism about mastering the friction that Clausewitz mentioned. In a crisis involving the dispersal of nuclear weapons and the anticipated request for their release from field commanders, the amount of friction in the system will be increased as Soviet attentiveness to NATO signals is raised. The NATO and Pact intelligence and warning systems might reinforce one another by amplifying feedback, in which the initial tendency of a process is amplified by the signals received from its various sensors and processed through its fusion centers. The NATO alert would lead to an initially higher Pact level of alert, which would lead to a further raising of NATO alert levels, and so on. This is not, however, a simple gradation. As the political and military restraints are taken off, the psychological expectations of commanders and political leaders change in not fully predictable ways. At each level of the system, some room exists for improvisation in the generalized instructions. Therefore, a paradoxical effect may occur. The organization for warning, assessment, and response *as a whole* may be unable to do anything other than initiate the standard operating procedures that have been previously established. But individuals within these organizations will have various reactions to what they understand policy to be. As policy is filtered through the hierarchy, it is interpreted through lateral channels of communication as well as vertical ones. The orders that unlock the nuclear codes and release the nuclear weapons from their storage sites will mean something very precise and discriminating to the members of the NATO Council and Military Planning Committee, or so they believe. Once these orders percolate through the bureaucratic maze and communications networks of the alliance, they will acquire other—and unintended—meanings for individual components of the organization.

Moreover, these disseminating orders may be intercepted by interested Soviet listeners and reacted to accordingly. The Soviets regularly listen in on NATO exercises; their SIGINT (signals intelligence) operations in Europe provide many ways of intercepting NATO alliance communications or those of individual member states. SIGINT systems are located in Soviet diplomatic establishments in eighteen West European countries.[53] The USSR maintains some sixty dedicated SIGINT ships and has numerous others with SIGINT collection capabilities.[54] Vehicular SIGINT operations conducted in Western Europe by the Soviet Union include direction finding (DF) for monitoring military and other unauthorized frequencies. Soviet and other East European SIGINT-equipped vehicles "have virtually unconstrained access throughout most of Western Europe," according to Desmond Ball.[55] The 1947 agreement among the United States, United Kingdom, France, and the Soviet Union allows the USSR to maintain three Soviet Military Liaison Missions in West Germany; these missions are said to provide thousands of intelligence collection opportunities to the GRU (Main Intelligence Directorate of the General Staff, from the Russian Glavnoye Razvedyvatel'noye Upravleniye) in a single year.[56] The U.S. European Command conducted a communications security assessment (COMSEC) after the October War of 1973. Included in the findings with regard to NATO communications security were the following:

The GRU and KGB SIGINT agencies were able to monitor combat readiness checks from the USCINCEUR (U.S. Commander in Chief, Europe) Airborne Command Post; the real-time status of deploying forces, such as the departure of the Fleet Ballistic Missile (FBM) submarines Kamehameha (SSBN-642) and Simon Bolivar (SSBN-641) from Rota following the declaration of DEFCON THREE on 25 October 1973; discussions relating to "contingency planning operations and potential task force compositions;" traffic concerning airlift departures from the continental United States (CONUS); the movement of "war material" from the ports of Nordham and Bremerhaven in West Germany; numerous communications of the movement of fuel and other logistic activity in the Mediterranean region; and other related air and naval activities.[57]

According to Benjamin F. Schemmer, editor of *Armed Forces Journal International*, writing in 1982:

The top level NATO C3 system is not just vulnerable; elements of it are so insecure that during the last major NATO exercise under Alexander Haig's tenure as Supreme Allied Commander, Europe, even the highly encoded traffic sent over a special communications net to NATO's nuclear units was intercepted so quickly by Soviet communications intelligence [COMINT] posts that the Russians broadcast a message in the *clear* on an open broadcast channel to the effect that, "NATO's going nuke."[58]

The Soviet capability to keep track of NATO alerting, release, and other activities would be combined with the vulnerability of the NATO European C^3 infrastructure to destruction with conventional weapons, and the confused Babel of communications and battlefield information systems deployed by NATO members. As to the former problem, vulnerability, C^3 facilities in the European theater can be attacked using conventional (perhaps chemical) weapons, special designation (Spetsnaz) forces, or radio-electronic combat. There are some sixty critical points in the command, control, communications, and intelligence (C^3I) networks in Europe that, if destroyed or put out of action, would prevent controlled and responsive NATO military operations.[59] Few of the European C^3I facilities have significant protection against nuclear blast or repeated conventional attacks. According to Desmond Ball, "The Soviet Union could easily destroy all but about a dozen sites in the whole European C^3I architecture with special forces using only conventional ordnance."[60] Thus, the probability of a selective and controlled NATO response to aggression would be small, and even alerts could be hard to manage successfully. As Ball has noted:

The present NATO C3I system is very far from this ideal. Its prevailing characteristics are more likely to be paralysis interjected with paroxysms. It is obviously impossible to predict how the system will in fact function—it will depend on the nature of the contingency, and there are no precedents for any of the situations of concern here. However, the system is so structured as to inhibit clear, coherent and timely decision-making at the outset of conflict, and then to rapidly generate escalation after a few days of intensive conventional conflict, followed very soon by a loss of any meaningful centralized control.[61]

There is implicit here a theme to which the last chapter returns: The friction that turns war plans into skeletal remnants of their original form, in conventional war, also afflicts the process of managing nuclear alerts and of using nuclear weapons in a selective and controlled way. The process by which friction upsets the prewar expectations of conventional war planners may differ from the process by which friction implodes the plans of nuclear crisis managers. For the moment, however, we are concerned with the tasking of nuclear forces as related to their presumed controllability. The provisional judgment is that NATO and U.S. forces that are NATO-tasked cannot provide the command systems to support a strategy that is heavily dependent on nuclear weapons for compellence.

The limits of command flexibility and fidelity under the plausible circumstances of war in Europe weigh against the case for theater missile defenses as significant improvements to deterrence stability. Were the levels of Soviet and U.S. offenses to be reduced drastically, the case for theater BMD might be improved in terms of its feasibility, but the case for its necessity as a deterrent would be weakened. This is the dilemma for advocates of missile defenses at theater or strategic levels: If necessary, they seem unattainable; if attainable, they seem unnecessary.[62] One might argue that, if NATO conventional forces were weak enough to be vulnerable to a Soviet blitzkrieg, and if that blitzrkieg depended heavily for its success on the prompt and effective use of conventional Soviet TBM, then an increment in NATO air defenses for Europe would be useful.[63] Both the antecedents and the consequents in this statement are open to challenge. The Soviet capability for a conventional blitzkrieg is not obvious, absent drastic force reductions by NATO or improvements by the USSR. And if this were the Soviet doctrine and the Soviet military leadership were persuaded of the feasibility of conventional aggression against Western Europe, then it is not obvious that the success or failure of that offensive would turn on the availability or timely use of conventional TBM. Should NATO conclude otherwise, affirm the antecedents, and deploy theater BMD to blunt the effectiveness of Soviet TBM, the effect may be to stimulate improvements in other arms of the Soviet ground forces and frontal aviation. Thus, given even the most pessimistic assumptions about future Soviet TBM capabilities, NATO weaknesses, and Soviet TBM-dependent blitzkrieg strategies, the net gain for NATO by deploying TBM in Europe remains to be demonstrated.

There is an issue even more daunting than these. The credibility of theater BMD for Western Europe is dependent upon what is anchored to those regional deployments on the other side of the Atlantic. If the Americans have not deployed robust strategic defenses with substantial competency against Soviet strategic ballistic missiles, then the deployment of Euro-strategic BMD can only suggest to the Europeans an intent of decoupling the fate of the United States from that of Western Europe. This issue is usually argued the other way around, and so bears further clarification. It is commonly assumed that a U.S. homeland BMD system will decouple the United States from Western Europe if the Americans have territorial defenses and the Europeans do not. But the Americans are not just defending themselves; they are defending Western Europe as well. Therefore, protection for the U.S. homeland does not guarantee the protection for Europe; that must still be provided for by U.S. punishment, rather than denial, capabilities. On the other hand, if Europeans have BMD but the Americans do not, then it might be argued that a war could be fought on the soil of Europe short of total destruction, but not on the soil of the United States. This point is missed by those who simply count the ratios of Soviet warheads to European versus U.S. aim points, and therefore argue that no defense will make war appear to be fightable in Europe. The Soviets cannot dedicate all their warheads to European targets, however, and it is therefore quite conceivable that robust Euro-strategic BMD could deny to the USSR limited strategic options against key military and command system targets on a theaterwide basis. This might be thought good by military planners in and of itself, but the upshot is bad for U.S.-European coupling unless the United States also has a robust system. Otherwise, the Americans have every incentive to cop out when the going gets tough. All of the above suggests that the conventional wisdom with regard to the relationship between coupling and defenses needs rethinking. Defenses for the United States without defenses for Europe leaves the situation pretty much as it is now: Assured destruction plus flexible nuclear compellence is still the deterrent of choice, although with improved damage limitation capabilities for North America, should deterrence fail. Defenses for Europe without defenses for the United States will create the erroneous impression of a fightable war in Europe without U.S. participation *unless* the Soviets are motivated by NATO theater BMD to offset them with offensive improvements, in which case the NATO BMD are expensive and superfluous.

Either way, the matter returns to the starting point: whether it is desirable or feasible for the United States to seek to change the basis of deterrence from offensive retaliation to defensive damage limitation. This larger issue, of which the preceding components are but pieces, must now be put into final focus.

DETERRENCE AND DEFENSE

Nuclear weapons are said to have turned strategy inside out. Offense pays and defense is feckless. This, as we have seen, is a misguided assessment. Offensive technologies are preeminent; therefore, defensive strategy pays dividends. There is no bonus for preemption compared to awaiting attack and then retaliating. The capability for second-strike ride-out is now shared by U.S. and Soviet military planners. This makes the hasty choice for war less likely.

The weakness of defensive strategy, based on the superiority of offensive technology and the threat of retaliation, is that it cannot promise to limit the consequences of war, should deterrence fail.[64] This was wrongly attributed to the mutual assured destruction (M.A.D.) doctrine of Robert McNamara, but McNamara was simply recognizing the realities of technology then and now. With offenses (in the sense of technologies) supreme and defenses innocent of competency, there was no expectation of meaningful damage limitation in a major U.S.-Soviet nuclear exchange. Mutual assured destruction made too much of quantifiable indicators with regard to the percentages of population and industry destroyed. For political leaders forced to make life-and-death decisions, the loss of even a few major cities to nuclear attack would begin another world. And the absence of city protection made it a M.A.D. world in fact as well as in theory.

Another weakness in defensive strategy was that it did not provide flexible options for response to less-than-all-out contingencies. This was judged problematical by McNamara himself from the time of his 1962 Ann Arbor speech until he retired from office. McNamara used assured destruction as a metric to limit the growth of U.S. forces beyond what was assumed to be the point of budgetary tolerance. He was not describing how the U.S. arsenal would actually be used if deterrence failed. To the contrary, he made it quite clear that the United States would fight a war in the traditional way, according to the classical strategy of attacking the opponent's forces first while sparing his cities for later destruction if necessary. By withholding attacks against cities and promptly attacking Soviet forces, the United States would be limiting damage to U.S. forces and society, while still holding out an incentive for the USSR to refrain from attacks on U.S. cities. In other words, damage to U.S. society was to be limited by denial capabilities, in the form of prompt offensive strikes against remaining Soviet forces, and by the creation of a suitable incentive structure, the hostage-making of Soviet society.[65]

The problem with this logic (of carrots and sticks to accomplish damage limitation along with postattack coercion) was that it appeared to the USSR not as a defensive strategy but as an offensive one. During the early 1960s, the size of U.S. strategic nuclear forces compared to Soviet forces was large. A U.S. damage-limiting and postattack coercion capability would appear very similar to a first-strike capability. As the Soviets approached strategic nuclear parity, they became less suspicious of the damage limitation components of U.S. strategy, and they could hardly deny their own interest in damage limitation via preemption and active defenses.[66] The superpower SALT I agreement did not, as was assumed by some U.S. observers, provide evidence that the Soviets had adopted M.A.D. as their preferred doctrine. But they recognized the existing balance between offensive and defensive technology and so declined to invest further in their own defenses, which could easily have been overwhelmed or circumvented. SALT did not affirm disinterest in damage limitation, but only in accomplishing it via the prevailing technologies of the early 1970s.

Politics makes strange bedfellows, and the interest in damage limitation by active defenses would return in the 1980s as a major agenda item for the Americans. President Reagan's March 23, 1983, speech called only for research and development, strictly speaking. But it was the president's aspiration and the secretary of defense's declaratory mission to find a deployable technology. A new debate over ballistic missile defenses ensued in the U.S. body politic, with candidate technologies having changed but the essential strategic issues remaining constant. Reagan's "strategic concept" of a nuclear-disarmed world appealed (1) to conservatives who distrusted the Soviets unless the United States were protected by an invulnerable space shield, and (2) to liberals dissatisfied with dependency on the balance of terror.[67] And the proponents of a denuclearized deterrent were joined by advocates of conventional force modernization on both sides of the Atlantic, not only to raise the nuclear threshold but also to remove it. McNamara, writing in the 1980s, now declared that he had always advised presidents against first-use of nuclear weapons and that nuclear weapons were without purpose except to deter the other side's first-use.[68]

The ABM debate of the late 1960s and early 1970s and the BMD debate of the 1980s had more to do with politics (in the lowest sense) than with strategy. It could not make sense for the Americans to advocate a nuclear-disarmed strategy for several reasons. First, as already noted, the United States is defending not just itself, but also allies without nuclear forces. Second, countries other than the United States and the Soviet Union now have strategic nuclear forces with significant countervalue capabilities, including two U.S. allies in Europe and the potential Soviet adversary in Beijing. Third, the superpowers' status as superpowers depends upon their nuclear weapons, and especially upon the size and diversity of their arsenals. To give those up in order to hide behind non-nuclear defenses would not be a "pacific" strategy with regard to the rest of the international order, but the reverse. Fourth, a weakening of the superpowers would make the outbreak of wars among their clients, allies, and fellow travelers more, instead of less, likely. Fifth, the knowledge of how to build nuclear weapons could not be disinvented. A country with this knowledge and a science and technology base the size of the U.S. or Soviet one could not be expected to forbear in the re-creation of a nuclear arsenal if needed.

Moreover, for the Europeans the decline of the United States as a nuclear guarantor would make Western Europe less likely to hang together in the face of Soviet intimidation. It would also draw it farther from its present course of evolution toward a true security community, in which peaceful resolution of disputes is assumed to be the only acceptable mechanism.[69] These two aspects of the U.S. nuclear umbrella for Europe are extremely important, separately and taken together. Europe will be more easily coerced absent a Soviet expectation of the prompt involvement of U.S. nuclear weapons in war. And the Europeans will be more inclined to get into defense- and security-related disputes among themselves after the United States has retracted its nuclear umbrella and, as a probable follow-on, reverted to a unilaterist globalism (without guarantees to Europe) at home.[70] We take for granted the absence of war in Europe since 1945 on account of the superpower hegemony of which the beneficiaries constantly complain, and the shackles of which they are constantly attempting to throw off. The truth is that the departure of the Soviets and the Americans back to the Urals and the Carolinas would not result in a united Europe but in a divided house. World War III would not be an implausible outcome shortly thereafter; without nuclear weapons, what would deter it?

Furthermore, we have seen that the Soviet perception of the scientific-technical revolution in military affairs admits the possible development, in the 1990s and beyond, of non-nuclear systems that can carry out missions now assigned to nuclear weapons. The implications for Soviet strategy are discussed elsewhere in this book, especially in the final chapter. It would be misleading to infer that the Soviet expectation is of a war or deterrent situation in which nuclear weapons are unimportant. Americans, reading their own apocalyptic visions of war into Soviet doctrine, take the statements of Soviet military writers and political leaders about nuclear war as tantamount to rejection of original sin. The Soviets have not rejected *preparedness* for nuclear war precisely because, according to their doctrine, the *Americans* (or NATO) are likely to start it. What could be more foolish than to expect one's potential adversary to withhold the most destructive weapons available, and to thereby surrender important political values? The Kremlin would not expect this of the United States even if the United States were a communist superpower instead of a capitalist one. They will certainly not expect it of capitalists, who, according to their doctrine, would only be using nuclear weapons in their death throes of desperation. And the deterrence of desperate capitalists cannot be accomplished by an arsenal that is vulnerable to surprise, including technological surprise. So the USSR will remain interested in strategic defenses as components of an offensive-defensive mix that will be needed to fight a war—a war that it is preferable to avoid but that may be unavoidable.[71]

The Dialectics of Offense and Defense

Critics of Clausewitz who have misread his work, including readers who were members of the German general staff, rebelled at his assumption that the defensive was the stronger form of war. More than that, some German military leaders of the nineteenth and twentieth centuries took from *On War* the notion that Clausewitz was an advocate of wars of annihilation.[72] Von Moltke (the elder) and Alfred von Schlieffen regard themselves as disciples of Clausewitz, yet they misunderstood his discussion of the relationship between war and policy.[73] Other Germans who could not abide Clausewitz simply ignored him or dismissed his importance. Clausewitz was regarded as a military philosopher, and therefore his work was considered less pertinent to the instruction of future general staff officers than the works of Schlieffen, which were regarded as practical.[74] Yet the dialectical relationship between offense and defense was at the heart of Clausewitz's philosophy of war. And we must always remember that it is a philosophy, which searches for the essence of things, and not just a training manual, which was apparently the preferred sort of reading for his successors.

The term "dialectical" as used in the preceding paragraph is not a reference to the dialectical materialism of Marx, but a broader expression of the fact that the conduct of offensive and defensive strategies, and of operations, is the mastery of diverse parts of a more inclusive whole. The side that will fight on the offensive must know when to shift to the defensive, and vice versa. Pure defense, according to Clausewitz, "would be completely contrary to the art of war."[75] A tactical battle is defensive if we await the appearance of the enemy in front of our lines and within range; a campaign is defensive if we wait until our theater of operations is invaded.[76] Regardless, "if we are really waging war, we must return the enemy's blows; and these offensive acts in a defensive war come under the heading of 'defense'—in other words, our offensive takes place within our own positions or theater of operations."[77] Assuming both sides have equal means in an engagement, defense is easier than offense because its object, preservation and protection, is easier. Preservation and protection are negative objectives. Although they may be easier to attain than positive ones, they do not add to the defender's capacity to wage war. A successful defense may change the potential balance of power in one's favor, but to realize that potential, the formerly defensive side would have to assume the offensive at some point. The defensive aim is easier because of its tacit acceptance of the military—and, therefore, political—status quo. As Clausewitz explains:

> If defense is the stronger form of war, yet has a negative object, it follows that it should be used only as long as weakness compels, and be abandoned as soon as we are strong enough to pursue a positive object. When one has used defensive means successfully, a more favorable balance of strength is usually created; thus the natural course in war is to begin defensively and end by attacking.[78]

Defenders and attackers benefit from different features of the combat environment. Defense enjoys the advantages of terrain; attack, the initiative and the potential for surprise.[79] Defenders are usually fighting on familiar home territory; attackers must operate far from their own theater of operation and their sources of supply.[80] This applies to conventional operations of Clausewitz's time and ours, but how applicable is it to the problems of contemporary nuclear deterrence?

The dialectical, and problematical, relationship between attack and defense has not changed, as we have already seen in this chapter. Defensive (retaliatory) deterrent strategies may be dependent on the same weapons systems that offensive (preemptive) strategies are: ballistic missiles armed with nuclear warheads. In addition, defensive and offensive strategies are defined by the political aim for which they are designed. Thus, the side that fears preemption in a nuclear crisis, and so shoots first, may be said to have acted defensively, albeit with weapons of mass destruction. On the other hand, preemption does not appear rational unless the first striker expects to escape from ruinous destruction in retaliation.

Would the deployment of territorial anti-nuclear strategic defenses by the Americans and Soviets, including bomber and missile defenses, end the dialectic of offense and defense in the nuclear gap? It is the supposition of the Reagan strategic concept that defenses based on non-nuclear technologies might eventually displace offensive nuclear weapons. Eventually, both superpowers would disarm to essentially zero long-range, strategic nuclear offensive weapons, while building non-nuclear defenses against the remnants. At some point, the remaining nuclear weapons would no longer present a credible threat to destroy the defenses *or* the targets that they were designed to protect. Having nothing to accomplish, swords would be sheathed, and shields would be triumphant.

According to Paul Nitze, in order to meet this anticipated progression, U.S. strategic defenses will have to meet two stringent requirements: marginal cost effectiveness and survivability.[81] The negotiation of nuclear offenses by future generations of non-nuclear defenses, even if feasible, is of questionable desirability from the U.S. and NATO European standpoint. This might seem contrary to military logic, according to which a defended U.S. homeland would make the U.S. president more likely, rather than less, to use nuclear weapons on behalf of allies. But that military logic is one-sided and ignores the likelihood that national territorial defenses deployed by one superpower would almost certainly be followed by essentially equivalent deployments by the other. And political logic suggests that the first side to break the assured destruction stalemate and deploy defenses will be viewed by its opponent as having violated an unspoken contract, one of deterrence by shared risk, and so having opened a Pandora's box of technological opportunism toward the denouement of strategic instability.

Nor can the United States operate as a unitary actor in this regard, in its relationship to the Soviet Union and possible Soviet countermeasures to U.S. anti-nuclear strategic defenses. The United States must consider both the deterrence of war against allies, including conventional, and their reassurance that another arms race is not going to undermine strategic stability. The temptation for both Americans and Soviets is to make what appears to be a Clausewitzian move (toward relative advantage in strategic nuclear, or non-nuclear, weapons technology) on the assumption that this temporary advantage can be exploited for future coercion. But for this exploitation to occur and for the balance of power to be changed in a meaningful way, more is required than workable defense technologies by one side that the other cannot match. The superior side would also have to preserve, or develop, some offensive means of coercion in order to supplement the defensive shield. Otherwise, the relationship between the two sides slips into permanent stasis. In the absence of *nuclear* offenses for coercion, conventional forces would be summoned. The side that sought relative advantage would be the side that deployed strategic non-nuclear defenses equivalent to those of the other superpower, plus superior general purpose forces for coercion and, if necessary, the fighting of campaigns and wars.

However, conventional swords in place of nuclear may suffice for Soviet future requirements, but not for Western. A conventional sword does not offer two things that a nuclear retaliatory force does, from the U.S. and NATO standpoint. First, it does not create indivisible risk. Conventional war can be lost in stages; while it is being lost, allies can be peeled off from the alliance like the outer skin of an onion.[82] Second, a conventional sword does not have the capacity to extend itself beyond the mean time/distance it takes to get troops into a theater of operations and to lose them there. In the U.S. case, the time/distance factors for deploying reserves to Europe will dictate that the amount of airlift and sealift are barely adequate to sustain combat in the relevant theater of operations, provided that NATO *mobilizes in time* and its navies immediately establish *control of the sea lanes of communication* (SLOCs) between the United States and Europe. Granted both of these assumptions, NATO still must defend its airfields and ports against plausible attacks that are mounted to disrupt the process of personnel and material reinforcement.

If conventional swords alone will not suffice because they are insufficiently deterring (for dependency on favorable scenarios), then nuclear swords suffer the reverse in costs and benefits. They are less usable in a discriminating and piecemeal way, but more destructive once used. Adversaries who believe that their opponents' conventional defenses are coupled to nuclear retaliation will be reluctant to light the fuse at all, because the detonation may not distinguish between victor and vanquished. On the other hand, those adversaries have to believe that the allies of desperate defenders, who would otherwise be swallowed up in conventional attacks, will be rescued by the use of weapons that, if used without limit, will destroy the very prizes being defended: the allied populations, territories, and social values.

The dilemma is that the Americans and Soviets, even if they had the requisite technology, could not rescue themselves from their conditions of nuclear hostage status without creating new hostage situations for their European allies. Since perfect defenses are out of the question, the best that can be expected are near-perfect, and these will obviously favor the owners at the expense of their allies and dependents. The dependents will then be hostage to a hostile superpower who is armed with offensive nuclear weapons, which may not threaten the other superpower but which can threaten them. Their only protection is to re-create the equality of risk that marked the predefense condition. But that equality cannot be re-created, for it has been turned into something relative rather than absolute. Once the Americans and the Soviets can distinguish meaningfully between the effects of limited nuclear war and total nuclear war, the protection provided for their allies by the superpowers' nuclear umbrellas will be less automatic than it is now. Non-nuclear strategic defenses for the super-powers redistribute risks for their allies; U.S. defenses especially do so for NATO European allies, for the same reasons that SALT II was perceived to have placed NATO Europeans in jeopardy by codifying parity. A change in superpower relationship from deterrence by punishment to deterrence by denial is not just a change in deterrence concept. It is also a change in the equation of risk sharing that binds the United States to Europe. Absent U.S. vulnerability to the same kind of nuclear destruction as that which threatens Western Europe, the United States will have less reason to consider Europe's quarrels its own. This is why the assumption that a defended U.S. homeland will lead to improved extended deterrence is misleading; the explanation lies in the Clausewitzian supremacy of shared political values and expectations to military defense commitments. Without the ties that bind created by shared risk and mutual vulnerability, the Americans need not, and might not, share in the war resulting from an East-West dispute over European issues.

The Clausewitzian insight works the other way, too, from Western Europe to North America. If Europeans do not perceive that Americans share the risk of nuclear destruction with them, then they may not care to partake of efforts to deter the Soviets and to project NATO power to the Middle East or elsewhere. Europeans who do not perceive that Americans need take part in their controversies will also feel free to develop their own national or European deterrents, to the detriment of crisis and arms race stability. Finally, Europeans who do not feel shared risk with Americans, and therefore shared commitments, may opt for a closer relationship with the Soviet Union; détente was, after all, one of the promises made by NATO to its members along with defense. And if the European members of NATO cannot get the combination of détente and defense that they expect from a trans-Atlantic framework of cooperation, then they will get it by mixing trans-Atlantic with East-West cooperation. To some extent this process has happened already, although it occurs fitfully, in the surges and declines of U.S. expressions of discontent with deterrence and European expressions of inadequately met needs for reassurance.

CONCLUSION

Anti-nuclear strategic defenses do not offer, any more than conventional deterrence can claim to offer, a plausible escape from nuclear revolution or nuclear deterrence. And if nuclear weapons are removed from the arsenals of major powers, the knowledge of how to make them remains in the scientific and military establishments of the major powers. The value of nuclear weapons is not that they are clean and surgical, but that they buttress a threat to use "weapons of mass destruction," as the Soviets say. From this threat major dividends can be obtained, although not without significant risks: forty years of peace in Europe in exchange for a threat of doomsday. Nuclear weapons have not been the only reasons for peace in Europe and between the superpowers. And doomsday has never been the only feasible outcome of a nuclear war. But the polarities of perpetual peace and doomsday have dominated the debate between advocates of more superpower reliance on nuclear deterrence and less.

So, too, has the debate over anti-nuclear defenses been a polarized one. And a correct understanding of the role of anti-nuclear defenses in future superpower strategy is not necessarily going to be found at some halfway point between the partisans of missile astrodomes and the defenders of strategic orthodoxy. U.S. and Soviet political agendas will be the determining factors in what can be deployed to support deterrence without seeming provocative of a larger arms race. The Soviets felt in the 1980s that they were being forced into a race over high technology with the Americans that put the Soviet deterrent and military scientific base at risk. The Reagan administration felt that the window of vulnerability and other purported Soviet advantages in the military balance would be exploited to the detriment of the West unless the United States opened the spigot on strategic modernization and research toward deployment of the next century's miracle weapons.

Of such misunderstandings are arms races and wars born. Seeing defense as a politically determined mission or function, instead of a set of technologies, brings us to judicious pessimism about any near-term overturning of the premises of nuclear strategy with wonder weapons. And were such a breakthrough in technology in the offing, it would not necessarily be stabilizing. Neither U.S. nor Soviet leaders can want a situation in which the political relationship holds out the prospect for improved détente, but in which the instruments of deterrence based on new technology create unstable expectations with regard to forbearance in time of crisis. The present situation of dependency on massive and redundant offenses for retaliation looks ghastly to anti-nuclear activists who have misunderstood the essential mission of nuclear weapons: to contribute to the avoidance of war, or to the quickest possible termination of it if deterrence fails. Dissuasion based on making war "winable" again may be in the cards, but not with nuclear weapons as the aces.

NOTES

1. Excerpts from the president's speech of March 23, 1983, appear in Arms Control Association, *Star Wars Quotes* (Washington, D.C.: Arms Control Association, 1986), Appendix.

2. See Fred S. Hoffman, Study Director, *Ballistic Missile Defenses and U.S. National Security*, Summary Report, Prepared for the Future Security Strategy Study (Washington, D.C.: October, 1983), and *The Strategic Defense Initiative: Defensive Technologies Study* (Washington, D.C.: April, 1984).

3. Carl Von Clausewitz, *On War*, ed. and trans. Peter Paret and Michael Howard (Princeton, N.J.: Princeton University Press, 1976), 358.

4. Clausewitz, *On War*, 357.

5. Clausewitz, *On War*, 357.

6. Clausewitz, *On War*, 357.

7. Clausewitz, *On War*, 363.

8. Clausewitz, *On War*, 370.

9. On dissuasion, see Edward N. Luttwak, *Strategy: The Logic of War and Peace* (Cambridge, Mass.: Belknap Press of Harvard University Press, 1987), 190–207.

10. The distinction between deterrence by denial and by punishment is explained in Glenn H. Snyder, *Deterrence and Defense: Toward a Theory of National Security* (Princeton: Princeton University Press, 1961), 3–16, 31, 33–40, 50. Pertinent excerpts appear in Robert J. Art and Kenneth N. Waltz, eds., *The Use of Force: International Politics and Foreign Policy* (Boston: Little, Brown, 1971), 56–76. Synder notes that the threat of denial action is likely to be appraised by the aggressor in terms of the deterrer's capabilities, while threats of punishment will be evaluated in terms of the defender's estimate of the aggressor's intentions. Thus, the threat of denial action, according to Snyder, is more credible on two counts: It is less costly for the deterrer to fulfill, and it may also prevent the attacker from making desired gains. Therefore, "While the making of a *threat* of nuclear punishment may be desirable and rational, its *fulfillment* is likely to seem irrational after the aggressor has committed his forces, since punishment alone may not be able to hold the territorial objective and will stimulate the aggressor to make counterreprisals." Snyder, *Deterrence and Defense*, 67.

11. Benjamin S. Lambeth, "Uncertainties for the Soviet War Planner," *International Security* 7, no. 3 (Winter 1982–1983): 139–66.

12. Lambeth, "Uncertainties," 157.

13. Paul H. Nitze, "Assuring Strategic Stability in an Era of Detente," *Foreign Affairs* 54 (1976): 207–33.

14. Clausewitz, *On War*, 528.

15. Clausewitz, *On War*, 528.

16. Clausewitz, *On War*, 370.

17. Clausewitz, *On War*, 370.

18. Clausewitz, *On War*, 370.

19. Samuel P. Huntington, "The Renewal of Strategy," *The Strategic Imperative: New Policies for National Security*, ed. Samuel P. Huntington (Cambridge, Mass.: Ballinger Publishing Co., 1982), 1–52.

20. See Stephen J. Cimbala, "NATO Strategy and Nuclear Weapons: A Reluctant Embrace," *Parameters* 18, no. 2 (June 1988): 51–62.

21. See Col. David M. Glantz, *Deep Attack: The Soviet Conduct of Operational Maneuver* (Fort Leavenworth, Kan.: Soviet Army Studies Office, 1987). A notional 1984 tank army tasked as an operational maneuver force for a front operation would have 1,300–1,500 tanks and SP guns, attacking in one or two echelons on attack sectors 16–24 kilometers wide (nuclear scared posture), over 4–6 invasion routes, with a depth of mission objective of 250 kilometers against a prepared defense, 300 kilometers against a partially prepared defense, and 350 kilometers against an unprepared defense. Glantz, *Deep Attack*, 123.

22. See Fritz Fischer, *Germany's Aims in the First World War* (New York: W. W. Norton, 1967), Ch. 23, 609–38.

23. Fischer, *Germany's Aims*, 625.

24. Fischer, *Germany's Aims*, 627.

25. See Jon Kimche, *The Unfought Battle* (New York: Stein and Day, 1968).

26. John J. Mearsheimer, *Conventional Deterrence* (Ithaca, N.Y.: Cornell University Press, 1983), 67–98. Mearsheimer analyzes the unwillingness of the British and French to attack Germany during the Phoney War as a failure of deterrence. As he notes,

> The assumption fundamentally underpinning Allied thinking, was, of course, that in the long run, an offensive would be possible because the balance of forces would shift decisively in their favor. Allied strength rested in a long war, in which they would attain the 'incontestable superiority of resources' that would allow them to defeat Germany. Despite the widespread acceptance of this assumption, there is no evidence that the Allies ever examined it in any detail.

Mearsheimer, *Conventional Deterrence*, 90–91.

27. Martin Van Creveld, *Supplying War: Logistics from Wallenstein to Patton* (Cambridge: Cambridge University Press, 1977), 142–80, esp. 152–53.

28. Luttwak, *Strategy*, 148.

29. Luttwak, *Strategy*, 149.

30. Luttwak, *Strategy*, 149.

31. John R. Southern, Carl G. Davis, and Melvin P. Edwards, "Army BM/C3 in the SDI Program," *High Technology Initiatives in C3I: Communications, Artificial Intelligence and Strategic Defense*, ed. Stephen J. Andriole (Washington, D.C.: AFCEA International Press, 1986), 358–69.

32. See Francis J. West, Jr., Jacquelyn K. Davis, James E. Dougherty, Robert J. Hanks, and Charles M. Perry, *Naval Forces and Western Security*, Special Report (1987; Cambridge, Mass.: Institute for Foreign Policy Analysis; New York: Pergamon-Brassey's, 1987).

33. According to the U.S. Office of Technology Assessment, "It cannot be emphasized too strongly that the ability to discriminate in this phase (midcourse) is essential to the feasibility of the whole space-based BMD concept." U.S. Congress, Office of

Technology Assessment, *Ballistic Missile Defense Technologies* (Washington, D.C.: U.S. Government Printing Office, 1985), 174.

34. William A. Davis, Jr., *Asymmetries in U.S. and Soviet Strategic Defense Programs: Implications for Near-Term American Deployment Options* (Cambridge, Mass. and New York: Institute for Foreign Policy Analysis and N.Y.: Pergamon-Brassey's, 1986).

35. See Theodore Jarvis, "Nuclear Operations and Strategic Defense," *Managing Nuclear Operations*, eds. Ashton B. Carter, John D. Steinbruner, and Charles A. Zraket (Washington, D.C.: Brookings Institution, 1987), 661–78.

36. Paul H. Nitze, "On the Road to a More Stable Peace," U.S. Department of State, *Current Policy* 657 (20 February 1985). This outlines the Reagan administration's "strategic concept" of moving in three phases from reliance upon nuclear offenses to U.S. and Soviet reliance upon nonnuclear defenses for security.

37. Richard Ned Lebow, *Between Peace and War: The Nature of International Crisis* (Baltimore: Johns Hopkins University Press, 1981).

38. Robert S. McNamara, *Blundering into Disaster: Surviving the First Century of the Nuclear Age* (New York: Pantheon Books, 1986), 57.

39. Raymond L. Garthoff, "Mutual Deterrence, Parity and Strategic Arms Limitation in Soviet Policy," *Soviet Military Thinking*, ed. Derek Leebaert (London: Allen and Unwin, 1981), 92–124.

40. Clausewitz, *On War*, 377, 384.

41. Ashton B. Carter, "Launch Under Attack," *MX Missile Basing*, U.S. Congress, Office of Technology Assessment (Washington, D.C.: U.S. Government Printing Office, 1981), Ch. 4.

42. See Jonathan E. Medalia, "Midgetman Small ICBM: Issues for Deterrence in the 1990s," *Challenges to Deterrence: Resources, Technology and Policy*, ed. Stephen J. Cimbala (New York: Praeger Publishers, 1987), 225–47 for an objective review of pertinent options and technologies.

43. President's Commission on Strategic Forces (Scowcroft Commission), *Report* (Washington, D.C.: 1983), 7–8.

44. President's Commission, *Report* 6. The commission's argument on behalf of unique properties inherent in ICBMs is worth quoting verbatim for what it implies about the policy commitments that drive the ICBM modernization program:

> ICBMs have advantages in command and control, in the ability to be retargeted readily, and in accuracy. This means that ICBMs are especially effective in deterring Soviet threats *of massive conventional or limited nuclear attacks*, because they could most credibly respond promptly and controllably against specific military targets and thereby promptly *disrupt* an attack on us *or our allies*.

(p. 8, emphasis added). This passage is extremely important, for it makes clear that the triad is less necessary as a hedge against Soviet attacks on North America, as it is a hedge against conventional and limited nuclear war in Europe, for which NATO conventional forces are (by implication) inadequate. In other words, the U.S. ICBM force modernization is being driven by the requirements for extended deterrence, to implement the "Schlesinger doctrine" and the "countervailing strategy." Former Secretaries of Defense Schlesinger and Brown served on the commission.

45. Paul Bracken, *The Command and Control of Nuclear Forces* (New Haven: Yale University Press, 1983), 94.

46. Martin Van Creveld, *Fighting Power: German and U.S. Army Performance, 1939–1945* (Westport, Conn.: Greenwood Press, 1982). See especially his discussion of the 1936 German army manual *Truppenfuhrung* with regard to issues of military doctrine. The manual notes that "war is an art," that "decision action remains the first prerequisite for success in war," and that "man is the fundamental instrument in war; other instruments may change but he remains relatively constant. Unless his behavior and elemental attributes are understood, gross mistakes will be made in planning operations and in troop leading." Van Creveld, *Fighting Power*, 28–31. Most notably, "In the training of the individual soldier, the essential considerations are to integrate individuals into a group and to establish for that group a high standard of military conduct and performance without destroying the initiative of the individual." Van Creveld, *Fighting Power*, 31.

47. Thomas C. Schelling, *Arms and Influence* (New Haven: Yale University Press, 1966), 69–80, esp. 78–80. It would also seem that denial capabilities may suffice for deterrence, but compellence may require denial and punishment capabilities. This implies, according to Snyder (Snyder, *Deterrence and Defense*, 3–16, 31, 33–40, 50) that compellence might require more assumptions about the adversary's intentions, with additional leeway for misperceptions.

48. Alexander L. George, David K. Hall, and William E. Simons, *The Limits of Coercive Diplomacy: Laos, Cuba, Vietnam* (Boston: Little, Brown, 1971), esp. Ch. 1 by George, "The Development of Doctrine and Strategy," 1–35.

49. Bracken, *Command and Control of Nuclear Forces*, 174.

50. Gregory F. Treverton, "Theatre Nuclear Forces: Military Logic and Political Purpose," *The Nuclear Confrontation in Europe*, eds. Jeffrey D. Boutwell, Paul Doty, and Gregory F. Treverton (London: Croom, Helm, 1985), 87–112.

51. Bracken, *Command and Control of Nuclear Forces*, 177.

52. See John M. Collins, *U.S.-Soviet Military Balance, 1980–85* (New York: Pergamon-Brassey's, 1985), 72; Catherine McArdle Kelleher, "NATO Nuclear Operations," *Managing Nuclear Operations*, ed. Carter, Steinbruner, and Zraket, 445–69; and Desmond Ball, *Controlling Theater Nuclear War*, Working Paper No. 138, Strategic and Defence Studies Centre, Research School of Pacific Studies, Australian National University, Canberra, October 1987. However, it is important to note that intelligence and warning systems would probably provide strategic warning of the possibility of attack well before it actually took place, and that certain measures of alert and readiness would be set in motion by the U.S. and NATO chains of command. Procedures for alerting U.S. nuclear forces were established by the joint chiefs of staff in the 1950s, consistent with the chain of command provided for in the Defense Reorganization Act of 1958. Five different defense condition (DEFCON) levels were established for U.S. forces: DEFCON 5 and 4 for normal peacetime position; DEFCON 3, troops on standby to await further orders; DEFCON 2, troops ready for combat; DEFCON 1, troops deployed for combat. The NATO chain of command for implementing alert measures runs from the Defense Planning Committee, to the Military Committee, to the three major NATO commanders (Supreme Allied Commander, Europe; Supreme Allied Commander, Atlantic; and Commander in Chief, Channel). There are five gradations in the NATO alert system, called alert conditions or LERTCONs. See Bruce G. Blair, "Alerting in Crisis and Conventional War," *Managing Nuclear Operations*, eds. Carter, Steinbruner, and Zraket, 75–120, esp. 77–78, 109–10. Blair notes that the formal chain of authorization running through the NATO command structure may be slower than the parallel chain of release running through the strictly U.S. command structure (109).

53. Ball, *Controlling Theater Nuclear War*, 22.

54. Desmond Ball, *Soviet Signals Intelligence (SIGINT): Vehicular Systems and Operations*, Reference Paper No. 159, Strategic and Defence Studies Centre, Research School of Pacific Studies, Australian National University, Canberra, February 1988, 1.

55. Ball, *Soviet Signals Intelligence*, 8.

56. Ball, *Soviet Signals Intelligence*, 9.

57. Ball, *Controlling Theater Nuclear War*, 25.

58. Benjamin F. Schemmer, "No NATO C3 'Check-Out Counter'," *Armed Forces Journal International* December 1982; 92, cited in Ball, Controlling Theater Nuclear War, 26.

59. Ball, *Controlling Theater Nuclear War*, 14.

60. Ball, *Controlling Theater Nuclear War*, 17.

61. Ball, *Controlling Theater Nuclear War*, 27.

62. A point made very well by Donald M. Snow, "Air Defense and Missile Defense: Good Ideas or Not?" *Strategic Air Defense*, ed. Stephen J. Cimbala (Wilmington, Del.: Scholarly Resources, 1989), 123–38.

63. For informed discussion of these issues, see Dennis Gormley, "Emerging Attack Options in Soviet Theater Strategy," *Swords and Shields: NATO, the USSR, and New Choices for Long-Range Offense and Defense*, eds. Fred S. Hoffman, Albert Wohlstetter, and David S. Yost (Lexington, Mass.: Lexington Books, 1987), 87–122, and Uwe Nerlich, Roles for Theater Ballistic Missile Defense in Europe Short Preparation Time Attack Scenarios," 239–60 in the same volume.

64. As Lawrence Freedman has noted, "By the early 1970s the adoption of flexible response and assured destruction together demonstrated a lack of confidence in the possibility of establishing and sustaining distinctive thresholds once nuclear weapons were in use." See Lawrence Freedman, "The First Two Generations of Nuclear Strategists," *Makers of Modern Strategy*, ed. Peter Paret (Princeton: Princeton University Press, 1986), 772. See also Lawrence Freedman, *The Evolution of Nuclear Strategy* (New York: St Martin's Press, 1981). This point about the coupling of flexible response and assured destruction is extremely important and has many implications. One is, as further developed in the text, that the U.S. end of the NATO connection was disinterested in flexible strategic warfighting on its own soil, but not unwilling to contemplate doing the same for Europeans in order to rescue a failed conventional defense. On the other hand, a capability for flexible nuclear warfighting was not available to the Americans until well into the 1970s, if then, and the Europeans remained disinterested, perceiving quite astutely its implications for decoupling. One might also note that a strategy of flexible nuclear warfighting plays to Soviet strengths as they are assessed by advocates of such U.S. and NATO strategies.

65. Alain C. Enthoven and K. Wayne Smith, *How Much Is Enough? Shaping the Defense Program, 1961–1969* (New York: Harper and Row, 1971), 175–84 provides McNamara's rationales for assured destruction. Assured destruction became controversial because of its presumed influence over U.S. arms-control strategy in the 1970s, and not as a result of its influence over actual targeting plans. See Desmond Ball, "Counterforce Targeting: How New? How Viable?" *Arms Control Today* 11, no. 2 (February 1981), reprinted with revisions in John F. Reichart and Steven R. Sturm, eds., *American Defense Policy* (Baltimore, Md.: Johns Hopkins University Press, 1982), 227–34.

66. See Stephen M. Meyer, "Soviet Nuclear Operations," *Managing Nuclear Operations*, eds. Carter, Steinbruner, and Zraket, 470–534, and Raymond L. Garthoff, "Mutual

Deterrence, Parity, and Strategic Arms Limitation in Soviet Policy," *Soviet Military Thinking*, ed. Derek Leebaert, (London: Allen and Unwin, 1981) 92–124. The Soviets are less dependent on preemption now than formerly as a result of force modernization, and they have options for preemption, launch under attack/launch on tactical warning, and second strike ride-out.

67. An example of the latter is Freeman Dyson, *Weapons and Hope* (New York: Harper and Row, Colophon Books, 1985).

68. McNamara, *Blundering into Disaster*.

69. For strong arguments to this effect, see Josef Joffe, *The Limited Partnership: Europe, the United States, and the Burdens of Alliance* (Cambridge, Mass.: Ballinger, 1987), 45–92.

70. Joffe, *Limited Partnership*, 173–208.

71. Benjamin S. Lambeth, "Soviet Perspectives on the SDI," *Strategic Defenses and Soviet-American Relations*, eds. Samuel F. Wells, Jr. and Robert S. Litwak (Cambridge, Mass.: Ballinger, 1987), 37–78.

72. See the discussion by Jehuda L. Wallach, "Misperceptions of Clausewitz's *On War* by the German Military," *Clausewitz and Modern Strategy*, ed. Michael I. Handel (London: Frank Cass, 1986), 213–39.

73. Williamson Murray, "Clausewitz: Some Thoughts on What the Germans Got Right," *Clausewitz and Modern Strategy*, ed. Handel, 267–86. And see Jehuda L. Wallach, *The Dogma of the Battle of Annihilation: The Theories of Clausewitz and Schlieffen and Their Impact on the German Conduct of Two World Wars* (Westport, Conn.: Greenwood Press, 1986).

74. Wallach, "Misperceptions," 217.

75. Clausewitz, *On War*, 357.

76. Clausewitz, *On War*, 357.

77. Clausewitz, *On War*, 357.

78. Clausewitz, *On War*, 358.

79. Clausewitz, *On War*, 363.

80. Clausewitz, *On War*, 365.

81. Paul H. Nitze, "On the Road to a More Stable Peace."

82. See Joffe, *Limited Partnership*.

7

STRATEGY AFTER
DETERRENCE: CONCLUDING
OBSERVATIONS

This book is concerned with what can be learned about the possible future of nuclear deterrence and military strategy on the basis of experience before and during the nuclear age. It argues that, strictly speaking, there is no such thing as "conventional deterrence." This is not just a quibble about terminology, for the connotatons of the term "deterrence" are extremely important. Here we focus on the immediate deterrence of an act of aggression that someone is seriously contemplating, not on the more general, although equally important, character of the longer-term balance of power and expectation of hostility among major powers.[1] In this context of immediacy, deterrence rests on the credible threat of excessive punishment as an instrument of dissuasion. And the term "excessive" in this context means not just in excess of what the prospective attacker might compare to a best case, but in excess of what the attacker might compare to a *worst case*.

There are other ways to dissuade potential attackers of their aggressive intentions, but these other approaches do not partake of deterrence properly understood. One can lead a potential aggressor to expect to attain victory at a cost that is higher than acceptable, although less than catastrophic. One can create in the minds of enemy leaders uncertainty about whether they will win or lose. Or one can threaten to impose unacceptable costs on a prospective attacker with a sufficient probability of success for dissuasion to work. Of these various approaches, only one is properly termed deterrence. Why the insistence upon such a narrow definition of deterrence when others have applied it to almost any situation involving the dissuasion of prospective attackers by potential victims of aggression?

The insistence on a narrower definition allows us to get at the heart of the concept—what distinguishes reliance upon deterrence for coercion from military capabilities for war fighting, of which *a side benefit is dissuasion*. Deterrence, unlike other forms of dissuasion, is based on a different "social contract" between potential military opponents. It is also based on a different notion of the relationship between force and policy, or war and politics.

The social contract on which deterrence rests is based on the exchange of hostages. It is a relationship between terrorist states, and it is based on terror as a medium of exchange. On an unprecedented scale, the lives of innocents are placed at immediate risk should either side stray over the boundary between peace and war. If this is what makes nuclear war as one form of deterrence seem so horrible, it is also what makes nuclear weapons credible as instruments of coercion on behalf of dissuasion. There are other ways to dissuade potential attackers, as we have noted. None of them involve an advance commitment to destroy the society of attacker and defender as a consequence of either having broken the peace. It would seem to follow that nuclear weapons have severed the connection between war and politics, and that reliance on nuclear deterrence is therefore a Faustian bargain.

But, if it follows that deterrence is only one form of dissuasion, and nuclear deterrence only one kind of deterrence, the disconnection of nuclear weapons from politics is more apparent than real. The actual hiatus occurs between strategic nuclear weapons deployed in abundant super-power arsenals and traditional forms of dissuasion that cannot be brought back—war. The non-renewability of war as a traditional form of dis-suasion is exacerbated for military traditionalists by the drift of Soviet policy and doctrine into a netherworld of at least temporary abstinence from the cold war. Without a potential opponent—and in the absence of resuscitation for traditional theories of warfare—military strategists, plan-ners, and government officials are left in a perilous state of uncertainty.

Deterrence based on nuclear weapons or other weapons of mass destruc-tion that promise to destroy the attacker's social values, no matter what the attacker's armies can accomplish in battle, is thus a perverse use of military technology in order to serve a good political aim. It follows that the most terrible weapons can contribute to the most durable peace. To this, traditionalists object that nuclear deterrence could fail as well, as nuclear weapons spread beyond the "big five" to Middle Eastern, South

Asian, and Latin American states. And so it could fail; but the outbreak of nuclear war between non-European adversaries does not change the character of dissuasion based on deterrence, nor does it change what makes this form of dissuasion different from other forms.

As noted above, one difference is that the outcome of the clash of arms in battle is judged less important than the deliberate taking of potential noncombatant hostages in peacetime. A second difference is that if deterrence fails, the defender is left with threats that may not be "implementable."[2] Over the years, military experts and policymakers have expressed serious doubts that any U.S. president would order the use of U.S. strategic nuclear weapons in significant numbers against targets in Europe or in the USSR, unless the Soviets had first struck targets in North America with their own nuclear weapons. Much of the paperwork that has burned the midnight oil in NATO has been designed to reassure skeptical Europeans on precisely this point: The United States is committed to doing the incredible for the seemingly (to Americans) ungrateful. The disproportionality of the threat to employ U.S. or other NATO nuclear weapons in response to Soviet conventional aggression in Europe has led to a variety of attempted escapes, as noted in previous chapters. These have included improved conventional defenses, political accommodation and détente between the blocs, restructurings of the U.S. and allied NATO nuclear arsenals, and declaratory policies to the effect that U.S. commitments cannot be doubted by the USSR because the Soviets can never be certain that the United States will *not* honor them.

The last point is worth a second glance. Why is it that a potential attacker in Europe, either the USSR from NATO's standpoint or vice versa, might hesitate to doubt the other superpower's commitment to "extended deterrence," using nuclear threats to protect allies? The extension of conventional deterrence in this fashion has been doubted frequently in history, as two world wars in this century give testimony. Notice the difference in reasoning. "The Soviets cannot be certain that the Americans will not honor their commitment to Western Europe." Compare this formulation to, "The United States needs to make certain to the USSR its commitment to the defense of Western Europe." The first formulation is a double negative: The Soviets have to reason, in the face of great difficulty, to devise a rationale for challenging the status quo. Whereas in the second case, the burden of proof is on the Americans to persuade the USSR that the United States will honor a commitment that is otherwise suspect.

The difference is that even a small probability of excessive (i.e., socially worst case) destruction is sufficient to dissuade a potential attacker who would otherwise insist upon a much larger probability. Deterrence as a form of dissuasion thus rests upon a different relationship between *probability and disutility* than do other forms. Probability can be close to zero as long as disutility remains beyond the realm of calculability and acceptability. Nuclear weapons deployed in their present numbers and with their current characteristics make this relationship unusually inflexible, but other weapons of mass destruction can and will be conceived. The disutility is not that of losing in battle but of losing the social values for which battle is undertaken, despite the success of those armed forces whose mission it is to defend the society and state.

The last sentence hints at another difference between deterrence, especially nuclear, and other forms of dissuasion. So far, two critical differences have been identified. Deterrence more than other forms substitutes the jeopardy of innocent hostages for the prospect of victory in battle and operates on a very different assumption about the relationship between probability and disutility compared to other forms of dissuasion. A third distinction, separating deterrence from other points along the spectrum of dissuasion, is that deterrence threatens to bring about a separation of state and society. It does this in several ways. First, it threatens massive destruction of social values apart from the verdict of combat arms. Second, the destruction may be hurled at the instruments of state control themselves, as has been advocated by planners in several U.S. administrations.[3] Third, the societal destruction attendant to major nuclear war might not be reparable during the lifetimes of the inhabitants of the victimized societies, and perhaps, according to some studies, never.[4]

Each of these three aspects delegitimizes the territorial state and its ruling government, however popularly based. To use the very apt terminology of Sheldon S. Wolin's analysis of Machiavelli's *The Prince*, deterrence creates a situation in which the state cannot provide for the *economy of violence*.[5] Undoubtedly, some of Wolin's readers reacted against that phrase when he first used it, for it has the timbre of an oxymoron. But the phrase is exactly the right rendering of Machiavelli's meaning. The prince was to be judged by how successfully he kept and developed the state. Having lost control of the state by force of arms, he had done his worst. Not for nothing was the urgent recommendation made by Machiavelli that aspiring princes should be preoccupied with the study of war. He was equally insistent that mercenary armies were less dependable than citizen militias. The mercenaries were more expendable, therefore less dependable: The economy for raising, equipping, and training armies was different from the economy of using them in war on behalf of the state.

Clausewitz contributed as well to an understanding of the issue of economy of violence, and the point is worth making on account of the many misreadings of Clausewitz on this issue. His formulation of "absolute war" is mistaken as a prescription for war without limit regardless of its appropriateness to time and place.[6] On the contrary, Clausewitz presented the construct of absolute war as an ideal type, against which actual war was plotted. *On War* emphasizes the constraints that policy must impose upon war. War was something with its own grammar, but not its own logic. No wonder general staffs including those in Germany have resisted this with varying degrees of success. The most successful gambit has been to tell policymakers that the military will handle all operational issues and the political leaders all political ones, as if the two can be neatly separated.

A nuclear deterrence relationship causes the political leadership to commit unprecedented interference into military operations, from the standpoint of military traditionalists. The reason is that misguided operational decisions may bring about decisive losses in the political realm, including the loss of social values and the decisive separation of society and state, in a very short time.[7] In a relationship of dissuasion based on conventional forces, a mistaken operational decision that leads to inadvertent war or escalation can be redeemed by policymakers who choose to exert their authority in order to control escalation. Policymakers do not always so choose. The worst tragedy of World War I is not only that it started, but that it continued long past the point at which the various regimes of Russia, England, France, Germany, and Austria-Hungary could have made any policy-relevant case for fighting. The Russian, German, and Austro-Hungarian regimes all fell victim to the insistence upon waging total war in the absence of any recipe for short and decisive victory.

Why did the protagonists of World War I persevere? Stubbornness and pride, not to mention inept military tactics, undoubtedly played a part.[8] The question of prevailing theories of dissuasion is a more subtle aspect, for dissuasion operates in war as well as before it. One answer to the stubborn perseverance of the combatants is that they foresaw only outcomes that did not exceed their assumed range of toleration: less, that is, than the entire loss of their regimes and empires. Thus, it was easy to be persuaded that, although prewar expectations of a short and decisive victory had been proved wrong, eventual triumph was still at hand—albeit in a long war if not a short one.

The World War I combatants recognized that they were in a relationship of dissuasion once war began, but they misunderstood the form of the relationship. They assumed that dissuasion was totally dependent on battlefield outcomes. In actual fact, they were participating in the first war in modern Europe in which the combatants were in a deterrence relationship before and during war. Deterrence, as noted earlier, is one form of dissuasion in which the survival of governments and peoples is hostage to the level and kind of destruction inflicted on both sides, regardless of who prevails in battle. World War I opened the door to this kind war, although leaders did not yet have weapons that could destroy entire societies in minutes.

But they did have weapons that, if used long enough and on a sufficiently widespread geographical canvas, would virtually destroy the economies, societies, and governments of the participants. One might argue that this did not matter, since no leader in July 1914 could have foreseen the hostage character of the various societies and economies. True enough, but the vulnerability of the various governments to coercion on the basis that their very legitimacy might be destabilized, and their existence threatened, was clearly established in the minds of European leaders of the early twentieth century. Austria-Hungary, fearing that the regime could not stand further reductions of her imperial glacis, squashed Serbia. Russia moved to the defense of Serbia despite the clear position of jeopardy into which any war with Austria-Hungary and its ally, Germany, would place the already enfeebled czarist regime. Germany's political aims in the years immediately preceding World War I were explicitly inclusive of ambitions to change the political map of Europe, and the threat to the survival and continuation of several foreign governments in their present form was not doubted by political principals in Europe and their intelligence establishments.[9]

World War II offered another illustration of leaders being in a deterrence relationship but not understanding that fact, whose wartime ambitions left no room for war limitation and whose objectives included the dismantling of the constitutions and social fabrics of their antagonists. The historical cases are worth citing as reminders that deterrence is not always nuclear, and the essence of deterrence is neither the absolute level of destruction nor the speed with which it can be carried out. What is special about a deterrence relationship is that the political control and social fabric of potential opponents can be undone despite the best possible performance by their respective armed forces in battle.

There remains a phenomenological issue. Can there be a deterrence relationship between adversary leaders who do not recognize that they have entered such a relationship, but prefer to imagine that they are still in a dissuasion situation of a different sort? In a dissuasion situation other than a deterrent one, leaders are in a politico-military "state of nature" in which skill and luck can combine to reward the side that has superior political and military leadership, planning procedures, technology, productive potential for war, and so forth. These things do not become irrelevant in a deterrent form of dissuasion, but their relationship to other variables is changed qualitatively. Today, leaders who are embarked on crisis decision making contemplate the prospect that the results of war may be out of their hands *no matter how carefully* they plan, execute, and contrive to prevail. Unacceptable punishment may befall the governments, societies, and economies of the winners and losers. By any standard, this was the outcome of World War I; thus, nuclear weapons did not create the potential decoupling of government and society, of polity and economy, in the aftermath of war.

What nuclear weapons did do, with dramatic visibility, was to make it apparent to policymakers and military technologists that they could no longer enter into wars with the believable exhortation that proper foresight, planning, and execution of plans could make even the worst case acceptable. Leaders prior to World War I could so exhort: Troops departed for the front amid wild cheers and well wishes in the expectation of something akin to an autumn punt. Leaders could conceal that the worst case was not only unacceptable, but also not within their power to control. They could not concede this point even after the futility of tactics on the Western front and the success of Germany over Russia on the eastern front made a negotiated settlement to the fighting seem apropos (to any historian looking backward from any vantage point in which the requirements of policy are judged to be superior to those of force).

Nuclear weapons have thus given to deterrence the visibility and clarity it has previously lacked. The failure of deterrence properly understood, of a war that escapes control and goes beyond the requirements of sensible policy into the destruction of entire regimes and societies, cannot now be masked as an accidental or *incidental aspect of combat*. Nuclear weapons make clear that deterrence is the essence of the threat posed by potential opponents to others, because nuclear weapons cannot be explained as anything other than weapons of terror. War becomes the infliction of savage destruction on innocents, and the way to prevent war is to make the implications of this fact palpable to leaders who doubt the strength of a nation's commitment to deterrence. The paradox is that this strategy is effective on account of its inhumaneness, intimidating for its lack of compassion, repugnant on account of its certain negligence of consequences. If one judges that national leaders are mostly prevented from choosing war by virtue of their inborn qualities, socialized propensities, or careful reckonings of the balance of power, then one might prefer other forms of dissuasion than deterrence—and especially nuclear deterrence. On the other hand, if one judges that leaders are at times sufficiently ambitious or desperate to wage war as long as the worst possible consequences can be veiled from their attentive and mass publics, then nuclear deterrence offers an ironical dividend.

That deterrence requires us to practice the worst in order to attain the best, or the better, among options in an imperfect world does not preclude the possibility of doing so at lower levels of armament. Neither the Americans nor the Soviets need weapons inventories of their present sizes and diversity in order to fulfill the requirements of deterrence. What is important is to understand what deterrence is all about in order that this strategy, if it is chosen at any level of armament, can be selected in full appreciation of its character. To summarize, the argument here has been that a deterrence situation is one in which (1) the societal values or political regimes of potential opponents are deliberately held hostage to threats of unacceptable and intolerable destruction, (2) threats to social values and regime stability of the opponent can be implemented even if the prospective deterrer is losing on the field of battle, (3) it is an accepted risk on the part of policymakers, even if the risk is imperfectly understood, that the war may escape their control if at least one side chooses to fight beyond the expectations of prewar plans and beyond the limits of societal and regime cohesion.

Clausewitz had experienced this kind of war, waged by Napoleon for the control of Europe's social and political destiny. He had seen Napoleon's wars evolve from campaigns of consolidation to preemptive attacks against potential opponents in Western Europe, and to the invasion of Russia in 1812, which brought about Bonaparte's first decisive reversal. Napoleon had thrown down not only a challenge of military dissuasion to those who might oppose him, but a challenge of a particular kind. Defeat in battle might be followed by dispossession of regime; dynasties were at imminent risk throughout Europe. Of course, in Napoleon's time and for many years thereafter, the opponent's armed forces had to be defeated in battle before his society could be devastated. But the development of strategic airpower and the increased range of navies ended this rule of thumb, of societal invulnerability prior to military defeat, long before nuclear weapons did. Theories of strategic air bombardment emerged, between World War I and World War II, which suggested that a sufficiently destructive attrition of the enemy's wartime economy would inflict intolerable suffering on his population and cause them to demand surrender of their reluctant government. This theory proved overly optimistic. But the uses of airpower by Britain and the United States against Germany and Japan in World War II did demonstrate that highly destructive attacks on social and economic values could no longer be prevented by forestalling military defeat of armies and fleets. Naval blockade and submarine warfare during both world wars also demonstrated that populations could be afflicted by economic hardship before their armies had been totally defeated.

In view of these arguments, conventional deterrence has not been exorcised completely. The demon must be readmitted, but on very strict terms—for it has assertive tendencies. Conventional deterrence is an influence relationship between potential adversaries in an immediate deterrence situation, which has the following features: (1) social and regime vulnerability as an explicit component of attacker or defender strategies, (2) vulnerability as independent of performance in battle, (3) risk of losing control over events as significant relative to the costs of fighting or of conceding the stakes at issue. Within these parameters, there certainly exists such a thing as conventional deterrence, for conventional wars have on many occasions satisfied these conditions. Nor does the attribution of conventional deterrence to prenuclear conflict situations preclude the simultaneous existence of other forms of dissuasion. Dissuasion is also based on the expectation of lost battles, of costs other than those inflicted by the opponent's military forces, and of operational and tactical uncertainties that can only be known more fully after a certain period of fighting has taken place.

One important distinction between a deterrent and nondeterrent dissuasion situation, however, is that in a deterrent situation the threat to lose control over events, with *strategic* consequences, is more explicit. The German chancellor on the verge of World War I refered to the "iron dice" that would inevitably roll the fate of Europe. Hitler invaded the Soviet Union on the anniversary of Napoleon's ill-fated invasion of Russia; neither had provided a coherent political or military objective beyond the operational-tactical.[10] Hitler postponed the invasion of England and attacked the USSR without having defeated his main opponent prior to that date. On the day of the Japanese attack on Pearl Harbor, Hitler gratuitously declared war on the United States, solving a large problem for Roosevelt and Churchill and ensuring Germany's ultimate defeat, for want of resources to fight a two-front war. Japan planned its attack on Pearl Harbor despite the availability of economic estimates that showed that it could not win a prolonged war against the United States.[11] This aspect of reliance upon uncertainty and unpredictability is a key distinction between deterrence and other forms of dissuasion. It may also be one of the weaknesses of deterrence theory when it is combined with nuclear weapons.[12] As Patrick M. Morgan has noted, with regard to authoritative formulations of U.S. nuclear deterrence strategy:

> If deterrence ultimately rests on hypersensitivity to the possibility of irrationality, great uncertainty, accident, and error, then anything that gives governments greater confidence in their ability to be cool and deliberate and to understand, control, and manipulate deterrence situations is counterproductive. But *this is precisely what classic deterrence theory set out to do.*[13]

Morgan points to an important contradiction in the logic of U.S. deterrence theory, but there is worse. Built on this contradiction is a greater one: the assumption that the rationality-of-irrationality theories that can prevent war will, if deterrence fails, allow nonetheless for its limitation. A theory that opts to prevent war by putting its chips not on prevalence in battle but on the manipulation of social risk is vulnerable to the distant mirror through which the opponent regards it. We must expect the opponent to be sufficiently rational to allow that we are somewhat irrational, and as a result he will hesitate to provoke us. Of course, we are supposed to be sufficiently rational to allow for his irrationality. This means that both sides are counting on their own coolness under fire along with a pretense of irrationality to serve as a timely reminder to the opponent that events may escape the control of both.

The Cuban Missile Crisis is sometimes cited as an example of successful deterrence in which the crisis management was handled according to the dictates of rational decision-making and without many of the artifacts of bureaucratic politicking, personal idiosyncrasy, and other distortions that might have provoked inadvertent war or escalation. However, the Cuban crisis can also be read another way, as an episode in which the superpowers almost lost control over events and in which both sides consciously manipulated the risk in order to bring the crisis to a head.[14] Materials now available with regard to the Soviet decision-making process during the "Caribbean crisis" emphasize how differently things were perceived in Moscow as compared to Washington. Whereas President Kennedy and his advisors saw the installation of Soviet MRBMs and IRBMs in Cuba as a direct and personal challenge to Kennedy's credibility and the U.S. reputation for power, Khrushchev saw the move as an expedient solution to his problem of strategic nuclear inferiority. In 1961, the United States had publicly disclosed its intelligence to the effect that the Soviet ICBM force lagged significantly in numbers and capabilities behind the U.S. force. The purpose of the disclosure was deterrence, but the result may have been to provoke Khrushchev to adventurism in order to redress the appearance of the balance.[15] His diplomatic assertiveness had been based on a willingness to brandish Soviet nuclear capabilities in public fora and to extract maximum propaganda leverage from merely adequate or deficient force balances.

With regard to the operation of deterrence, there was some analogy between the U.S. position in West Berlin during the 1950s and 1960s and the Soviet position in Cuba. Neither could be defended by conventional forces alone in the face of actual attack. Each required the "extended deterrence" through willingness to escalate into a retaliatory response involving more than U.S. forces stationed in Berlin, or Soviet forces in Cuba.[16] However, this extended deterrent need not be nuclear. Some U.S. participants in the Cuban Missile Crisis have contended that it was the overwhelming superiority in conventional forces on the part of the United States that could be brought to bear in the immediate theater of operations (the threat of an air strike and/or invasion of Cuba) that was instrumental in forcing Khrushchev to back down. Other participants and scholars have placed more importance on the superior numbers of U.S. strategic nuclear weapons and delivery systems relative to Soviet in 1962. For the political principals, Kennedy and Khrushchev, what seemed to matter most was the risk that events would get beyond their control and result in direct superpower conflict, including possible nuclear war.[17]

What these sources on the Cuban Missile Crisis indicate is that nuclear deterrence, conventional deterrence, and conventional dissuasion were all operating together, although not necessarily with consistency or in harmony with policymakers' aims. Nuclear deterrence was used by Kennedy to deter any launch of Soviet missiles from Cuba against any target in the Western hemisphere. Nuclear deterrence probably also prevented Khrushchev from responding to the U.S. move with a countermove against West Berlin, and Khrushchev's own nuclear weapons served to enforce U.S. prudence in the operation of the blockade and in the reluctance to attack Cuba with regular military forces. Conventional deterrence operated also. The United States was obviously aware of the concerns of its allies in Europe that Soviet pressure on Berlin could extend into war involving

NATO, during which the outcomes of the first battles would be determined by the relative strengths of conventional forces. Even without nuclear escalation in Europe, the collateral damage attendant to such a war in Germany or elsewhere in Central Europe was a powerful persuader for the Soviets and Americans. Conventional dissuasion operated too, as a result of the battlefield losses attendant to any American invasion of Cuba, any Soviet military move on Berlin which met a Western military response, and in the aftermath of any U.S.-Soviet naval encounter in the Caribbean or Atlantic. The relative strength of the U.S. Navy compared to the Soviet one, especially in territorial waters favorable to the former, allowed conventional dissuasion (prospect of immediate naval losses by the USSR) to be supported by conventional deterrence (invasion of Cuba with an outcome almost certainly favorable to the Americans, despite costs which the Americans would have preferred to avoid if possible).

Two levels of the distinction between deterrence relationships and other types of dissuasion have been proposed. At the first level—applied decision-making—three attributes of deterrence were defined: social and regime vulnerability as explicit components of threats, societal and regime vulnerability as independent of battlefield performance, and feared loss of control by the opponent used as a manipulative instrument. At a second and more theoretical level deterrence can be distinguished from other forms of dissuasion according to the following attributes. First, deterrence involves the creation of terror by the threat to victimize noncombatants and regimes along with the destruction forces. Second, deterrence rests on an inversion of the influence relationship between probability and disutility in expected war outcomes. This means that deterrence counts on a deterree whose mind can be fixed on his or her *maximum expected losses* and not on the expected probability that the threat can and will actually be carried out.

A third aspect of the theory of deterrence which sets it apart from other kinds of dissuasion is that it depends on the successful management of a logical contradiction. Each side *must fear the other's loss of control more than it fears its own loss of resolve* for deterrence to hold. For if it fears its own loss of resolve more, it will not be deterred but provoked into demonstrating that resolve by inflexible bargaining or preemptive attack. On the other hand, the fear of the other side's loss of control *must not be made so apparent to the other side* that they, feeling that we have abandoned hope of their self-control, have decided to strike first as the "least worst" option.[18] Each party to a deterrence crisis, including a nuclear one, must assume in particular that the policy-making machinery of government cannot be subverted by the instruments of war into a premature mobilization tantamount to war, as happened in July and August, 1914. The instruments of war preparedness became the proximate causes of war because leaders could not assume that the dogs of war and escalation had been leashed in other capitals, and so they embarked on competitive mobilization designed to culminate in war.[19]

This case is often treated differently and with some validity, as a case of failed dissuasion. The various sides sought to pose the threat not only of devastating retaliation against governments and social fabrics should war break out. They also counted on their military machines to prevail on the field of battle, and promptly.[20] The point is that the dissuasive threats not based on deterrence (as explained here, of losing in battle) did not suffice to prevent war. There was also necessary a deterrent threat of unacceptable social losses, apart from the fortunes of battle. Such a threat was either not made sufficiently clear or was not believed with sufficient strength.

The argument here is that deterrence, whether based on the threat to use conventional or nuclear forces, is similar in character. Nuclear weapons make the threat seem more obviously hideous, but the reliance on the cardinal attributes of societal destruction, rationality of irrationality, and other aspects of deterrence did not begin with the atomic bomb. They began in the appreciation by leaders and planners that terror for use in coercion may meet the requirements for economy of violence in war or during crisis better than dissuasive threats not based on terror. Dissuasive threats not based on terror may not be sufficiently convincing; in the case of conventional dissuasion one may have to show one's cards, so to speak, by occasional forceful demonstrations.

No one desires even a demonstrative application of nuclear weapons. They are therefore the ideal instruments of terror, of what has been called deterrence and described as if it were a polar alternative to war. It is not. It is a psychological form of warfare; one that, if deterrence is to be credible, calls for plans ready-made to execute. The advocates of nuclear deterrence underscore the risks of execution as being so great that powers will always draw back from the brink. The critics of nuclear deterrence point out that in past non-nuclear deterrence episodes, powers have slipped over the brink. Not all failures of dissuasion are deterrence failures, for some result from excessive optimism about combat capabilities or from other nondeterrent causes. But the story of conventional dissuasion includes a sufficient number of deterrence failures, too; the lesson is that nuclear deterrence, having the same blood type, cannot be assumed immune to the disease.

Deterrence before the nuclear age was a dirty business. But it was a dirty business within a state of nature in which potential enemies could still pretend that superiority in combat or resoluteness in diplomacy would allow for a decision that masked the inhumaneness of deterrence. The opponent who failed to yield would either be coerced into retiring from the field or disarmed into doing so. The costs might be bloody, but no one could say before war began exactly what the costs might be. If only leaders were more enlightened, then crises would not develop. If they did, then superior forces would settle the issue. The spectators who happened not to live in the immediate theater of military operations would be spared any direct consequences. Nuclear weapons remove the veil from deterrence, revealing its essential ugliness for all prospective suitors. Coercion aimed at social dislocation and governmental disestablishment was never anything other than extortion. That extortion can work under some conditions is a regrettable paradox of international relations as well as other relations. But nuclear weapons combined with deterrence as an influence mechanism make apparent the transition from "innocent" state of nature to an informed complicity with the nuclear Leviathan. The freedom to choose other options has been traded for security on the cheap, financially and strategically. What is so appealing about nuclear deterrence is that it makes deterrence seem automatic, when in fact it is hard work. New technology, doctrine, and decision-making styles in the Soviet Union and in Western Europe will undoubtedly make the work even harder for U.S. leaders and planners in the future.

MODIFYING THE CONTRACT

It would not do to end on so pessimistic a note. After all, contracts can be modified, including metaphorical ones and ones based on shared understandings in the international realm rather than on coercion or violence. These understandings are covenants of a sort, or "regimes" in contemporary terminology. Regimes are stable expectations between two or more nations with regard to the consistent performance of obligations or fulfillment of commitments.[21] These expectations need not be codified into law or formal treaty, although they sometimes are. The expectations are clustered around one or more issue areas that are functionally related. Theorists of international economic "interdependence" have posited that these issue-clustered regimes have a significant impact on the behavior of state actors in international politics. And although national security is thought to be the preserve of the most autarchic of political leaders, they cannot isolate it from the currency of interdependence. There are too many issues in which it makes more sense to upgrade common interests than to play a zero-sum game.[22]

Arms control is the obvious way to use the politics of interdependence to modify the contract binding states to accept the wrath of nuclear Leviathan for coercion or violence. However, this arms control must be accomplished at several levels. First, and most obvious, the nuclear forces of the superpowers must be limited in size and character. Second, the military doctrines of the Americans and Soviets must be studied within a truly comparative frame of reference. Unlike episodes of the past, the study of Soviet military doctrine should not be conducted as a means to enlarge the U.S. defense budget. An improved understanding of Soviet military doctrine by Western analysts, and of Western doctrine by Soviets, is an intrinsic benefit.[23] Third, the proliferation of nuclear weapons to states that do not now have them should be discouraged, and the Soviets and Americans have established for this purpose what can justifiably be called a security regime on nonproliferation. Regrettably, not all nuclear-armed states are so inclined, but the force of U.S.-Soviet agreement on this issue has brought others to heel (South Africa apparently shelved plans to develop a ready-made nuclear arsenal after a clandestine test was discovered by Soviet spaceborne detectors and the information passed to concerned Western sources—and this during the Brezhnev era).

U.S.-Soviet explicit and tacit agreements have established limits on vertical proliferation of nuclear weapons, also. The two sides' strategic nuclear offensive forces have been constrained within quantitative limits on launchers and numbers of reentry vehicles by two SALT agreements. The ABM Treaty of 1972 limited both superpowers to missile defense deployments at two sites (later reduced to one) and prevented deployment modes other than fixed, land-based ones. The numbers of ABM launchers were also limited, and the deployment of missile defense radars was constrained by location and orientation in order to prevent deployment of comprehensive BMD systems. It would be too much to say that the Soviets in signing the ABM Treaty had adopted U.S. notions of assured destruction or mutual assured destruction.[24] But it does not exaggerate to argue that the Americans and Soviets agreed to modify the terms under which the arms race had been conducted prior to 1972. The Soviet position in the 1960s had been stated with some heat by Premier Kosygin at Glassboro in 1967: Defense is moral, offense is immoral.[25] The Soviets had changed position by the time of SALT I, motivated by the desire to stabilize competition in offensive forces and recognizing that limiting defenses was going to be a necessary trade-off.[26]

It is worth noting that the United States and the Soviet Union could, at least in theory, have taken a different approach to the development of regime norms on arms limitation. They could have taken the conceptual approach articulated by the Soviets in the latter 1960s: Drastically reduce offenses and build up defenses. This approach was later recommended by President Reagan in the 1980s and explained in government releases as the new U.S. "strategic concept." According to Paul H. Nitze, special U.S. ambassador for arms control and a highly regarded expert on the subject for decades, the U.S. strategic concept envisioned three stages in which strategic offensive forces would be gradually disarmed and defenses based on non-nuclear weapons gradually built up.[27] This strategic concept was either too late or too early for its time; the United States might have found a receptive audience in the Kremlin two decades earlier, but not in the early to mid-1980s. Instead, the Soviets rejected this new strategic concept on the grounds that it represented backpedalling from previous understandings about how the arms race would be conducted. Whether that accretion of understandings and precedents is properly called regime, or something else, is less important than the impact of precedent for future policy. Reagan's vision of a nuclear-disarmed world ran into the Soviet vision of incremental adjustment of nuclear balances at the margin. The Soviet vision was the result of decades of experience in negotiating with the Americans and experience in negotiating within the government of the USSR.[28]

David W. Tarr, drawing upon the analysis of Condoleezza Rice, Alexander George, and others, has suggested that the currently prevalent U.S.-Soviet arms-control regime has three core attributes or shared understandings about how to conduct the nuclear arms race.[29] First, parity and the perception of intent to continue it on both sides is important to maintaining stable equilibrium in the arms race (arms-race stability) and to preventing first-strike fears from developing in a crisis (crisis stability). Second, both U.S. and Soviet forces should be invulnerable to disarming first strikes. Some U.S. analysts think that the Soviets also acknowledge that it is desirable to maintain both sides' societies as vulnerable to second strikes, but the Soviet acceptance of the ABM Treaty does not necessarily signify this.[30] Soviet behavior during the "SALT decade" and subsequently does signify that their political and military leaderships now accept the fact of mutual deterrence and the impossibility for either side to have nuclear superiority in the form of a first-strike option that would avert unacceptable retaliation.[31]

Third, most arms-control experts in the United States and the larger number of U.S. and Soviet officials who have negotiated arms-control agreements now accept that limitations on, or reductions of, offenses must be tied to constraints against defenses. This flies in the face of conventional military wisdom and against the U.S. coalition in favor of missile defenses and other expansion of active and passive defenses. However, absent former President Reagan and some of the more dedicated aficionados of his entourage, there seems little informed opposition to the preservation of deterrence based on offensive retaliation, although at reduced levels. At Reykjavik in 1986, Reagan almost demolished NATO alliance consensus on arms control by impulsive agreement in principle to the objective of total denuclearization on a global basis. He was only saved from the consequences of his own instincts by his insistence that SDI could not be bargained away. Afterward, Reagan planners went on with the design for a START agreement that would, if implemented, carry out nominal 50 percent reductions in existing levels of strategic warheads deployed by the two superpowers on strategic nuclear delivery vehicles (6,000 accountable warheads distributed among land-based missiles, sea-based missiles, and bomber-delivered weapons). START counting rules as developed under Reagan and handed over to Bush would favor bomber-delivered weapons compared to those carried by land- and sea-based ballistic missiles during marginal trade-offs to meet the reduced ceilings.[32]

The Reagan administration also contradicted another component of the emerging superpower arms-control regime when it insisted on the elimination of mobile missiles in preliminary START negotiations. This was thought to be peculiar by some, since the survivability of mobile land-based missiles was judged by experts to be superior to that of silo-based ones. Moreover, Reagan also handed over to Bush the Solomon decision to keep warm development lines for two new mobile, land-based missile configurations: MX based in rail garrison deployments, and Midgetman based on road-mobile transporter-launchers. Adding to the difficulty of those seeking START agreement building upon precedent, the Soviets had begun deployment of strategic land-based missiles (ICBMs) by the time Reagan left office, and the USSR planned to deploy mobile SS-24 ICBMs on railcars and road-mobile SS-25 ICBMs among its next generation of land-based missiles.[33] The Soviet mobile ICBMs were a response in part to the improved hard target capabilities of U.S. forces being programmed for the 1990s, including MX/Peacekeeper, Trident II (D-5), and advanced strategic cruise missiles, along with a modernized U.S. bomber fleet.

Another extension of the U.S.-Soviet arms-control regime occurred with the signing of the INF Treaty in December 1987. An entire category of superpower weapons was eliminated: land-based missiles with ranges between 500 and 5,500 kilometers. The agreement surprised U.S. proponents of "double zero," who had expected that the Soviets would not accept such drastic reductions in their modern SS-20 IRBM force, which they had begun to deploy in 1977. It also left the Americans, with regard to subsequent dealings among U.S. NATO allies, with painful prices for success in arms control. Now the remaining short-range nuclear forces deployed in Western Europe would make the West Germans feel "singularized," and German resistance to SNF modernization would be even stronger than before. It was not the first time that improvements in the superpower arms-control regime resulted in disquiet within NATO Europe: As the Americans and Soviets have moved toward nuclear détente, some Europeans have always expressed the reservation that they will be left out in the cold. This was the point of former West German Chancellor Helmut Schmidt's concern, expressed pointedly in 1977, that the superpowers' strategic nuclear arsenals neutralized one another. Therefore, he contended, equality in the balance of those forces intended specifically to threaten Europe must be sought apart from the equilibrium of U.S. and Soviet strategic nuclear forces.[34]

By this time, the U.S. and Soviet leaderships had established a sufficient degree of shared understanding on arms control to be aware of the difficulties attendant to even two-way agreements relative to a single level of the military balance: strategic nuclear arms. By the 1980s, the Soviets had all but given up the idea of restricting U.S. "forward-based systems" capable of nuclear delivery on the grounds that they were functionally equivalent to U.S. strategic nuclear forces capable of striking the Soviet homeland. From the Soviet standpoint it had been a telling point in arms-control negotiations for decades that U.S. FBS and Chinese, British, and French nuclear weapons were all targeted against the USSR or its military forces deployed outside its borders. This was quite reasonable as a perspective, but there was no hope of getting the United States to negotiate on this basis (even if it wanted to, the French and British would have none of it). Therefore, the Soviets sought compensation in the deployment of theater-range systems, including the modernized SS-20s. These were so much more capable than their predecessors (SS-4 and SS-5 land-based medium- and intermediate-range missiles) that they alarmed NATO, which responded with a two-track solution: Seek reductions in Soviet deployments through re-introduction of an old NATO idea from the

1950s—medium-range missiles deployed in Europe capable of reaching into Soviet territory. Some 108 Pershing II ballistic missiles and 464 ground-launched cruise missiles (GLCMs) were slated for deployment to begin in December 1983, the initiation of which caused the USSR to walk out from the INF and START negotiations until Reagan's second term.

Both the Soviet and U.S. INF modernizations had violated a "regime norm" in contemporary nomenclature, and they were somewhat surprised to find that they had done so. When the United States had deployed Thors and Jupiters in Europe in the 1950s they sparked much less controversy, although they were technically obsolete by the early 1960s and eventually gave way to ICBMs based in North America. The U.S. Jupiter missiles deployed in Turkey became hostages to the Soviets in the negotiations to end the Cuban Missile Crisis. But there was not the uproar among political constituencies in Western Europe and among a broad public against the U.S. and NATO deployments of the 1950s compared to the 1980s. Enhanced visibility of nuclear issues as a result of Reagan rhetoric was one cause of controversy, but not the entire explanation. Elites also jumped on the bandwagon of opposition to the "572" deployments, including some of those who had indicated a need for reductions in Soviet INF deployments but who preferred to see that come about through the carrot of arms control without the stick of threatened new deployments by NATO.

What had happened in the interim between the 1950s and the 1980s, among other things, was the development of regime expectations between the blocs as a result of Helsinki and follow-on accords that thawed the political temperature of Europe, and of U.S.-Soviet arms-control agreements previously reached. The precedents set by arms-limitation and confidence-building/war-averting agreements signed by the superpowers in the 1960s and 1970s made the NATO case for new deployments seem weaker than the case for arms control without new deployments. The confidence-building/war-averting agreements included the Direct Communications Link (Hot Line) begun in 1963 and its subsequent upgrades and modernizations with satellite transmission and facsimile capabilities; agreements on notification of nuclear test launches that would carry either Soviet or U.S. delivery systems and reentry vehicles outside national territory; SALT protocols against interference with "national technical means," including satellite reconnaissance; agreements during the 1970s on how to handle notification of nuclear accidents and to avoid incidents at sea; and, during the same decade, the first of many confidence- and security-building measures (CSBMs) in Europe calling for notification of military exercises with the potential to conduct offensive operations and

surprise attacks. The durability of many of these precedents in the con-
fidence-building/war-averting regime was underscored in the 1980s when
further agreements, such as those reached at Stockholm in 1986, required
notification of exercises above a certain level instead of leaving it to peer
pressure from the other bloc and the participating NN (nonaligned and
neutral) nations. The precedents for progressively more constraining
measures with regard to monitoring of prohibited force deployments were
further developed with the very intrusive inspection provisions attendant
to the INF Treaty, including Soviet acceptance of on-site, challenge
inspections of military production facilities.[35]

These developments toward the creation of arms-limitation and confidence-building regimes will have their counterparts in conventional
force reductions and in related confidence-building measures in Central
Europe, and perhaps from the Atlantic to the Urals (the ATTU region), if
optimistic expectations about the eventual conclusion of the NATO-Warsaw Pact Conventional Armed Forces in Europe (CFE) are proved valid.
The CFE negotiations have seen serious proposals tabled by both sides for
the delineation of concentric zones, radiating outward from the center of
Europe and ultimately encompassing the entire ATTU region, within
which limits would be placed on the numbers of deployed tanks, armored
troop carriers and fighting vehicles, artillery, and other components of
surprise attack and large offensive operations.[36] The intrusive inspection
provisions established for the INF agreement have set a precedent for
further definition of verification and monitoring procedures of the kind
that might be required to implement any CFE agreement. The Bush
administration indicated in the spring of 1989 a desire to nail down an
agreement on conventional force reductions and related confidence-building measures as soon as possible, for reasons of deterrence and reassurance
within the Western alliance. The reassurance problem was that the West
German leaders were reluctant to proceed with short-range nuclear force
modernization, which would appear to their electorates to leave them
singularized with regard to Soviet nuclear coercion. On the other hand,
the U.S. and British leaderships were loath to postpone SNF modernization on account of the forces lost to the INF agreement and the desire
not to have the Soviets mistake NATO's nuclear resolve. A compromise
was reached in May 1989 under which the matter of SNF would be
deferred temporarily until after the next West German elections and until
the Soviets had been nailed down to a prompt timetable for CFE. This plan
would get conventional force reductions moving prior to the initiation of
SNF modernization, thus reassuring the Americans (about unfavorable

conventional balances in the aftermath of INF) and the West Germans (about their unique exposure to nuclear blackmail).

In Europe, the fate of conventional arms control was as important to the development of security regimes as were the nuclear and space talks. The likelihood was that any war would begin not by direct nuclear aggression but by the use of conventional forces, followed by nuclear escalation. Therefore, the use of regime change to reduce the risks and costs of war would have to include the reduction of perceived vulnerability to conventional invasion, and not only the perceived vulnerability of NATO. The Soviet Union had been conditioned by its historical experience to expect that military unpreparedness in the initial period of war could have nearly catastrophic consequences.[37] The reduction of nuclear arsenals in some ways compounded the problem of conventional stability, as did the development of high-technology non-nuclear weapons for deep attack. The time urgency felt by decision makers in a crisis could lead to conventional preemption as well as nuclear. Therefore, the question of conventional deterrence or other forms of dissuasion without the use of nuclear weapons was intertwined with that of nuclear deterrence in Europe.

CONVENTIONAL DISSUASION AND NUCLEAR DETERRENCE

The last observation, that dissuasion in Europe is a two-sided problem with conventional and nuclear forces in the balance, returns us to the fundamental conceptual problem. That problem is the ubiquitous use of the term "deterrence" to apply to all kinds of politico-military influence relationships; deterrence means all things to all people. The preference here is that deterrence be treated as one form of dissuasion, and nuclear deterrence as one form of deterrence. The essence of deterrence, and especially of nuclear deterrence, is that it creates the expectation on the part of potential attackers that they will suffer unacceptable losses of social values and regime control, even if they prevail in battle. Other forms of dissuasion may be related to deterrence, but they have a different center of gravity. When we say that leaders are "deterred" from waging war, we ought to mean that unacceptable social and political costs, which their armed forces cannot prevent, weigh heavily on their minds as they stumble toward the brink of war. When a leader who cares about deterrence asks military advisors for their advice, a favorable response with regard to expected outcomes in battle is a necessary, but not sufficient, stimulus to plump for war.

The substitution of conventional deterrence (meaning dissuasion) for nuclear deterrence is, according to the distinctions laid down in the preceding paragraph, full of significant risks with regard to stability in Europe and in superpower relations otherwise. This is so for theoretical as well as practical reasons. In terms of theory, there are at least three crucial distinctions between the influence models of conventional dissuasion and nuclear deterrence.

First, nuclear deterrence depends upon a large component of "rationality of irrationality," of the "threat that leaves something to chance," on the shared risk of escalation due to a loss of control over events.[38] Conventional dissuasion, on the other hand, requires that combat stability, cohesion, and control be maintained at a level superior to that of the opponent and that the potential aggressor so anticipates. The dependency of nuclear deterrence and escalation theories on the loss of control is evident in the disinterest of NATO in developing a fully survivable, multinational theater-nuclear force designed for a war of counterforce attrition with the Soviet strategic and theater-nuclear forces targeted against Western Europe.[39]

Second, the issue of control is handled differently by the assumptions on which theories of nuclear deterrence are built, compared to the assumptions made in conventional dissuasion. One aspect of this is the distinction between central control and peripheral control. The former refers to the control of policymakers over the broad choices among politico-military options; the latter, to the actual military planning and operations that must be done to implement the options.[40] The relationship between central and peripheral control is very indirect in situations of conventional dissuasion. The military tradition on not skipping echelons down the chain of command, and the related tradition of civilian noninterference with the detailed operations of forces in combat, weighs heavily when nuclear deterrence is not in the picture. But when nuclear deterrence is involved, the assumption of distance between central and peripheral control is no longer tenable. Now, widely deployed armies, fleets, and tactical air forces become burning fuses that can ignite a larger, and catastrophically destructive, war.

We know far less than we should about the Soviet view of these matters. Would the Soviet Politburo, defense council, and general staff be more inclined than NATO to withhold nuclear release until the last possible moment, and then to grant to front commanders a great deal of latitude in the selection of targets? In peacetime, Soviet strategic nuclear forces other than ICBMs are apparently maintained at lower levels of alert readiness compared to U.S. bombers and ballistic missile submarines. These lower levels of readiness may indicate Soviet confidence in their ICBMs for coverage of prompt retaliatory launch targets. It may also suggest a certain wariness about the control of alerted bombers and surged submarines compared to ICBMs. Soviet confidence in peripheral control over bombers and SLBMs during crisis and early wartime operations might be even lower than in peacetime. Lower levels of readiness for prompt launch by bombers and SLBMs compared to Soviet ICBMs follows naturally from their basing modes and technical attributes (as in the U.S. case). In addition, the Soviet political and military leadership apparently regards a massive U.S. nuclear "bolt from the blue" as a planning contingency of low probability compared to other possible paths to nuclear war. On the other hand, an important Soviet study published in 1982 described the basis of U.S. deterrence strategy as one of planning for nuclear first attack. And the possibility of a conventional surprise attack is taken very seriously, as Soviet reactions to NATO exercises and Warsaw Pact exercises and training suggest.[41]

Third, with regard to concepts and theory that distinguish conventional dissuasion from nuclear deterrence, the notion of partial victory is quite acceptable in situations of conventional dissuasion and war. Col. Gen. M. A. Gareyev, writing as deputy chief of the Soviet general staff in 1985, referred to this possibility of partial victory in the context of modern military operations, and in critique of some of his predecessors among Soviet military theorists.[42] Gareyev's point was that the Soviet military doctrine of the Khrushchev years had anticipated that any war with the West would inevitably be nuclear and global. In that context, the possibility of limited and partial victory seemed remote. Under present conditions, according to Gareyev, the excess of Soviet and U.S. nuclear arsenals neutralize one another and create the possibility of limited war with partial victory below the nuclear threshold. This is perhaps a Soviet version of Glenn H. Snyder's stability-instability paradox with regard to the relationship between nuclear deterrence and conventional dissuasion.

On the other hand, one of the principal components of nuclear deterrence, especially of extended deterrence, is the absence of the possibility of partial victory and the sharing of ultimate risks by the nuclear protector and the protected. As Josef Joffe has noted, the "first commandment" of extended deterrence under conditions of nuclear parity is that no party to an alliance can be allowed the status of a sanctuary.[43] This is precisely what worries the West Germans now that long- and shorter-range INF are being removed and destroyed from NATO and Pact arsenals. The Germans are concerned that the rest of NATO Europe will be "sanctuarized" while the FRG is "singularized." This is an intra-European variant of the question whether the United States would agree to place at nuclear risk the survival of New York or Chicago for Bonn or Paris. Notice, too, that the French theory of proportional deterrence, of threatening to "tear an arm off" a potential attacker, was an effort to compensate for the risk that the United States would attempt to limit a war to Europe and to sanctuarize North America. It was a strategy designed to deny the option of partial victory or defeat within the context of the Western alliance.

U.S. extended nuclear deterrence is judged necessary by NATO on account of its perceived deficiency in conventional forces. But as noted above, one cannot make up for deficiencies in conventional dissuasion by improving the credibility of nuclear deterrence. This does not mean that nuclear *weapons* are irrelevant to the dissuasion of aggression in Europe. Just the opposite is the case. However, they play both deterrent and other dissuasive roles. The theater-nuclear forces deployed by NATO are deterrents insofar as, and only as long as, they are connected to the U.S. strategic nuclear deterrent. They contribute to other-than-deterrent forms of dissuasion in the same way that conventional forces do once they are used on the battlefield and provided that their battlefield use is contained short of uncontrollable expansion. The Soviets must fear both the containment (if their battlefield losses exceed those of NATO) and the escape from containment (if the use of battlefield and other theater-nuclear weapons goes beyond the immediate theater of operations and into the Soviet homeland).

Three differences between conventional dissuasion and nuclear deterrence as models of influence have been noted. A second task is to ask how stability can be preserved in a multipolar power system of the future, which may be less dependent on nuclear deterrence and more reliant on conventional dissuasion for the prevention of war.

The historical record of multipolar, balance-of-power systems prior to the nuclear age is not encouraging in this regard. Essentially, these systems preserved stability in two ways, if the eighteenth- and nineteenth-century balance-of-power systems in Europe are indicative. First, the great powers were willing to fight many small wars in order to avoid having to fight a larger one. Second, the powers were willing to wage war on the periphery of the Euro-centered state system instead of coming into direct conflict in the center of the system.[44] Thus, stability was not necessarily correlated with peace. The dynamics of multipolar power systems of the past may not provide the necessary components of stability for the multipolar systems of the future. Where is the "periphery" in the 1990s and beyond, and what are "small" wars? Ironically, the increased dependency on conventional dissuasion instead of nuclear deterrence for stability may reduce the differences between small and larger wars, and between the center and periphery of the international system. Both technological and political forces push in this direction, of convergence between center and periphery, and of blurring the difference between small and larger wars. States outside the main security zones of the superpowers are now acquiring limited arsenals of nuclear or high-technology conventional weapons, and the isolation of their value conflicts from the European state system is not guaranteed, as is evident in the Middle East wars of 1967 and 1973.

The difference between deterrence (especially nuclear deterrence) and conventional dissuasion, and the difficulties of maintaining stability in multipolar systems defy proper analysis unless a third set of questions can be addressed. The third issue is the nature of stability itself, and the relationship between deterrence or other forms of dissuasion and stability. Is stability the product of successful dissuasion, or is dissuasion made possible by the existence of stability? There is also the need to distinguish military from political stability. Military stability can be defined with more precision: It is the absence of a condition in which the instruments of war become the proximate causes of war, and in particular, in which the expected value of striking first greatly exceeds the expected value of striking second.[45] Political stability is more complicated.

Three kinds of political stability can be distinguished. The first is the absence of war. The second is the absence of any expectation of war. The third is the existence of a true security community within which there are no value conflicts for which the use of force or coercion is deemed an acceptable solution. These three points on a spectrum of relative stability can be aligned with their respective characteristic forms of military dissuasion. A true security community makes military dissuasion unnecessary, as between the United States and Canada. The intermediate zone, involving no immediate expectation of war although preparedness is still prudent, requires passive forms of dissuasion including passive forms of nuclear deterrence. The first zone, in which there is an absence of war but not the absence of any expectation of war, requires the use of more active forms of dissuasion including deterrence for stability. This is especially the case if Case One is marked by alliance commitments that are not to destabilize but to stabilize the system.

The preceding typology of political stability conditions, with corresponding degrees of activeness and passiveness in dissuasion, raises another issue. What is the role of nuclear deterrence, among a spectrum of deterrence and other dissuasive options, in a Case One condition: the absence of war but the expectation that war is possible and, under some conditions, likely? A speculative but plausible answer is that the role of nuclear deterrence becomes a residual one: It takes a back seat to conventional dissuasion and is regarded as a last resort for the prevention of anticipated enemy moves or for the compellence of adversary compliance with cease-and-desist orders. The paradox may be that the residual political status of nuclear deterrence compared to conventional dissuasion may require the use of active forms of nuclear deterrence, meaning compellence, once policymakers have decided that deterrence is the preferred form of influence.[46] This outcome is likely because conventional dissuasion will now be expected to discourage some of the coercion and aggression that were formerly deterred by nuclear threats.

For what would this nuclear compellence under the assumption of residual deterrence be undertaken? In the past, the answer might have been to compel an aggressor to cease and desist from an attack before escalation got out of control, or before he was forced to suffer unacceptable losses. In theory, compellence would still have these missions. But more and more, the future role of nuclear compellence, especially in NATO, will be to deter the mobilization, concentration, and deployment of conventional forces from a defensive posture into an offensive one during a period of crisis and tension.[47] The confrontation of conventional high-technology forces in Central Europe, even after significant reductions in size and offensive capability, still leaves open the question of surprise and preemption by the side that mobilizes first. If this assumption of nuclear compellence as a future brake on mobilization and deployment of forces is correct, then it follows that the focus of studies on escalation control and deescalation may shift from the period after war has broken out to the period before war starts. Although the U.S. study of crisis management has a long tradition in academic literature, the benefits were limited on account of the short times and immediate catastrophes associated with scenarios of superpower nuclear war. If the Americans and Soviets become less dependent on nuclear deterrence and more dependent on conventional dissuasion (of which conventional deterrence is one very special form), then the problem of crisis management may not seem as forbidding, or the costs of failure so absolute. The importance of developing confidence- and security-building measures (CSBMs), which would provide additional time for deliberation, transparency of capabilities, and clarification of intentions for the two sides during a crisis, would be increased in a model of dissuasion less dependent upon nuclear deterrence. Although the costs of nuclear deterrence failure seem to argue for CSBMs more urgently in nuclear crisis management than in other cases, the development of nuclear crisis relevant CSBMs is limited by the small number of historical cases from which to draw. Conversely, despite the complexity of conventional force structures and command systems compared to strategic nuclear forces of the superpowers, the opportunity for CSBMs might be larger in the conventional case. In case of good-faith cooperation by one side that is disappointed by the actions of the other, the losses are less than catastrophic if the failure of confidence-building measures leads to inadvertent war or deliberate attack. There is still time and opportunity to retrieve the situation prior to the unacceptable loss of social values, however dreadful the losses in battle might be.

Finally, although the difference between conventional dissuasion and nuclear deterrence has been stressed here, there may be ironical similarities at the level of individual and group psychology of decision making. This is a tentative hypothesis only. Conventional dissuasion depends on the expected outcome of battle. The essence of the expected outcome of battle rests upon the cohesion or disintegration of primary groups under fire.[48] The essence of successful nuclear deterrence rests on the balance between cohesion and disintegration of decision-making groups of principal policymakers and their advisors. Research supports both assertions, but with a caution. In battle, the objective of each side is to preserve its own cohesion but to bring about disintegration of the opponent's. In nuclear crisis management, both sides would want to preserve the opponent's decision-making cohesion as long as possible, unless the opponent were judged to be irrational. But in that exceptional case, the opponent would be beyond deterrence—or would it be more correct to say, beyond dissuasion?

NOTES

1. See Patrick M. Morgan, *Deterrence: A Conceptual Analysis*, 2nd ed. (Beverly Hills, Calif.: Sage Publications, 1983), Ch. 3.

2. I believe this is James R. Schlesinger's term.

3. Desmond Ball, "The Development of the SIOP, 1960–1983," *Strategic Nuclear Targeting*, eds. Desmond Ball and Jeffrey Richelson (Ithaca, N.Y.: Cornell University Press, 1986), 57–83.

4. Carl Sagan, "Nuclear Winter and Climatic Catastrophe: Some Policy Implications," *Foreign Affairs* 62 (Winter 1983/1984: 257–92. The nuclear winter thesis became controversial in the scientific community on technical grounds, but its most interesting implication was that even "light" strategic nuclear war might have unacceptable climatic effects for both sides.

5. Sheldon S. Wolin, *Politics and Vision* (Boston: Little, Brown, 1960), 220–35, cf. Niccolo Machiavelli, *The Prince*, ed. and trans. Robert M. Adams (New York: W. W. Norton, 1977), 185–94.

6. Jehuda L. Wallach, *The Dogma of the Battle of Annihilation: The Theories of Clausewitz and Schlieffen and Their Impact on the German Conduct of Two World Wars* (Westport, Conn.: Greenwood Press, 1986) makes the case for misconstruction of Clausewitz's understandings of the relationship between force and policy. See also Michael I. Handel, ed., *Clausewitz and Modern Strategy* (London: Frank Cass, 1986) and Michael Howard, *Clausewitz* (New York: Oxford University Press, 1983).

7. Bruce G. Blair, *Strategic Command and Control: Redefining the Nuclear Threat* (Washington, D.C.: Brookings Institution, 1985), Ch. 3.

8. See John Keegan, *The Face of Battle* (New York: Viking Press, 1976), Ch. 4.

9. On Germany's war aims, see Fritz Fischer, *Germany's Aims in the First World War* (New York: W. W. Norton, 1967).

10. For an appraisal of Hitler's aims, see Erich Von Manstein, *Lost Victories* (Chicago: Henry Regnery Company, 1958).

11. Roberta Wohlstetter, *Pearl Harbor: Warning and Decision* (Stanford, Calif.: Stanford University Press, 1962).

12. This thesis is argued by Richard Ned Lebow, *Nuclear Crisis Management* (Ithaca, N.Y.: Cornell University Press, 1987). See also Morgan, *Deterrence*, Ch. 5.

13. Patrick M. Morgan, *Deterrence: A Conceptual Analysis* (Beverly Hills, Calif.: Sage Publications, 1983), 123.

14. Graham T. Allison, *Essence of Decision: Explaining the Cuban Missile Crisis* (Boston: Little, Brown, 1971). See also Richard Ned Lebow, "The Cuban Missile Crisis: Reading the Lessons Correctly," *Political Science Quarterly* 98 (Fall 1983): 447–78. On manipulation of risk, see Thomas C. Schelling, *Arms and Influence* (New Haven, Conn.: Yale University Press, 1966), Ch. 3.

15. For an account of Soviet decision making during the Cuban missile crisis, see Raymond L. Garthoff, *Reflections on the Cuban Missile Crisis*, rev. ed. (Washington, D.C.: Brookings Institution, 1989), esp. 6–42.

16. See Richard K. Betts, *Nuclear Blackmail and Nuclear Balance* (Washington, D.C.: Brookings Institution, 1987), 110–11.

17. McGeorge Bundy, *Danger and Survival: Choices about the Bomb in the First Fifty Years* (New York: Random House, 1988), 391–462.

18. For these and other paradoxes of nuclear crisis decision making, see Paul K. Davis, *Studying First-Strike Stability with Knowledge-Based Models of Human Decisionmaking* (Santa Monica, Calif.: RAND Corporation, 1989).

19. On the historical events leading to the outbreak of World War I, see Rene Albrecht-Carrie, *A Diplomatic History of Europe since the Congress of Vienna* (New York: Harper and Row, 1958), Ch. 8.

20. See Jack Snyder, *The Ideology of the Offensive: Military Decision Making and the Disasters of 1914* (Ithaca, N.Y.: Cornell University Press, 1984).

21. On the concept of regime applied to international relations, see Robert O. Keohane and Joseph S. Nye, *Power and Interdependence*, 2nd ed. (Glenview, Ill.: Scott, Foresman and Co., 1989).

22. A zero-sum game is one in which the wins and losses of all players sum to zero. Thus, one player's gain is automatically another's loss. I am grateful to David W. Tarr for insights and references pertinent to this entire section.

23. In this regard, the development of journals such as the *Journal of Soviet Military Studies* in the United States and a new cadre of Soviet civilian analysts of military and defense problems are most welcome. See, for example, "Perestroyka sovetskoy voennoy

nauki v zerkalc zapadnoy press" (Perestroika in Soviet military science through the mirror of the Western press"), *Voyenno-Istoricheskiy zhurnal* (*Military historical journal*) no. 3 (1989): 85–91.

24. See John Newhouse, *Cold Dawn: The Story of SALT* (New York: Holt, Rinehart and Winston, 1973).

25. Robert S. McNamara, *Blundering into Disaster: Surviving the First Century of the Nuclear Age* (New York: Pantheon Books, 1986), 57.

26. For Soviet views of SALT and its implications for mutual deterrence, see Raymond L. Garthoff, "Mutual Deterrence, Parity and Strategic Arms Limitation in Soviet Policy," *Soviet Military Thinking*, ed. Derek Leebaert (London: Allen and Unwin, 1981), 92–124.

27. Paul H. Nitze, "On the Road to a More Stable Peace," U.S. Department of State, *Current Policy* 657 (20 February 1985).

28. On the Soviet approach to arms control, see Michael MccGwire, *Military Objectives in Soviet Foreign Policy* (Washington, D.C.: Brookings Institution, 1987), Ch. 11, esp. 266–282.

29. The author gratefully acknowledges the opportunity to read a paper by David W. Tarr on this subject from which the taxonomy is drawn, although Tarr is not responsible for its application here.

30. See Garthoff, "Mutual Deterrence," and, for Soviet analysis of U.S. doctrine, Alexey G. Arbatov, *Lethal Frontiers: A Soviet View of Nuclear Strategy, Weapons, and Negotiations* (New York: Praeger, 1988).

31. There are clear trends in this regard, from Brezhnev's "Tula speech" of 1977 to the present. See Raymond L. Garthoff, "New Thinking in Soviet Military Doctrine," *The Washington Quarterly* 11 (Summer 1988): 131–58. See also Maj. Gen. William E. Odom, "The Soviet Approach to Nuclear Weapons: A Historical Overview," *Annals of the American Academy of Political and Social Science* 469 (September 1983): 117–35; Joseph D. Douglass, Jr. and Amoretta M. Hoeber, *Soviet Strategy for Nuclear War* (Stanford: Hoover Institution Press, 1979); Notra Trulock III, "Soviet Perspectives on Limited Nuclear War," *Swords and Shields: NATO, the USSR, and New Choices for Long-Range Offense and Defense*, eds. Fred S. Hoffman, Albert Wohlstetter, and David S. Yost (Lexington, Mass.: Lexington Books, 1987) 53–86; and Edward L. Warner III, *Soviet Concepts and Capabilities for Limited Nuclear War: What We Know and How We Know It* (Santa Monica, Calif.: RAND Corporation, 1989). However, these are Western sources. For Soviet comments, see Marshal N. V. Ogarkov, *Istoriya uchit bditel' nosti* (History teaches vigilance) (Moskva: Voyenizdat, 1985), 68, 73–77. An explicit no-first-use commitment is made by Ogarkov, 77. See also his comments on limited nuclear war, 89. Compare his concluding chapter in *Istoriya* with Marshal of the Soviet Union Sergey Akhromeyev, "Doktrina predotvrashcheniya voyny, zashchity mira i sotsializma" ("Doctrine for the prevention of war, the defense of peace and socialism"), *Problemy Mira i Sotsializma* (Problems of peace and socialism) 12 (December 1987): 23–28. See also Marshal N. V. Ogarkov, *Vsegda v gotovnosti k zashchite Otechestva* (Moskva: Voyenizdat, 1982), 46.

32. Michele A. Flournoy, "START Thinking about a New U.S. Force Structure," *Arms Control Today* July/August 1988: 8–14.

33. U.S. Department of Defense, *Soviet Military Power: Prospects for Change, 1989* (Washington, D.C.: U.S. Government Printing Office, 1989), 45.

34. Schwartz, NATO's Nuclear Dilemmas, 214.

35. According to the INF Treaty, parties are to update data and provide notifications required by the treaty through the Nuclear Risk Reduction Centers, established September 15, 1987 (Article IX, 2). Each party has the right to conduct inspections for thirteen years after the treaty enters into force: twenty inspections per year for the first three years, fifteen per year for the next five years, and ten per year for the last five years (Article XI, 5). The parties established a Special Verification Commission to resolve questions of compliance: They are to use the risk reduction centers to exchange data, provide notifications of inspections and other notices, and to provide and receive requests for cooperative meaures (Article XIII, 1).

36. See U.S. Department of State, *Military Confidence- and Security-Building Measures in Europe: Strengthening Stability through Openness* (Washington, D.C.: U.S. State Department, April 1989).

37. S. P. Ivanov, *Nachal' nyy period voyny* (Moscow: Voyenizdat, 1972). Available in U.S. Air Force Soviet Military Thought Series, U.S. Government Printing Office.

38. Thomas C. Schelling, *Arms and Influence* (New Haven, Conn.: Yale University Press, 1966), Ch. 3; Thomas C. Schelling, *The Strategy of Conflict* (Cambridge, Mass.: Harvard University Press, 1960), Ch. 8.

39. For an argument to this effect, see Paul Bracken, *The Command and Control of Nuclear Forces* (New Haven, Conn.: Yale University Press, 1983), Ch. 5.

40. John J. Mearsheimer, *Conventional Deterrence* (Ithaca, N.Y.: Cornell University Press, 1983), Ch. 2.

41. Richard K. Betts, "Surprise Attack and Preemption," *Hawks, Doves and Owls: An Agenda for Avoiding Nuclear War*, eds. Graham T. Allison, Albert Carnesale, and Joseph S. Nye, Jr. (New York: W. W. Norton, 1985), Ch. 3.

42. M. A. Gareyev, *M. V. Frunze: Voyennyy teoretik* (Moskva: Voyenizdat, 1985), published as M. A. Gareev, *M. V. Frunze: Military Theorist* (New York: Pergamon-Brassey's, 1988), 217.

43. For further discussion, see Joseph Joffe, *The Limited Partnership: Europe, the United States and the Burdens of Alliance* (Cambridge, Mass.: Ballinger Publishing Co., 1987) 145 and passim.

44. Geoffrey Blainey, *The Causes of War* (New York: Free Press, 1973).

45. This definition of military stability is a composite. See Schelling, *Strategy of Conflict*, Ch. 9; Morgan, *Deterrence*, Ch. 3; and Leon V. Sigal, *Nuclear Forces in Europe* (Washington, D.C.: Brookings Institution, 1984), Ch. 1 for distinctions among strategic, crisis, and arms race stability.

46. Schelling, *Arms and Influence*, 69–91 discusses compellent threats.

47. I am indebted to Leon Sloss for this suggestion.

48. See Keegan, *Face of Battle*, Ch. 5.

SELECTED BIBLIOGRAPHY

Allison, Graham T. *Essence of Decision: Explaining the Cuban Missile Crisis*. Boston: Little, Brown, 1971.

Allison, Graham T., Albert Carnesale, and Joseph S. Nye, Jr., eds. *Hawks, Doves and Owls: An Agenda for Avoiding Nuclear War*. New York: W. W. Norton, 1985.

Art, Robert J., Vincent Davis, and Samuel P. Huntington, eds. *Reorganizing America's Defense: Leadership in War and Peace*. New York: Pergamon, 1985.

Ball, Desmond. *Can Nuclear War Be Controlled?* Adelphi Papers No. 169. London: International Institute for Strategic Studies, Autumn 1981.

Ball, Desmond, and Jeffrey Richelson, eds. *Strategic Nuclear Targeting*. Ithaca, N.Y.: Cornell University Press, 1986.

Bellamy, Chris. *The Future of Land Warfare*. New York: St Martin's Press, 1987.

Betts, Richard K. *Nuclear Blackmail and Nuclear Balance*. Washington, D.C.: Brookings Institution, 1987.

Bialer, Seweryn. *The Soviet Paradox: External Expansion, Internal Decline*. New York: Alfred A. Knopf, 1986.

Blainey, Geoffrey. *The Causes of War*. New York: The Free Press, 1973.

Blair, Bruce G. *Strategic Command and Control: Redefining the Nuclear Threat*. Washington, D.C.: Brookings Institution, 1985.

Boutwell, Jeffrey D., Paul Doty, and Gregory F. Treverton, eds. *The Nuclear Confrontation in Europe*. London: Croom Helm, 1985.

Bracken, Paul. *The Command and Control of Nuclear Forces*. New Haven, Conn.: Yale University Press, 1983.

Byely, Col. B., et al. *Marxism-Leninism on War and Army*. Moscow: Progress Publishers, 1972.

Carter, Ashton B., John D. Steinbruner, and Charles A. Zraket, eds. *Managing Nuclear Operations*. Washington, D.C.: Brookings Institution, 1987.

Cimbala, Stephen J. *Nuclear Strategizing*. New York: Praeger Publishers, 1988.

Clausewitz, Carl von. *Vom Kriege* [On war]. Edited and translated by Michael Howard and Peter Paret. Princeton, N.J.: Princeton University Press, 1976.

Dailey, Brian D., and Patrick J. Parker, eds. *Soviet Strategic Deception*. Lexington, Mass.: Lexington Books, 1987.

Daniel, Donald C., and Katherine L. Herbig, eds. *Strategic Military Deception*. New York: Pergamon Press, 1981.

Davis, Paul K. *Studying First-Strike Stability with Knowledge-Based Models of Human Decisionmaking*. Santa Monica, Calif.: RAND Corporation, 1989.

Donnelly, Christopher N. "Soviet Operational Concepts in the 1980s." In *Strengthening Conventional Deterrence in Europe: Proposals for the 1980s*, 105–36. Report of the European Security Study. New York: St Martin's Press, 1983.

Donnelly, Christopher N., et al. *The Sustainability of the Soviet Army in Battle*. The Hague: SHAPE Technical Center, 1986.

Einhorn, Robert. "The Emerging START Agreement." *Survival* 30, (September/October 1988): 387–401.

Erickson, John. *The Road to Berlin*. Boulder, Colo.: Westview Press, 1983.

Erickson, John, Lynn Hansen, and William Schneider. *Soviet Ground Forces: An Operational Assessment*. Boulder, Colo.: Westview Press, 1986.

Freedman, Lawrence. *The Evolution of Nuclear Strategy*. New York: St Martin's Press, 1981.

Gareyev, M. A. *M. V. Frunze: Voennyy teoretik* (M. V. Frunze: Military theorist). Moscow: Voyenizdat, 1985.

Garthoff, Raymond, L. *Detente and Confrontation*. Washington, D.C.: Brookings Institution, 1985.

Glantz, David M. *Deep Attack: The Soviet Conduct of Operational Maneuver*. Fort Leavenworth, Kan.: Soviet Army Studies Office, 1987.

Gottfried, Kurt, and Bruce G. Blair. *Crisis Stability and Nuclear War*. New York: Oxford University Press, 1988.

Hines, John G. "How Much Is Enough for Theater War? The Soviet Approach to Sufficiency of Conventional Forces in Europe." Appendix X in U.S. Congress, General Accounting Office, *NATO-Warsaw Pact Conventional Force Balance*, pp. 35–47. Washington, D.C.: General Accounting Office, 1988.

Hines, John G., and Phillip A. Petersen. "The Changing Soviet System of Control for Theater War." *International Defense Review*, 3 (March 1986). (Reprinted with revisions in Stephen J. Cimbala, ed., *Soviet C3*, pp. 191–219.) Washington, D.C.: AFCEA International Press, 1987.

Hines, John G., Phillip A. Petersen, and Notra Trulock III. "Soviet Military Theory 1945–2000: Implications for NATO." *Washington Quarterly* 9, no. 4 (Fall 1986): 117–37.

Hoffman, Fred S., Albert Wohlstetter, and David S. Yost, eds. *Swords and Shields: NATO, the USSR and New Choices for Long-Range Offense and Defense*. Lexington, Mass.: Lexington Books, 1987.

Hungington, Samuel P., ed. *The Strategic Imperative*. Cambridge, Mass.: Ballinger Publishing, 1982.

Ikle, Fred Charles. *Every War Must End*. New York: Columbia University Press, 1971.

Ivanov, S. P. *Nachal'nyy period voyny* (The initial period of war). Moscow: Voyenizdat, 1974. (Reprinted in U.S. Air Force, Soviet Military Thought Series. Washington, D.C.: U.S. Government Printing Office, undated.)

Jervis, Robert. *The Illogic of American Nuclear Strategy*. Ithaca, N.Y.: Cornell University Press, 1984.

Jervis, Robert, Richard Ned Lebow, and Janice Gross Stein. *Psychology and Deterrence.* Baltimore, Md.: Johns Hopkins University Press, 1985.

Joffe, Joseph. *The Limited Partnership: Europe, the United States and the Burdens of Alliance.* Cambridge, Mass.: Ballinger Publishing, 1987.

Knorr, Klaus, and Patrick M. Morgan, eds. *Strategic Military Surprise.* New Brunswick, N.J.: Transactions Books, 1983.

Lebow, Richard Ned. *Between Peace and War: The Nature of International Crisis.* Baltimore, Md.: Johns Hopkins University Press, 1981.

———. *Nuclear Crisis Management: A Dangerous Illusion.* Ithaca, N.Y.: Cornell University Press, 1987.

Lee, William T., and Richard F. Staar. *Soviet Military Policy since World War II.* Stanford, Calif.: Hoover Institution, 1986.

May, Ernest R., ed. *Knowing One's Enemies: Intelligence Assessment before the Two World Wars.* Princeton, N.J.: Princeton University Press, 1984.

MccGwire, Michael. *Military Objectives in Soviet Foreign Policy.* Washington, D.C.: Brookings Institution, 1987.

Mearsheimer, John J. *Conventional Deterrence.* Ithaca, N.Y.: Cornell University Press, 1983.

Meyer, Stephen M. "Soviet Nuclear Operations." *Managing Nuclear Operations,* Edited by Ashton B. Carter, John D. Steinbruner, and Charles A. Zraket. pp. 470–534. Washington, D.C.: Brookings Institution, 1987.

Meyer, Stephen M. *Soviet Theater Nuclear Forces, Part II: Capabilities and Implications.* Adelphi Papers, no. 188. London: International Institute for Strategic Studies, Winter 1983–1984.

Miller, Steven E., ed. *Strategy and Nuclear Deterrence.* Princeton, N.J.: Princeton University Press, 1984.

Morgan, Patrick M. *Deterrence: A Conceptual Analysis.* Beverly Hills, Calif.: Sage Publications, 1983.

Ogarkov, N. V. *Istoriya uchit bditel' nosti* [History teaches vigilance]. Moscow: Voyenizdat, 1985.

———. *Vsegda v gotovnosti k zashchite Otechestva* [Always in readiness to defend the fatherland]. Moscow: Voyenizdat, 1982.

Panov, B. V., et al. *Istoriya voyennogo iskusstva* [The history of military art]. Moscow: Voyenizdat, 1984.

Paret, Peter, ed. *Makers of Modern Strategy.* Princeton, N.J.: Princeton University Press, 1986.

Quester, George. *The Future of Nuclear Deterrence.* Lexington, Mass.: Lexington Books, 1986.

Reznichenko, V. G., I. N. Vorob'yev, and N. F. Miroshnichenko. *Taktika* [Tactics]. Moscow: Voyenizdat, 1987.

Schelling, Thomas C. *Arms and Influence.* New Haven, Conn.: Yale University Press, 1966.

———. *The Strategy of Conflict.* Cambridge: Harvard University Press, 1960.

Schwartz, David N. *NATO's Nuclear Dilemmas.* Washington, D.C.: Brookings Institution, 1983.

Scott, Harriet Fast, and William F. *Soviet Military Doctrine: Continuity, Formulation and Dissemination.* Boulder, Colo.: Westview Press, 1988.

Smoke, Richard. *War: Controlling Escalation.* Cambridge: Harvard University Press, 1977.

Sokolovskiy, V. D. *Voyennaya strategiya* [Military strategy]. Moscow: Voyenizdat, 1962.

Trulock, Notra. "Soviet Perspectives on Limited Nuclear Warfare." *Swords and Shields: NATO, the USSR and New Choices for Long-Range Offences and Defense*, edited by Fred S. Hoffman, Albert Wohlstetter, and David S. Yost, 53–86. Lexington, Mass.: Lexington Books, 1987).

Vigor, P. H. *Soviet Blitzkrieg Theory.* New York: St Martin's Press, 1983.

Wardak, Ghulam, comp., and Graham Hall Turbiville, Jr., gen. ed. *The Voroshilov Lectures: Materials from the Soviet General Staff Academy.* Vol. I: *Issues of Soviet Military Strategy.* Washington, D.C.: National Defense University Press, 1989.

Whaley, Barton. *Codeword Barbarossa.* Cambridge, Mass.: MIT Press, 1973.

Yurechko, John J. "Command and Control for Coalitional Warfare: The Soviet Approach." *Signal* (December 1985): 34–39. Reprinted in Stephen J. Cimbala, ed., *Soviet C3*, 17–34 (Washington, D.C.: AFCEA International Press, 1987).

Zhurkin, V., S. Karaganov, and A. Kortunov. "Vyzovy bezopasnosti: staryye i novyye" (Challenges to security: Old and new) *Kommunist* 1 (1988): 42–50.

INDEX

LITERATURE CITED

ABOUT THE AUTHOR

STEPHEN J. CIMBALA is professor of political science at Pennsylvania State University's Delaware County Campus in Media, Pennsylvania, where he teaches courses in international relations, foreign policy, defense studies, and intelligence. Cimbala has contributed to the literature of national security and defense studies on the topics of deterrence, arms control, nuclear strategy, intelligence, and Soviet military policy. His recent works include *Nuclear Endings* (Praeger, 1989) and *Uncertainty and Control: Future Soviet and American Strategy.*